This book presents the history of the first two religious sects successfully launched in seventeenth-century Massachusetts, where it was illegal to participate in any faith other than the legally established congregationalism of the Puritan founders of the colony. Taking a comparative approach, the author examines the Quaker meeting in Salem and the Baptist church in Boston over more than a century. The work opens with the dramatic events surrounding dissenters' efforts to gain a foothold in the colony. *Quakers and Baptists in Colonial Massachusetts* then locates sectarians within their families and communities, examines their beliefs and the changing nature of the organizations they founded, and discusses their interactions with the larger community and its leaders. The book deals with the religiosity of lay colonists, finding that men and women responded to these sects differently. It also analyzes sociological theories of sectarian evolution, the politics of dissent, and changes in beliefs and practices.

Quakers and Baptists
in colonial Massachusetts

Quakers and Baptists
in colonial Massachusetts

CARLA GARDINA PESTANA

The Ohio State University

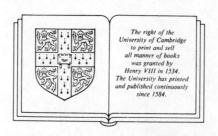

The right of the
University of Cambridge
to print and sell
all manner of books
was granted by
Henry VIII in 1534.
The University has printed
and published continuously
since 1584.

CAMBRIDGE UNIVERSITY PRESS

Cambridge
New York   Port Chester   Melbourne   Sydney

Published by the Press Syndicate of the University of Cambridge
The Pitt Building, Trumpington Street, Cambridge CB2 1RP
40 West 20th Street, New York, NY 10011, USA
10 Stamford Road, Oakleigh, Melbourne 3166, Australia

First published in 1991

Printed in the United States of America

Library of Congress Cataloging-in-Publication Data
Pestana, Carla Gardina.
Quakers and Baptists in colonial Massachusetts /
Pestana, Carla Gardina.
p.   cm.
Includes index.
ISBN 0-521-41111-4
1. Society of Friends – Massachusetts – History.   2. Baptists –
Massachusetts – History.   3. Massachusetts – Church history.
4. Massachusetts – History – Colonial period, ca. 1600–1775.
5. Church and state – Massachusetts – History.   I. Title.
BR555.M4P47   1991
286'.13'09744 – dc20   90-28973
                                                             CIP

British Library Cataloguing in Publication Data
Pestina, Carla Gardina
Quakers and Baptists in colonial Massachusetts.
1. Massachusetts. Quakers. Baptists, history
I. Title
286.1744

ISBN 0-521-41111-4 hardback

For Donald

Contents

Preface

During most of the period covered by this book, the English began the calendar year on March 25. Because the remainder of Europe had already adopted the Gregorian calendar, the English regularly followed a practice of dual dating for the period from 1 January through 24 March. What we would consider 1 March 1660, they thought of as 1 March 1659/60. Their practice of providing both years has been utilized here for the sake of clarity. In addition, most early New Englanders avoided the use of month names – which they considered pagan – and instead numbered the months. They would have rendered 1 March 1659/60 as 1st day 1st month 1659/60. To avoid confusion, all months have been given their "pagan" names.

Quotations from colonial sources have been left as in the original except that the letters of the alphabet have been changed as necessary to follow modern usage. Seventeenth-century publications typically had extremely long titles. The ends of these have regularly been lopped off without the insertion of ellipses.

Where Knowledge of a woman's family history is needed to follow a discussion, the full name – including any maiden name or previous married names – is provided. For those cases in which a name is not known, brackets, [   ], indicate the omission.

While working on this project, I have incurred many debts. The American Council of Learned Societies and the National Endowment for the Humanities provided leave from teaching duties with the Fellowship for Recent Recipients of the Ph.D. An exchange program between the Huntington Library and the British Academy made a research trip to London possible. Short-term fellowships at the American Antiquarian Society (the Kate D. and Hall J. Peterson Fellowship), the Henry E. Huntington Library (the Frank Hideo Kono Memorial Fellowship), and the John Carter Brown Library financed visits to those archives. The Ohio State University provided various forms of assistance, including leave time with a College of Humanities' Special Research Assignment and the Department of History's Faculty Development Quarter as well as research support through the College of Humanities' Grant-in-Aid and the Graduate School's University Small Grant programs. A Charlotte W. Newcombe Doctoral Dissertation Fellowship from the Woodrow Wilson National Fellowship Foundation freed me from having to seek employment during my last year of graduate study. At Cambridge University Press, Frank Smith moved my manuscript quickly through the review process.

Research for this project was conducted at various repositories, where staff members provided assistance. These included the libraries of the Massachusetts Historical Society, New England Historical and Genealogical Society, Essex Institute, Lynn Historical Society, American Antiquarian Society, and Rhode Island Historical Society, as well as the John Carter Brown Library, Henry E. Huntington Library, British Library, Boston Public Library, Houghton Library, Widener Library, Friends' Library at Swarthmore College, James P. McGill Library at Haverford College, Library of the Society of Friends of the Friends' House in London, William Andrew Clark Memorial Library, Dr. Williams's Library in London, Massachusetts Archives Library at the State House, University Research Library at the University of California at Los Angeles, and the William Oxley Thompson Memorial Library at the Ohio State University. In addition, I consulted court, probate, and deed records in the public repositories of three Massachusetts counties – Essex, Middlesex, and Suffolk – as well as court records in the new facility on Columbia Point in Boston, the Massachusetts Archives. Peter Drummey of the Massachusetts Historical, Norman Fiering of the John Carter Brown, and Martin Ridge of the Huntington libraries, as well as Robert Middlekauff and Prudence Bakman, formerly at the Huntington and the Essex Institute libraries, respectively, made special efforts on my behalf, for which I remain grateful.

I have had the good fortune to receive advice and encouragement from able and generous scholars. My graduate school adviser, Gary Nash, has a well-deserved reputation as an incisive critic. I had the benefit not only of the close readings he gave my work, but also of his invariably astute insights about navigating the shoals of graduate school and launching oneself into academia. I found that I could rely on Joyce Appleby for both an encouraging word and thought-provoking ideas about my material. Ruth Bloch and Jon Butler helped me to begin thinking about how to transform my dissertation into this book, and both of them have continued to advise me on the project. Christine Heyrman, E. Brooks Holifield, and Richard Sheils also thoroughly critiqued the revised manuscript. Edwin Gaustad, Stephen Marini, Randolph Roth, Leila Rupp, and, especially, Kathleen Myers read portions of this work. My graduate student, Raymond Irwin, assisted me in preparing the manuscript for publication.

Finally, my loved ones have helped in less direct but no less important ways. My extended family may have wondered about the wisdom of pursuing a Ph.D. in history, especially after I had explained my prospects for employment; their good-natured concern has been a constant source of encouragement. Don, who has made this work possible by making my life as a graduate student and an assistant professor enjoyable, maintains that it has been no sacrifice. For that, I am especially grateful.

Abbreviations used in the footnotes

Sources

BTR	*Reports of the Record Commissioners of the City of Boston . . . Records Relating to the Early History of Boston.* 39 vols. Boston, 1876–1909
CMHS	*Collections of the Massachusetts Historical Society*
CSMC	*Publications of the Colonial Society of Massachusetts, Collections*
ECPR	Essex County Probate Records. Essex County Courthouse, Salem, Mass.
EIHC	*Essex Institute Historical Collections*
EQC	George Francis Dow and Mary G. Thresher, eds. *Records and Files of the Quarterly Courts of Essex County, Massachusetts, 1636–1686.* 9 vols. Salem, Mass.: Essex Institute, 1911–21, 1975
MAE	Massachusetts Archives, Bound Manuscripts, Ecclesiastical. Judicial Archives at the Massachusetts Archives, Boston, Mass.
MCC	Middlesex County, County Court Records (including the "Folio Collection"). Judicial Archives at the Massachusetts Archives, Boston
MCPR	Middlesex County Manuscript Probate Records. County Courthouse, Cambridge, Mass. Microfilm
NEHGR	*New England Historic Genealogical Register*
NEQ	*New England Quarterly*
PMHS	*Proceedings of the Massachusetts Historical Society*
RIHSC	*Rhode Island Historical Society Collections*
RIYM	Society of Friends. Rhode Island Yearly Meeting Records. New England Yearly Meeting Archive. Rhode Island Historical Society Library, Providence, R.I.
RMB	Nathaniel B. Shurtleff, ed. *Records of the Governor and Company of the Massachusetts Bay in New England.* 5 vols. in 6. Boston, 1853–4. Reprint. New York: AMS Press, 1968
SCC	Suffolk County Records. Judicial Archives at the Massachusetts Archives, Boston
SCPR	Suffolk County Manuscript Probate Records. Boston Public Library, Boston. Microfilm

Abbreviations used in the footnotes

SMM   Society of Friends. Salem Monthly Meeting Records. New England Yearly Meeting Archive. Rhode Island Historical Society Library, Providence, R.I. (only the men's monthly meeting records are extant before 1767; for the records beginning in 1767, references distinguish between men's and women's meetings)

SQM   Society of Friends. Salem Quarterly Meeting Records. New England Yearly Meeting Archive. Rhode Island Historical Society Library, Providence, R.I.

WMQ   *William and Mary Quarterly*

Archives

AAS   American Antiquarian Society, Worcester, Mass.
ANTS   Franklin Trask Library, Andover Newton Theological Seminary, Newton, Mass.
LHS   Lynn Historical Society, Lynn, Mass.
LSF   Library of the Society of Friends, Friends' House, London
MA   Massachusetts Archive, Boston
MHS   Massachusetts Historical Society Library, Boston
NEHGS   New England Historical Genealogical Society Library, Boston
RIHS   Rhode Island Historical Society Library, Providence, R.I.

Introduction

History of dissent and the orthodox response, 1630–55

The founders of colonial Massachusetts spent their first decades in the New World working to erect a godly commonwealth in accordance with their understanding of God's plan for his people. They struggled to forge an orthodox consensus informed both by their concerns as Puritan reformers within the Church of England and by the needs arising from their attempt to organize righteous churches in the wilderness. As they labored to create institutions that would promote spiritual purity and social stability, the leaders of Massachusetts confronted challenges on two fronts. Accused of excessive timidity by those with a more radical vision and of extremism by those who believed a more modest reformation appropriate, the colony's leaders attempted to chart a middle course through these conflicting options.

In doing so, they staked out a position within the Anglo-Puritan community that they would attempt to defend in ensuing years. The earliest of these threats arose during the initial decade of settlement, as two reputedly godly residents led movements denouncing what they saw as the colony's failure to implement divine directives. In responding to the criticisms of Roger Williams and Anne Hutchinson, the colony's leaders declared their unwillingness to embrace the separatism and mysticism these radicals advocated. The second significant threat to the emerging New England way came from the presbyterian branch of the English Puritan party, whose reform program departed less decisively from the Anglican church. Far from finding Massachusetts orthodoxy too timid, Presbyterians thought the colonial establishment too radical. This challenge proved more difficult to overcome because presbyterianism – which by the 1640s had powerful advocates in England – shared much common ground with the orthodox establishment and its proponents were not as easily dismissed as Williams and Hutchinson had been. Although the leaders of the Bay colony would eventually make some compromises with their presbyterian brethren, they continued to maintain a position between them and the radical Puritan faction. Their efforts to create stable and godly communities succeeded remarkably well, in spite of such criticisms.

Only toward the end of the civil war and interregnum years would the architects of the New England way confront the far more serious threat posed by the introduction of radical sectarianism. Since the late 1640s, England had witnessed an unprecedented rise in religious and political extremism. The ominous growth of radicalism in England had further encouraged colonial leaders to make peace with their presbyterian brethren. The Bay colony, long sheltered from these stormy developments, finally felt their full force with the arrival of Quaker witnesses in the colony in 1656. In the late 1650s, as the English gentry was beginning to suppress radical activity at home, indigenous radicalism would become a major problem in orthodox New England for the first time. The response of the Bay colony to first the Quakers and later the Baptists was shaped by its previous experiences in dealing with the criticisms of Roger Williams, Anne Hutchinson, and the Presbyterians of old and New England. In some respects, the defenders of orthodoxy inadvertently paved the way for the creation of local sectarian movements.

The first sustained opposition to the nascent establishment coalesced around the promising young minister Roger Williams, who became teacher of Salem Church in 1634. Williams advocated that all the Bay colony churches declare their formal separation from the Church of England. In making this argument, he was promulgating a view that had guided the creation of a number of independent congregations in England as well as among English exiles on the European continent and in neighboring Plymouth Plantation.[1] Adopting a position usually associated with the separatist stance, Williams also objected to the idea that a magistrate should suppress dissent, coerce church attendance, or otherwise protect religion. The concern for church purity that underlay both of these views also led Williams to advocate the veiling of women at worship service, which he believed was a practice of the primitive churches. For his offensive ideas and his refusal to keep them to himself, the magistrates banished Williams in 1636. At that time, he traveled south to what would become the Rhode Island and Providence Plantations, where his belief in "soul liberty" would turn that settlement into "the Sinke into which all the Rest of the Colonyes empty their Hereticks."[2]

Anne Hutchinson, the leader of the second movement to disrupt the Bay colony in the 1630s, would be forced to follow Williams south two years later, after the government banished her for her objectionable views. A substantial matron, Hutchinson criticized the preaching of many of the colony's ministers, for she believed that they were encouraging a dangerous reliance on human activity in bringing about salvation.[3] She voiced these objections in private

---

[1] The best discussion of Williams's views on these issues remains Edmund S. Morgan, *Roger Williams: The Church and the State* (New York: Harcourt, Brace & World, 1967).

[2] John Woodbridge, Jr., to Richard Baxter, in "Woodbridge–Baxter Correspondence," ed. Raymond Phineas Stearns, *NEQ* 10 (1937): 573.

[3] The literature on Hutchinson is voluminous. For a brief summary of her views, see E. Brooks

meetings held in her Boston home, meetings attended by both men and women who came to hear her discuss the weekly sermons. The informal doctrinal discussions in which the Hutchinsonians so eagerly participated were a continuation of English Puritan practices, but their opponents believed that the doctrines upheld in the Bay colony's churches – unlike those of the Anglican church – did not deserve the critical comment of the laity.[4] Furthermore, Hutchinson's ministry raised questions about the proper role of lay people in the church, and the fact of her gender framed the issue in particularly controversial terms. Ousting Hutchinson necessitated a political struggle, for her male supporters included a number of powerful colonists. But the General Court was eventually able to banish her, along with some of her followers, in 1637. Boston Church excommunicated her the following spring, after which she left the colony.

In rejecting Williams and Hutchinson, colonial leaders were not dismissing the concerns for church purity and biblical primitivism, the desire for an intense spiritual experience, or the eagerness to have the laity take an active role in the religious affairs that had inspired the dissent of these rebels. Rather, their vision of orthodoxy was designed to steer a middle course between the radical positions these dissidents advocated and the more conservative views of the Anglican church.[5] The colony's "non-separatist" congregationalism, as Perry Miller called it, rejected the ceremony, hierarchy, and inclusiveness of the Church of England while continuing to hold out hope for the reformation of the national church. Although the experience with Hutchinson suggested that lay participation in public religious discourse should be carefully monitored, the ministry recognized the importance of lay involvement in the governing of individual

---

Holifield, *Era of Persuasion: American Thought and Culture 1521–1680* (Boston: Twayne, 1989), 116–18.

[4] A number of scholars have argued recently that Hutchinson was reacting to the changes Puritanism was experiencing in the New World; see Harry S. Stout, "Word and Order in Colonial New England," in *The Bible in America: Essays in Cultural History*, ed. Nathan O. Hatch and Mark A. Noll (New York: Oxford University Press, 1982), 20, 23–6, 31–3; Amy Schrager Lang, *Prophetic Woman: Anne Hutchinson and the Problem of Dissent in the Literature of New England* (Berkeley and Los Angeles: University of California Press, 1987), 37, 33. Andrew Delbanco goes farther, arguing that Hutchinsonians were upholding true Puritanism; *The Puritan Ordeal* (Cambridge, Mass.: Harvard University Press, 1989), especially 203–4.

[5] William K. B. Stoever, *A Faire and Easie Way to Heaven: Covenant Theology and Antinomianism in Early Massachusetts* (Middletown, Conn.: Wesleyan University Press, 1978). The founders had to suppress allegiance to Anglicanism in the town of Weymouth, which had been settled in the 1620s, prior to the Puritan migration; see William Hyde, "The Early History of Weymouth," in *History of Weymouth, Massachusetts*, 4 vols. (Boston, 1923), 1:98–100. Some scholars have misread the evidence as involving a fight over Baptist views; compare David Benedict, *A General History of the Baptist Denomination in America* (New York, 1850), 369, to Isaac Backus, *History of New England*, ed. David Weston, 2 vols. (Newton, Mass., 1871; reprint ed., New York: Arno, 1969), 1:93–4; the latter was originally published as *A History of New England With Particular Reference to the Denomination Called Baptists*, 3 vols. (Boston, 1777–96). Weston's addition to note 2, page 94, encourages this misreading.

congregations. Furthermore, Bay colonists placed more emphasis on the autonomy of each congregation than did their brethren who supported the Scottish
presbyterian system. The practices of limiting church membership to those who
appeared to be among the elect and of limiting political participation to those
men who were church members were intended to ensure the purity of the
church as well as the godliness of the civil government.[6] Like Williams and
Hutchinson, the architects of Massachusetts orthodoxy justified their system
with reference to scriptural example. They hoped, in the aftermath of these
incidents, that the godly impulses toward purity, piety, lay involvement, and
biblicism could subsequently be contained within the church order erected in
the colony. Regardless, they were resolved to thwart any attacks on that order
in the future, just as they had in the cases of Williams and Hutchinson.

While the establishment did succeed in giving expression to the radical impulses inherent in the Puritan movement to the satisfaction of most colonists,
the temptation to leave the orthodox fold to satisfy a desire for further church
purity, lay activism, and strict biblicism remained. "Anabaptism" – which one
minister declared "the Vexation and Clog of Reformation ever since the beginning of it" – was the most popular choice among colonists who felt this temptation during the years after Williams and Hutchinson had been dispatched.[7]
Anabaptists, as Baptists were then derisively called, limited church membership
to adult believers.[8] Typical sectarians, they viewed these pure churches as necessarily estranged from the sinful, larger society. As a result, they denied the
state any power over matters of conscience, which gave rise to their support for
freedom of religion. Seventeenth-century commentators criticized anyone who
strove for greater church purity than they themselves considered necessary by
linking them with the Anabaptist heresy: Tarred with that brush by Anglicans
and Presbyterians, the founders of Massachusetts accused separatists in turn.[9]

The defenders of New England orthodoxy appreciated that the Baptist faith
could snare the godly colonist, acknowledging that the scriptural basis for infant
baptism was complicated. They were sympathetic to those who "scrupled" infant baptism and only urged them to keep their uncertainties private. However,
the public advocacy of Baptist views – whether opposition to infant baptism or
the more pronounced support for adult baptism – demanded the attention of

---

[6] In fact, the Bay colony's position on this issue was too extreme for some people – such as Thomas
Hooker, founder of Connecticut – who were otherwise in agreement with the system.

[7] Jonathan Mitchell, *An Answer to the Apologetical Preface Published in the Name and Behalf of the
Brethren that Dissented in the Late Synod* (Cambridge, 1664), 6. Anabaptism was somewhat akin to
the separatism of Williams; he would become a Baptist briefly in 1639.

[8] Baptist beliefs are reviewed in Philip F. Gura, *A Glimpse of Sion's Glory: Puritan Raidicalism in
New England, 1620–1660* (Middletown, Conn.: Wesleyan University Press, 1984), 94–6.

[9] John Winthrop suggested that Roger Williams had been a closet Anabaptist in his separatist
phase; see *Winthrop's Journal, "History of New England" 1630–1649*, ed. James Kendall Hosmer,
2 vols. (New York: Scribner, 1908), 1:297.

the authorities, who were concerned to prevent other colonists from being infected.

Only a small number of cases of Anabaptism – twenty-six – have come to light for the period between 1639 and 1654.[10] Some of these dissidents were undoubtedly influenced by the burgeoning Baptist movement in England and Rhode Island.[11] At the same time, they continued and extended a tradition within the Bay colony itself of lay support for the more radical aspects of Puritanism. The first person known to have been publicly associated with believer's baptism in the colony was William Walcott; he was, appropriately, a Salem resident who soon traveled to Providence to join with Williams, his former minister, in the newly founded Baptist church there.[12] The most spectacular conversion became public in 1653, when Harvard president Henry Dunster began freely espousing Baptist views; like William Walcott, Dunster left the colony in search of spiritual fellowship and freedom to practice his newfound faith.[13] Because those publicly associated with antipedobaptism were few, un-

---

[10] Only one known case occurred in 1639 (rather than two, as has been generally believed, see note 12). In addition, the 1638 case involving Seth Sweetser did not, in fact, take place; see note 59. After the 1639 case, instances of Anabaptist sentiment appear in the records again in 1642, peaking in 1646 with a total of eight. Subsequently, cases dropped off rapidly, recurring only in 1649 (2), 1651 (3), and 1653 (2). The peak in 1646 may have resulted from a concerted effort to root out antipedobaptists in that year, which also witnessed the passage of a new heresy law and the meeting of the Cambridge Synod. The vast majority of cases (20) occurred in Essex County, especially Salem and Lynn (16 of the 17 for which the town of residence can be determined). Marblehead, Watertown, Charlestown, Cambridge, Boston, Reading, and Hingham had at least one each.

See *EQC*, vol. 1; Ernest W. Baughman, "Excommunications and Banishments from the First Church in Salem and the Town of Salem, 1629–1680," *EIHC* 113 (1977): 97–8; Gura, *Glimpse of Sion's Glory*, 110–11; William G. McLoughlin, *New England Dissent, 1630–1833: The Baptists and the Separation of Church and State*, 2 vols. (Cambridge, Mass.: Harvard University Press, 1971), 16–17; Joseph B. Felt, *The Ecclesiastical History of New England*, 2 vols. (Boston, 1862), 2:12, 46; Thomas Cobbet, "A Brief Answer to a Scandalous Pamphlet," appendix to *The Civil Magistrates Power in Matters of Religion* (London, 1653), 39; and Middlesex County Court Records, trans. David Pulsifer (1851), Judicial Archives at MA, 1:37, 45, 51 [hereafter cited as Pulsifer Transcript]. Also see "The Autobiographical Memoranda of John Brock, 1636–1659," ed. Clifford K. Shipton, *Proceedings of the American Antiquarian Society*, n.s., 53 (1943): 101, for the timing of the increase in the heresy.

[11] Baptist tracts were circulating in Massachusetts by at least the mid-1640s; see John Cotton, "To The Reader," in *The Grounds and Ends of the Baptisme of the Children of the Faithfull* (London, 1647), n.p.; *Winthrop's Journal*, ed. Hosmer, 2:257.

[12] Gura, *Glimpse of Sion's Glory*, 105–6; Sidney Perley, *The History of Salem, Massachusetts, 1626–1716*, 3 vols. (Salem: Essex Institute, 1924–8), 1:271–2. Gura has Walcott joined in this stance by William Wickenden; however, according to the work Gura cites for this information, Wickenden had already removed to Providence when he publicly embraced the position. See Samuel Gorton, *Simplicities Defence against Seven-Headed Policy* (1646), reprinted in Rhode Island Historical Society, *Collections* 2 (Providence, 1835), 109n.

[13] Jeremiah Chaplin, *Life of Henry Dunster: First President of Harvard College* (Boston, 1827). Typically, the authorities would attempt to dissuade the openly heterodox; failing that, they urged

organized, and generally willing to cooperate with the measures taken to rid the colony of their views, their dissent did not pose a significant threat during the 1640s or 1650s. Only after the orthodox faith introduced modifications in its own practice of the ordinance of baptism would this scattered Anabaptist sentiment coalesce into a sectarian movement.[14]

During the 1640s, the major challenge to the standing order in Massachusetts – and one that shaped its response to the handful of Anabaptists in its midst – was mounted by the increasingly powerful presbyterian branch of the English Puritan movement. Beginning in the late 1630s, religious reformers who advocated reorganizing the Church of England along the lines of the Scottish national church criticized the congregational system in New England's largest colony. According to these critics, individual congregations should be subservient to a centralized presbytery that made decisions regarding church polity and doctrine. Furthermore, Presbyterians rejected the effort to create pure churches composed only of "visible saints," arguing instead that church membership should be available to any reputedly upright person. Adopting these practices would have moved the churches of Massachusetts back in the direction of Anglicanism, with its hierarchic structure and its inclusive parish system of membership. In both private correspondence and published treatises, English Presbyterians and New English Congregationalists debated their respective church orders vigorously for a decade.[15] The debate took on added urgency after civil war broke out in 1642, because these critics of New England orthodoxy temporarily gained ascendance in England. Emboldened by the success of their allies at home, colonists with presbyterian sympathies attempted to pressure the government into modifying the standing order, especially the church membership requirement for the franchise. Two Bay colony churches inclined toward presbyterianism, and ministers from the other churches struggled over how to maintain congregational autonomy while suppressing the unconventional practices of these churches.[16]

them to keep silent. For those who continued intransigent, an effort was made to persuade them to leave of their own volition. Dunster's particularly well documented case proceeded in this way. Banishment, provided for by a 1642 law, was not used until a Baptist church was actually gathered in the colony in the 1660s. Of the twenty-six cases previously discussed, only two colonists – William Witter of Lynn and Christopher Goodwin of Charlestown – are known to have made their objectionable beliefs public again. Presumably, the others were successfully dissuaded, silenced, or persuaded to leave.

[14] The distinction between dissidents and sectarians, developed by Jon Butler, is applicable here; the former – like the radicals of the pre-1656 era – are only critical of the prevailing system, while sectarians – who would organize after 1656 – erect a new one. See his "The Origins of American Denominational Order," American Philosophical Society, Transactions 68 (1978), 8.

[15] For a summary of the points at issue, see Perry Miller, The New England Mind, vol. 2: From Colony to Province (Cambridge, Mass.: Harvard University Press, 1953; Boston: Beacon, 1961), 68–81. A good example is discussed by Larzer Ziff, Introduction, in John Cotton on the Churches of New England (Cambridge, Mass.: Harvard University Press, 1968), 31–4.

[16] John J. Waters, "Hingham, Massachusetts, 1631–1661: An East Anglican Oligarchy in the New

The presbyterian challenge was clearly pivotal during the 1640s. Although Philip Gura has argued that the radical Puritan threat continued to shape orthodoxy throughout this period, the radical influence was – for the time being – less than the conservative one.[17] Largely in response to the presbyterian critique, the Massachusetts establishment codified its ecclesiastical system in the Cambridge Platform, and leading ministers issued significant statements outlining congregational polity.[18] The vigorous church admission procedures instituted in the 1640s under the guidance of John Cotton were developed partially in response to the Presbyterians' comparatively inclusive policy.[19] The criticisms made by their more conservative brethren even encouraged orthodox efforts to root out and punish Baptists, for Presbyterians claimed that the New England way – with its restricted church membership and high level of lay involvement – fostered Anabaptism.[20] And the trend toward limiting the role of the laity, which had begun in the aftermath of the Hutchinson affair, continued during these years; restricting opportunities for lay members to speak during worship services served to weaken allegations of congregational radicalism.[21] With various radical tendencies within the Puritan movement decisively rejected during the 1630s, the major battle of the 1640s was fought on the other front, against the advocates of a comparatively hierarchic and inclusive church order. The skirmishes against Anabaptists were minor by comparison during these years.

If the criticisms of Presbyterians were distressing to Bay colony leaders, the failure of that party to retain control of England led to still more ominous developments, which raised the specter of radicalism and anarchy. In the late 1640s, events in England took a troubling turn, in the view of the godly ortho-

World," *Journal of Social History* 1 (1968): 351–70; Williston Walker, *The Creeds and Platforms of Congregationalism* (New York, 1893; Philadelphia: Pilgrim Press, 1960), 138–9, 159–71.

[17] See Gura, *Glimpse of Sion's Glory*. Besides those who took heterodox positions on baptism and the few people who were influenced by the Gortonists, he cites very few cases of radical activity in Massachusetts from the late 1630s until the arrival of the Quakers in 1656.

[18] The text of the Cambridge Platform is provided in Walker, *Creeds and Platforms*, 194–237. John Cotton, *The Way of Congregational Churches Cleared* (London, 1648).

[19] Normal Petit, *The Heart Prepared: Grace and Conversion in Puritan Spiritual Life* (New Haven, Conn.: Yale University Press, 1966), 161.

[20] Robert Child et al., Remonstrance and Petition, in *The Hutchinson Papers*, 2 vols. (Boston, 1769; reprint ed., Albany: Publications of the Prince Society, 1865), 1:221; Robert Mascall to Captain James Oliver, 25 March 1669, in Backus, *History*, 1:311–13.

[21] David D. Hall, *The Faithful Shepherd: A History of the New England Ministry in the Seventeenth Century* (Chapel Hill: University of North Carolina Press, 1972), 90–4, 110–11. James F. Cooper disagrees with Hall on the impact of the Hutchinsonian controversy but finds a decline in the lay role eventually; see "Anne Hutchinson and the 'Lay Rebellion' against the Clergy," *NEQ* 61 (1988), 392–7. Also see Barbara Ritter Dailey's account of the Bachiler party in "The Itinerant Preacher and the Social Network in Seventeenth-Century New England," in *The Dublin Seminar for New England Folklife: Annual Proceedings 1984*, ed. Peter Benes (Boston: Boston University Press, 1986), 45.

dox on the other side of the Atlantic. By that time, the presbyterian effort to redesign the English national church had foundered. The rise of a plethora of radical movements, the execution of the king, and Oliver Cromwell's policy of toleration all contributed to the creation of an unprecedented situation in England, one that was alien to the colonists in orthodox New England. Having recently defended themselves against charges of fostering radicalism with their congregationalist church order, Bay colonists suddenly found themselves denounced for their conservative intolerance. According to one of their radical critics, repressive New England was becoming old at the same time as increasingly tolerant old England was becoming new.[22] The leaders of the Bay colony watched events in their homeland with fascination and alarm, safeguarded their policy of intolerance against all assailants, and shored up their defenses against dissent. Through it all, they thanked God that the civil and religious system that they had erected prevented their colony from sliding into the anarchy that had overtaken England.

In the decisively different context of Massachusetts, the impact of radicalism was comparatively limited. Some scholars, most recently Philip Gura and David Lovejoy, have argued that the "free aire of the New World" encouraged the expression of the full spectrum of radical views.[23] Although in tolerant Rhode Island colonists were free to embrace Anabaptism, Gortonism, and Quakerism, orthodox New England did not foster such extremism. Popular radicalism in the areas under orthodox control was generally limited to the occasional case of hostility to some aspect of the established faith, with opposition to infant baptism the most focused criticism made. Regions on the periphery of the colony were more likely to be "infected" with heterodox views, presumably as a result of extensive contact with radicals in the settlements that bordered on Massachusetts, Connecticut, and New Haven.[24]

The unprecedented situation in the British Isles fostered an outpouring of subversive sentiments while circumstances in the orthodox New England colonies militated against such a development. The growth of extremism in England occurred with the downfall of the increasingly repressive Laudian Church of England and in the context of failed Puritan efforts to establish a reformed national church in its place.[25] The "internal dynamic" of the Puritan movement

---

[22] John Clarke, *Ill Newes from New-England* (London, 1652), title page.

[23] Gura, *Glimpse of Sion's Glory;* David S. Lovejoy, *Religious Enthusiasm in the New World* (Cambridge, Mass.: Harvard University Press, 1985).

[24] Stephen Foster makes this observation with regard to the Quakers; "English Puritanism and the Progress of English Institutions, 1630–1660," in *Saints and Revolutionaries: Essays on Early American History,* ed. David D. Hall, John M. Murrin, and Thad W. Tate (New York: Norton, 1984), 32.

[25] William Haller made the point that once they had failed to reform the Church of England, the Elizabethan Puritans began inadvertently to lay the groundwork for more radical positions by criticizing the church hierarchy and advocating lay initiative in spiritual affairs; *The Rise of Puritanism* (New York: Columbia University Press, 1938), esp. ch. 5.

might propel people completely out of mainstream Puritanism into the Baptist faith and even – perhaps – beyond it, as scholars have argued, particularly with regard to civil war and interregnum England.[26] But the successful institutionalization of a Puritan polity could provide an adequate forum for the expression of potentially radical tendencies.[27] In Massachusetts, where Puritan reformers were in control from the outset, the largest identifiably disgruntled element in the population was concerned to protect traditional features of the New England way against innovations suggested by the ministry. For instance, the laity – comparatively uninterested in exploring the sectarians' more extreme version of the pure church – cared passionately about the purity of their congregational churches.[28]

Observing events in England with horror, the defenders of orthodoxy in the Bay colony moved to prevent the heresies rampant there from infecting their colony. Never complacent, they refused to rely solely on the orthodox inclinations of the populace in their campaign to protect the New England way. Their traditional strategies for dealing with dissent were fortified during these years with new legislation specifically outlawing Anabaptism (1644), the works of John Reeves and Lodowick Muggleton (1654), Quakerism (1656), and a host of less specific threats.[29] The authorities briefly and unsuccessfully tested a new approach when they sent troops beyond the borders of the Bay colony to arrest Samuel Gorton and some of his followers in 1643. After sentencing the group to hard labor in seven towns, the magistrates were distressed to find that the "Gortonists" had succeeded in leading a number of residents astray with their views. Although apparently few colonists were permanently lost to this heresy, the incident underscored the wisdom of removing heretics who could not be silenced.[30] By the mid-1650s, the standing order had developed successful

---

[26] James Fulton Maclear, "The Making of the Lay Tradition," *Journal of Religion* 33 (1953): 113–36, esp. 119, 129; Alan Simpson, *Puritanism in Old and New England* (Chicago: University of Chicago Press, 1955), ch. 1; Hugh Barbour, *The Quakers in Puritan England* (New Haven, Conn.: Yale University Press, 1964), ch. 1; David D. Hall, "Understanding the Puritans," in *The State of American History*, ed. Herbert J. Bass (Chicago: Quadrangle, 1970), 331–2.

[27] The situation in seventeenth-century Amsterdam, where English residents were free to choose among nonseparating congregationalist, separatist, and Anabaptist options, was similar to Massachusetts in this respect; see Keith Sprunger, "English Puritans and Anabaptists," *Mennonite Quarterly Review* 46 (1972), 113–28.

[28] Foster, "Progress of English Institutions," 9; also see Baird Tipson, "Samuel Stone's Discourse Against Requiring Church Relations," *WMQ*, 3d ser., 46 (1989): 790–4. Lay opposition to the halfway covenant – discussed later – was also based on this concern.

[29] *RMB*, 2:85; 3:356; 4, pt. 1:277–8; also 3:98–102, 259–60.

[30] Robert Emmet Wall, *Massachusetts Bay: The Crucial Decade, 1640–1650* (New Haven, Conn.: Yale University Press, 1972), ch. 4. Only Eleanor Truslar of Salem is known to have been punished for holding Gortonist views (*EQC* 1:68). John Endecott was possibly referring to her when he suggested that an example be made of a vocal Gorton supporter in Salem; see Endecott to John Winthrop, 22 April 1644, in *Winthrop Papers*, vol. 4: *1638–1644* (Boston: Massachusetts Historical Society, 1944), 456.

mechanisms of suppression and was primed to respond vigorously to the Quaker witnesses who would arrive shortly.

Establishment concern to protect the colony from radical influences may have fueled a trend toward conservatism in orthodox church polity. During the civil war and interregnum years, the churches curtailed opportunities for lay preaching, the power of the ministry increased, and synods that met to establish a common position on points of doctrine and practice became a frequent occurrence. In addition, ministers and lay elders meeting in these synods seriously broached the possibility of expanding church membership to include the grandchildren of the elect – an innovation that tended toward the more inclusive practices of Presbyterians and Anglicans.[31]

Arguably, these changes could be explained as the result of the institutionalization of the Puritan faith in the process of becoming an established church, as some scholars – most notably H. Richard Niebuhr – have suggested.[32] The changing attitude toward lay discussions of doctrinal matters offers one case in point. In England, where Puritans attempted to practice their faith in the context of an established church indifferent if not hostile to their cause, private meetings (which were not always conducted under ministerial oversight) were of paramount importance. Lay people became accustomed to discussing theological matters and, somewhat inadvertently, learned to be critical of those in official positions in the church hierarchy. Anne Hutchinson may have assumed that such discourse would become all the more possible in a Puritan-run colony, and she exercised the critical faculties that had previously been turned against the Laudian clergy in her attacks on the colony's ministers. But, in the context of a Puritan religious establishment, such practices subverted – rather than supported – godliness. In New England, the ministers who had encouraged English conventicles either opposed unsupervised lay discussion or worked to shift lay gatherings from a focus on doctrinal to devotional matters.[33] The changing nature of Puritanism in the early years of the Bay colony can be explained largely with reference to the process of a reform movement becoming an establishment.[34]

---

[31] See the works cited in note 21 as well as Hall, *Faithful Shepherd*, generally. For the discussions of baptism during this period, see Robert G. Pope, *The Half-Way Covenant: Church Membership in Puritan New England* (Princeton, N.J.: Princeton University Press, 1969), ch. 1.

[32] See especially H. Richard Niebuhr, *The Kingdom of God in America* (New York: Harper & Row, 1937), ch. 5. Pope has dealt with the halfway covenant in this way; see *Half-Way Covenant*, 261–2.

[33] See Thomas Cobbet, *A Just Vindication of the Covenant and Church-Estate of Children of Church-Members* (London, 1648), A2v–A3; also see *Records of the Colony or Jurisdiction of New Haven . . . 1653, to the union* (Hartford, Conn., 1858), 244, 245.

[34] Stephen Foster puts this process in a transatlantic perspective in "The Godly in Transit: English Popular Protestantism and the Creation of a Puritan Establishment in America," in *Seventeenth-Century New England*, ed. David D. Hall and David Grayson Allen (Boston: The Colonial Society of Massachusetts, 1984), esp. 211–15, 237.

Still, the specter of religious turmoil in England did provide further impetus for these changes. The need to protect the colony from radical outsiders, rather than from sizable numbers of rebels already present within the colony, added urgency to the reforms advocated by the defenders of orthodoxy.[35] This focus on the dangers of nonresident radicalism would prove well founded. Quaker missionaries – proponents of one of the most distressing of the new heresies – would launch an "invasion" that led to the "convincement" of a few dozen colonists after 1656.

In the process of strengthening its defenses against foreign subversion, the establishment inadvertently prepared the way for the rise of sectarianism within the colony. Two of the sects active in England would be successfully planted in the Bay colony during the seventeenth century. The colonists who would join the Quaker or Baptist movements in the decades after 1656 were reacting against changes that were taking place within the orthodox establishment. While the Quakers were disaffected in a general way by the institutionalization that occurred in the New World setting, the Baptists criticized specific features of orthodoxy, particularly changes in the ordinance of baptism. Once the English Puritan movement had matured into a New English religious establishment, the stage was set for the development of the modest but tenacious sectarian movements of the era after 1657. The story of religious radicalism in colonial New England was not ending while events in England were taking a more conservative turn, as Philip Gura has argued, but rather, only beginning.[36]

The emergence of the Quaker and Baptist movements

Despite similarities in their legal status and the timing of their emergence within Massachusetts, the Quaker and Baptist movements related to the orthodox community in diametrically opposed ways. Espousing Quakerism entailed a fairly thorough rejection of the established faith, for the Quakers dismissed many beliefs basic to English Puritanism. In contrast, Baptists retained most of the beliefs and practices of the orthodox churches. They disagreed vehemently on such significant but secondary matters as who ought to preach or receive baptism. Unlike the Baptist faith – which had a marginal existence in England before the founding of the Bay colony – Quakerism arose in the early 1650s in response to the disruption caused by civil war.[37] Among the most extreme of

---

[35] In *Glimpse of Sion's Glory*, Gura gives the impression that radicals were constantly active everywhere in New England between 1629 and 1660. Separating his evidence for agitation within the confines of the Bay colony from that occurring outside of it and noting the limited success of the nonresident radicals who visited the colony to proselytize gives a different picture of the extent of radicalism among the laity in Massachusetts.

[36] Gura, *Glimpse of Sion's Glory*, 13.

[37] On early English Baptists, see A. C. Underwood, *A History of the English Baptists* (London: Kingsgate, 1947); D. Mervyn Himbury, *British Baptists: A Short History* (London: Kingsgate,

the civil war sects, the initially disorganized Quakers shocked English and New English Puritans as well as most Baptists by minimizing the role of Scriptures, elevating the potential worth of human nature, and advocating preaching by women and children. Of necessity, this alien sect was introduced to the colony by Quaker missionaries. Baptists arrived at their dissenting views without similar encouragement from their English counterparts. While resident Anabaptists remained in dialogue with orthodoxy – however heated these debates might become – Quakers resolutely turned away from the discussion.

Embracing Quakerism necessitated a renunciation of the faith of the larger community. The Quakers did share a few characteristics with their orthodox neighbors, most notably the millennialism many Puritans had in common with more radical groups.[38] To a limited extent, Anne Hutchinson's concern for free grace can be compared to the Quaker emphasis on the light within. Although the two concepts are theologically different and the Quakers rejected fundamental beliefs that Hutchinson and her detractors shared, the desire for a mystical union with God was similar in both the Hutchinsonian variant of Puritanism and Quakerism.[39] The early Quakers, however, dismissed predestination and the reliance on Scriptures – two tenets basic to Puritanism in old and New England – in favor of a universally shared inner light that offered guidance superior to that found in the Bible. Furthermore, Quakerism provided the faithful with a role in religious observances unprecedented in New England, far beyond even what Hutchinson had suggested. To one orthodox opponent, the Quaker faith seemed so bizarre that he concluded that it must require adherents to "cast off all attendances to ordinances, as public preaching, praying, reading the Scriptures, and attending to times of God's worship, and then wait for the communication of this power [or light within]." Salem magistrate William Hathorne was certain that, under such circumstances, "it will not be long that the Devil will appear."[40] In belief and practice, the Quaker faith represented a

---

1962); and J. F. McGregor, "The Baptists: Font of All Heresy," in *Radical Religion in the English Revolution*, ed. J. F. McGregor and B. Reay (Oxford University Press, 1984), 23–63. The standard work on the early Quakers – who have been more extensively studied – is William C. Braithwaite, *The Beginnings of Quakerism* (New York: Macmillan, 1923), and the most recent is Barry Reay, *The Quakers and the English Revolution* (London: Temple Smith, 1985).

[38] See Reay, *Quakers and the English Revolution*, ch. 5; also J. F. Maclear, "New England and the Fifth Monarchy: The Quest for the Millennium in Early American Puritanism," *WMQ*, 3d ser., 32 (1975), 223–60.

[39] James Fulton Maclear, " 'The Heart of New England Rent': the Mystical Element in Early Puritan History," *Mississippi Valley Historical Review* 42 (1956): 621–52. Hutchinson's positions were similar to (if not the same as) those of John Cotton, while the Quakers were beyond the pale as far as all Puritan divines were concerned. Theodore Dwight Bozeman would have us revise this view to account for similarities between Hutchinson and the Quakers and differences between the former and her adversaries in Massachusetts; see *To Live Ancient Lives: The Primitivist Dimension in Puritanism* (Chapel Hill: University of North Carolina Press, 1988), 367–8.

[40] Quoted in George E. Ellis, *The Puritan Age and Rule in the Colony of Massachusetts Bay, 1629–1685* (Boston, 1888), 452n.

radical departure from – rather than, as scholars once argued, a continuation of – the established faith in Massachusetts.[41] Residents who abandoned orthodoxy to join this mystical, millennialistic movement took an extreme step, arguably even more so than did their counterparts in England, where the world seemed to have been "turned upside down."

The colonists who became Quakers clearly experienced disaffection from the orthodox establishment. Most of the convinced Quakers in New England lived beyond the bounds of orthodoxy: in Rhode Island, with its history of radicalism; in separatist Plymouth, with its chronic ministerial shortage; on Long Island, with its ethnically and religiously diverse population; and, eventually, on the eastern frontier, in New Hampshire and Maine.[42] The greater willingness of people in these regions to become Quakers was linked to the fact that the periphery had earlier drawn those who were uninterested if not outright opposed to the orthodox experiment.[43]

Within the Bay colony, the overwhelming concentration of Quakers resided in Salem, where separatist, Hutchinsonian, Anabaptist, Gortonist, and possibly even proto-presbyterian sentiments, taken together, had been more strongly expressed than in any other town.[44] Founded on the eve of the Great Migration, Salem gathered its church without the advice and counsel of the leading divines who would shortly begin arriving in the colony. With this freedom, the saints of Salem had displayed a sympathy for more radical practices than the colonial majority would eventually sanction. In addition, Salem incorporated a sizable group of migrants who had been living in the region previously and who did not necessarily share the religious proclivities of most later settlers. These cir-

---

[41] An emphasis on similarities can be traced to Geoffrey F. Nuttall, who presented Quakers, Baptists, and separatists as well as Presbyterians and Independents (or Congregationalists) as Puritans; *The Holy Spirit in Puritan Faith and Experience* (Oxford: Blackwell Publisher, 1946). Gura follows him in this in *Glimpse of Sion's Glory*. The literature making the case for discontinuity between Puritans and Quakers is larger and growing. See especially Melvin B. Endy, Jr., "Puritanism, Spiritualism and Quakerism: An Historiographical Essay," in *The World of William Penn*, ed. Richard S. Dunn and Mary Maples Dunn (Philadelphia: University of Pennsylvania Press, 1986), 281–301; also Bozeman, *To Live Ancient Lives*, 364–8.

[42] Cotton Mather explained that Quakerism was successful in such "sinful areas" because "it advances and exaults man"; *Little Flocks Guarded Against Grievous Wolves* (Boston, 1691), 108.

[43] For a small group of settlers with radical inclination who could not find a permanent residence within the Bay colony – despite years of trying one town after another – see Dailey's account of the Bachiler party in "The Itinerant Preacher and the Social Network," 39–42. That group was unusual in moving around within the colony for as long as it did.

[44] In addition to the incidents previously discussed involving Williams and separatism, Anabaptism, and Gortonism, Salem residents were second only to Bostonians in numbers that supported Hutchinson (see Emery Battis, *Saints and Sectaries: Anne Hutchinson and the Antinomian Controversy in the Massachusetts Bay Colony* [Chapel Hill: University of North Carolina Press, 1962], 304–28). Samuel Symonds reported support among some Salem residents (especially young men and women) for the remonstrance; Symonds to John Winthrop, 6 January 1646–7, in *Winthrop Papers*, 5:125.

cumstances may have helped to polarize the town on issues that other communities found easier to resolve. Efforts to bring Salem firmly within the orthodox fold had shown signs of success in the 1650s. During the period just before
the Quaker invasion, the town had been relatively untroubled by extremism.
However, Richard Gildrie has suggested that political factionalism and the inadequate ministrations of the aging and infirm pastor, Edward Norris, contributed to the disillusionment of some townspeople.[45] Opposition to the gradual circumscription of the role of the laity within the church may have also been
a factor in leading some residents to welcome the opportunities presented by
the Quaker faith.[46] For whatever combination of reasons, some thirty Salem
residents would form the nucleus of the Quaker movement in that region,
founding the first and most stalwart meeting within the confines of New England's least tolerant colony.

While the Quaker movement introduced an unfamiliar, even alien faith into
the colony, the Baptist movement resulted from the maturation of a dissenting
tradition that had long been a minor presence in Massachusetts. In choosing to
become a Quaker, a colonist turned away from many of the issues that had
concerned the laity in New England. Recreating the godly communities of biblical times, ensuring the purity of the gathered church, and maintaining a balance between ministerial authority and lay activism were not urgent matters in
the Quaker meeting. The Baptists, however, continued to be involved in the
quest for biblical primitivism, a pure gathered church, and an appropriate role
for the laity. In this respect, William McLoughlin's observation that Quakerism
was imported while the Baptist movement was indigenous to New England is
accurate.[47] Hence, of all the converts admitted to Cambridge Church during
the late 1630s and early 1640s, Charles Cohen found that no one gave a more
impassioned and Christocentric conversion narrative than William Hamlet; this
future Baptist convert may have been particularly emphatic about the importance of a pure community of the godly as well.[48] The Baptist faith arose out of

---

[45] Richard P. Gildrie, *Salem, Massachusetts, 1626–1683: A Covenant Community* (Charlottesville:
University Press of Virginia), 129–30. The link between political infighting and Quaker convincement was not direct, however; in a 1667 petition from thirty-five Salem Farms residents
who sought to be relieved from watch in Salem town – which Gildrie cites to connect the two
developments – only one Quaker (John Smith) was among the signatories. See *Essex Antiquarian*
2 (1898): 27–9.

[46] In 1675, Salem minister John Higginson reported that he and his predecessor Edward Norris
had both been accused of presbyterianism and taking away the church's liberties; see *CMHS*,
4th ser., vol. 8 (1868): 276.

[47] McLoughlin, *New England Dissent*, 5–7, 50.

[48] Charles Lloyd Cohen, *God's Caress: The Psychology of Puritan Religious Experience* (New York:
Oxford University Press, 1986), 236–9. His admission to the Baptist church occurred in about
1670; see Record Book of the First Baptist Church, Boston, 1669–71 [hereafter Baptist Record
Book], on deposit at ANTS; and Backus, *History*, 1:327.

a dialogue with orthodoxy, the Quaker faith out of a rejection of the terms of that discourse.

In keeping with the Baptists' continuing concern about issues important to the orthodox community, the impetus to gather a Baptist church arose directly out of an objectionable reform being adopted by the established churches – the "halfway covenant."[49] Every major synod from 1646 through 1662 grappled with the ordinance of baptism, trying to determine the eligibility of those grand-children of church members whose parents had not become full church mem-bers in their own rights. Initially, these children had been denied the ordinance, but the synod of 1662 finally concluded that the policy ought to be reversed. The decision resulted in the first major breach within orthodox ranks, as min-isters disagreed publicly and one Boston church split over it. Many lay people joined the defeated ministerial faction in objecting to the decision as a threat to church purity.

Some of those most dismayed by the decision reassessed their commitment to the established faith entirely. As one colonist opposed to the reform and supportive of the newly gathered Baptist church informed the authorities, what "you were about at the synod" that authorized the baptism of the grandchildren of church members was "to make [an] Anabaptist."[50] According to those who became Baptists from 1665 on, the orthodox churches, which had been flirting with error when they sanctioned the baptism of any children, had completely undermined their claims to purity with the decision to extend baptism even farther. The halfway covenant, which troubled many lay people, drove a few of them out of the orthodox churches altogether.

Arguably, the advocates of the reform found themselves between a rock and a hard place when it came to sectarianism and the halfway covenant. The pas-sage of time and the failure of a younger generation to make the same commit-ment to the church that their parents had forced the defenders of orthodoxy to face the Presbyterians' question: How could they expect widespread religious participation in a church dedicated to exclusivity? As one lay critic described the circumstances of the children of church members under the system that prevailed during the first years, "they dealt with children here as the people [deal] with their young shoates in Virginia, to take them up and marke them and then turne them into the woods."[51] To extend the analogy to children who were not baptized because their parents were not members, these young hogs were not even marked before being put out to fend for themselves. The halfway covenant was designed to keep as many colonists as possible involved in the church – so that they would not be left to their own devices like the shoates in

---

[49] On the reform, see Pope, *Half-Way Covenant.*
[50] John Thrumble, quoted in "The Baptist Debate of April 14–15, 1668," ed. William G. Mc-Loughlin and Martha Whiting Davidson, *PMHS* 76 (1964): 117.
[51] Woodbridge to Baxter, 575.

Virginia – at the same time as it maintained purity by reserving full membership to the visible saints. If Quakers left the orthodox fold alienated from the established faith, then the growing number of uninvolved colonists could be seen as potential Quaker converts themselves, should their disinterest grow into disillusionment. As the General Court observed – with a touch of snobbery – in one of its anti-Quaker pronouncements, the sect appealed to the "simpler, or such as are less affected to the order & government in Church and commonwealth."[52] An organized alternative faith in the colony gave added urgency to the need to bring another generation under the care of the church.

But if the halfway covenant was designed to draw the inactive into the church, it risked driving away those who were deeply committed to the principle of a pure church. In a move intended in part to guard against the threat posed by one sectarian group, the establishment exacerbated the objections of other colonists, who then created a second sectarian alternative. That the losses on either front were ultimately so few suggests the wisdom of the orthodox decision. Still, the frustration felt by the ministry was understandable, since its efforts to strengthen the churches under its care contributed to the emergence of Anabaptism.[53]

Quakerism helped to set the stage for the Baptist movement as well. The people who became Baptists were concerned over Massachusetts's official intolerance as well as its too liberal church admission standards. During the Quaker invasion, the potential for brutality against dissenters who refused to be silenced or ejected was brought into stark relief by the stubbornness of both the magistrates and the Quaker witnesses. The traditional association of Baptists with the principles of religious toleration made that faith appealing to people dismayed by the Quaker executions.[54] Because Quakerism was planted in Massachusetts first and because it then contributed to the emergence of a full-blown Baptist movement there, the founding of the Salem Quaker meeting has been dealt with first in the chapters that follow. Antipedobaptist sentiment had been sporadically expressed in the colony for over a decade when the first Quaker witnesses arrived but did not come together to form the basis of a sect until Quakers had been meeting in Salem for eight years.

Although the emergence of these sectarian movements can be linked to the halfway covenant, the persecution of the Quakers, a general disillusionment with the orthodox establishment, and the efforts of traveling Quaker missionaries, the two sects did not arise directly out of previous radical agitation within

---

[52] *RMB* 4, pt. 1:346.

[53] Many orthodox leaders believed that discussing the issue without reaching a conclusion was especially likely to foster an upsurge in Anabaptist sentiments among the laity; see, e.g., Samuel Whiting and Thomas Cobbet to John Eliot and Samuel Danforth, 2 August 1654, Curwen Family Manuscript Collection, AAS.

[54] Samuel Hooten, Something Concerning my travell, in *The Friend: Religious and Literary Journal* 77 (1904): 204–5.

the colony.[55] The vast majority of sectarians lacked a personal history of radicalism. The documentation necessary to determine those who were Roger Williams's most ardent followers in Salem is no longer available.[56] However, since only a handful of Quakers had been adults during the 1630s, few could have been active in that controversy. In any case, those Salem residents most dedicated to Williams's cause had long since joined him in Providence. No future convert to either sect in Massachusetts had been identified as a supporter of Anne Hutchinson or as having been infected by the Gortonists, although a few Quakers were related to people who had been.[57] Instead, two of the first Quaker converts, Cassandra and Lawrence Southwick, had testified against a neighbor with Gortonist tendencies. Only one man had previously voiced opposition to infant baptism; over a decade later, Michael Shafflin went on to become a Quaker rather than a Baptist.[58] The father of one convert may have been a Baptist church member in England before coming to the colony in 1638; if so, he found the orthodox church at Charlestown acceptable and joined it upon arriving in the colony.[59] Some of the first Baptists, but none of the Quakers, had been active in radical religious movements in civil war and interregnum England.[60] By comparison to these few, indirect ties to the colony's stunted

[55] This summary of previous radical activity on the part of first-generation sectaries was developed by checking the names of all those known to have been members of the Quaker meeting or the Baptist church during the first decade against the records documenting support for various radical positions. Possibly, a few of those infected by Gortonism have gone undetected; only one Salem resident thus infected was named in the records, possibly because she was so dedicated that an example was made of her.

[56] The Salem Church records were copied into a new book, with all references to the Williams imbroglio deleted, early in John Higginson's ministry; see Baughman, "Excommunications," 89–90.

[57] Most notably, Elizabeth Freestone Turner Gardner lived as a girl in Boston with her aunt, Anne Hutchinson; see George E. McCracken, "The Salem Gardners: Comments and Clues," *American Genealogist* 30 (1954): 160–1, for those family ties. The father of William King was disarmed as a Hutchinson supporter; James Savage, *A Genealogical Dictionary of the First Settlers of New England*, 4 vols. (Boston, 1860–2), 3:27. Eleanor [ ] Phelps Truslar had been tried for her Gortonist views in 1644; her son became a Quaker thirteen years later; *EQC* 1:68. For another possible Gortonist–Quaker link, see Barbara Ritter Dailey, "Root and Branch: New England's Religious Radicals and Their Transatlantic Community, 1600–1660" (Ph.D. diss., Boston University, 1984), 279–81.

[58] *EQC* 1:68, 99.

[59] The evidence that Seth Sweetser was a Baptist in England is contained in a 1772 letter; John Davis to Isaac Backus, 3 August 1772, Backus Collection, ANTS. McLoughlin (*New England Dissent*, 14n.) read the letter, which lists Sweetser as the first Baptist in the region and then goes on to describe in a general way punishments to which early Baptists were subjected, to mean that Sweetser publicized his views upon arriving in the colony and was then punished. However, the *Records of the First Church in Charlestown* (ed. James F. Hunnewell [Boston, 1880], 9, 47) reveal that he became a church member and had his child baptized in Charlestown.

[60] Five had definitely been Baptists in England; Baptist Record Book, 28 May 1665. Another three may have been. Mary Greenliefe, whose husband had fought under Cromwell and whose daughter, Rooksby, was apparently named for a major who died in the Battle of Dunbar, may have brought

radical tradition, twenty-four of those initially involved in both sects (fourteen Quakers and ten Baptists) had previously been members of one of the colony's established churches.[61] This paucity of links to earlier radicalism indicates how successfully the authorities had removed radicals who could not be dissuaded. With the introduction of Quakerism, that would change irrevocably.

The history of sectarianism

Most frequently, scholars have treated these sects as catalysts that brought about changes in the larger community. Perry Miller's explication of the "New England mind" revealed that colonial leaders frequently presented the sects as a sign of the decline of New England society. Following Miller, many scholars have listed the emergence of the Quakers and Baptists among those developments that signaled the fragmentation of a once unified society.[62] Alternatively, some historians have viewed the sects as harbingers of religious diversity and champions of religious liberty. In emphasizing this aspect of the sects' impact, William McLoughlin, Jonathan Chu, and others have carried on a historiographical tradition inaugurated by Whig historians in the nineteenth century.[63] These two interpretations make up two sides of the same analytical coin, depending on whether the introduction of sectarianism is judged from the perspective of the founders – who hoped to establish a colony free of competing spiritual options – or from the perspective of later generations of liberals – who advocated the separation of church and state in the United States.

The history of sectarianism cannot be fully presented in a linear narrative that moves from uniformity and intolerance to diversity and liberty. Diversity as well as a modicum of tolerance were relatively quick in coming to Massachusetts Bay; it is arguable whether the first three decades of any new settlement – no matter how successfully launched – can supply the standard against which

the sectarian inclinations so common in the New Model Army with her to New England; James Edward Greenleaf, *Genealogy of the Greenleaf Family* (Boston, 1896), 75–6. Isaac Hull and his wife joined the Baptist church so soon after its founding that they may have already held Baptist views upon their arrival in Salem three years earlier; Perley, *History of Salem*, 2:316.

61 These generalizations are based on the prosopography discussed in Chapter 3. Eighteen of the twenty-four were men (ten of them Quakers), and six were women (four Quakers).

62 Miller, *Colony to Province*, 2: esp. ch. 9; Hall, *Faithful Shepherd*, 228–33, 236–7; Harry S. Stout, *The New England Soul: Preaching and Religious Culture in Colonial New England* (New York: Oxford University Press, 1986), 186. While these scholars focus on the colonists' perception that decline had occurred, some have argued that it did, in fact, occur and that sectaries were a major cause of it; see, e.g., Gildrie, *Salem*, 130–7, 140.

63 McLoughlin, *New England Dissent*; Jonathan M. Chu, *Neighbors, Friends, or Madmen: The Puritan Adjustment to Quakerism in Seventeenth-Century Massachusetts* (Westport, Conn.: Greenwood, 1985). The prevailing attitude among nineteenth-century scholars can be found in George Bancroft, *History of the United States: Colonization*, 3 vols. (Boston, 1834–40; 10th ed., 1843), 1:449–52; on Roger Williams as the heroic defender of liberty, see 367–77.

all its subsequent history should be judged.[64] The ministerial elite that developed the declension theme had to meld it with a veneration for the ancestors in order to give their criticisms credence. Colonial leaders responded creatively to the collapse of their policy of enforced uniformity, developing strategies that were intended – and may well have served – to increase popular identification with orthodoxy. Decrying declension, whether real or imagined, helped to shape their society.

In addition, greater toleration and diversity would not continually prove a boon for sectarians. Both the Quakers and Baptists would find that the liberalization of Massachusetts society posed problems for them. By equating sectarianism with other forces for change – such as economic growth, religious liberalism, and anglicization – the Whig interpretation associates sects with developments they did not necessarily foster, welcome, or benefit from. As we shall see, many factors affected how the two sects responded to the changing nature of colonial society.

As they struggled with the problem of long-term survival, the Quakers and Baptists of Massachusetts confronted the classic dilemma of a sect. Sociological theories posit that sects tend to lose their initial radicalism, becoming more routinized or more like churches over time. Robert G. Pope has applied this concept to the established churches in the Bay colony with regard to the halfway covenant.[65] The two sects first founded in Massachusetts did not follow a uniform path to routinization, which sociologists have come to appreciate was often the case.[66] Even two sects in the same historical context experienced the general process in divergent ways. More important than their shared status as sects were their beliefs, the social bases of their communities, and their relationships to the orthodox establishment. The history of the Quakers and Baptists in Massachusetts attests to the complexity of the process of sectarian evolution.

Shifting attention from the sects' role in introducing diversity – whether welcomed or not – to the history of the sects themselves, the Salem Quakers and the Boston Baptists have received only superficial treatment by scholars thus far.[67] General histories of American Quakerism usually give a detailed

---

[64] Darrett Rutman's work raises this issue with particular force, since his Puritans hardly disembarked before decline began; see "God's Bridge Falling Down: 'Another Approach' to New England Puritanism Assayed," *WMQ*, 3d ser., 19 (1962): 408–21; and idem, *Winthrop's Boston: Portrait of a Puritan Town, 1630–1649* (Chapel Hill: University of North Carolina Press, 1965).

[65] For a summary of the classic sociological literature on routinization and the sect–church typology, associated with Max Weber and Ernst Troeltsch, respectively, see Michael Hill, *A Sociology of Religion* (London: Heinemann, 1973). On Pope, see his *Half-Way Covenant*, 261–2.

[66] For example, see the work of Bryan Wilson, especially *Religious Sects: A Sociological Study* (New York: McGraw Hill, 1970).

[67] On Friends in Gloucester, see Christine Leigh Heyrman, *Commerce and Culture: The Maritime Communities of Colonial Massachusetts, 1690–1750* (New York: Norton, 1984), 95–104, 125–30, and idem, "Specters of Subversion, Societies of Friends: Dissent and the Devil in Provincial

account of the missionary invasion of 1656–61 and concentrate on Pennsylvania for the later colonial period.[68] Only the small Boston weekly meeting – one of three belonging to the Salem Monthly Meeting during the colonial period – has been the subject of extended examination, in a recent history by Cambridge Friend George Selleck. Arthur Worrall has written about the meetings north of the middle colonies, providing an overview that includes the Salem Monthly Meeting along with numerous others.[69] Baptist historiography has not been as fully developed as that for the Society of Friends. William McLoughlin's *New England Dissent*, the only twentieth-century history to deal with the Boston Baptists, focuses on the legal and political aspects of their history. No other account of the sect has been produced, and McLoughlin's study remains the major secondary source on all early New England Baptists.[70] Given the number of community studies produced in the past twenty years, surprisingly little is known about these sectarian enclaves.

As a community study of another sort, an examination of the Quakers and Baptists adds to our understanding of popular religion in early Massachusetts. Scholarly interest in lay religiosity has increased during the past decade, influenced by a debate within New England Puritan studies as well as by trends in European historiography. In reaction to intellectual histories of Puritanism, most notably Perry Miller's magisterial study of "the New England mind," a generation of social historians argued that the mind of the ordinary colonist could not be apprehended through an explication of the thought of the ministerial elite. At the same time, early modern European scholars began uncovering evidence of unbelief, anticlericalism, and occult practices, which indicated that lay belief diverged sharply from that advocated by the clergy.[71] While Keith Thomas has developed this view with regard to England, Christopher Hill has

---

Essex County, Massachusetts," in *Saints and Revolutionaries*, 38–74. In Salem, see Gildrie, *Salem*, 130–7.

[68] For example, Rufus M. Jones with Isaac Sharpless and Amelia M. Gummere, *The Quakers in the American Colonies* (London: Macmillan Press, 1911).

[69] George A. Selleck, *Quakers in Boston, 1656–1964: Three Centuries of Friends in Boston and Cambridge* (Boston: Todd, 1976). Arthur J. Worrall, *Quakers in the Colonial Northeast* (Hanover, N. H.: University Press of New England, 1980).

[70] Unfortunately, McLoughlin's account of the social history of sectarianism contains minor errors, which other scholars have repeated; see, e.g., the previous discussion of Seth Sweetser in note 59. Gura (*Glimpse of Sion's Glory*, 106) cited the Sweetser case to show that, even before a Baptist church had been founded in the region (in Providence in 1638/9), adherents of the sect were agitating in Massachusetts. For an earlier history of the Boston church, see Nathan E. Wood, *History of the First Baptist Church of Boston* (Philadelphia, 1899).

[71] For a recent exchange on the issues raised in the first instance, see George Selement, "The Meeting of Elite and Popular Minds at Cambridge, New England, 1638–1645"; David D. Hall, "Toward a History of Popular Religion in Early New England"; and Darrett B. Rutman, "New England as Idea and Society"; all in *WMQ*, 3d ser., 41 (1984), 32–51. On the second instance, see Jon Butler, "The Future of American Religious History: Prospectus, Agenda, Transatlantic Problematique," *WMQ*, 3d ser., 42 (1985), 171–7.

highlighted the religious radicalism of many of the English civil war and inter-regnum era movements.[72] Historians of colonial America have begun grappling with these issues. In a study of the regular weekly preaching of New England ministers, Harry Stout has argued that they continually addressed issues of importance to the laity. Charles Cohen and Charles Hambrick-Stowe have analyzed the spirituality of orthodox church members; Cohen, in particular, looks at how lay and ministerial beliefs intersected.[73] For those outside of the orthodox fold, the lack of evidence creates special difficulties. Jon Butler and David Hall have taken opposing positions on the importance of unbelief and occult practices. According to Butler, colonial society exhibited some of the same tensions that Thomas and others found in Europe between folk attitudes and those beliefs officially sanctioned by the clergy. Hall has maintained that New Englanders, at least, shared a common religious culture, which he defines broadly enough to include Quakers as well as Baptists.[74]

Despite growing scholarly interest in popular religion, little work has been done on the sectarian alternatives that reshaped the spiritual landscape of Massachusetts in the years after 1656. Otherwise ordinary colonists decisively declared their views when they left the orthodox fold to associate themselves with an illegal sect. By coming together to form a Quaker meeting and a Baptist church, they created communities that competed with those that had previously occupied the uncontested center of colonial life. Although colonial sectarian movements were tied to the events in England analyzed by Christopher Hill, the reasons that Massachusetts colonists chose sectarianism were bound up with their experiences in the New World. Changes in church polity fostered the Baptist movement, while a more general disillusionment with the New England way gave rise to the Quaker meeting in Salem. Quakers and Baptists went on to create unique communities, shaped by their beliefs and their relationship to colonial society. Undaunted by serious obstacles, they organized spiritual alternatives where none had previously existed.

These sects revealed the beliefs of other colonists as well. In their response to the sectaries in their midst, nonsectarian colonists indicated their attitudes toward orthodoxy, dissent, and toleration. The majority clearly stated its relative lack of interest in the cause championed by sectarians when they chose not to join with them in their dissent. In addition, in their interactions with Quakers

---

[72] Keith Thomas, *Religion and the Decline of Magic* (New York: Scribner, 1971); Christopher Hill, especially *The World Turned Upside Down: Radical Ideas During the English Revolution* (London: Temple Smith, 1972).

[73] Stout, *New England Soul;* Charles E. Hambrick-Stowe, *The Practice of Piety: Puritan Devotional Disciplines in Seventeenth-Century New England* (Chapel Hill: University of North Carolina Press, 1982); Cohen, *God's Caress,* especially 170–6, 183–200; also, Selement, "Meeting of Minds."

[74] Jon Butler, *Awash in a Sea of Faith: Christianizing the American People* (Cambridge, Mass.: Harvard University Press, 1990), ch. 3. David D. Hall, *Worlds of Wonder, Days of Judgment: Popular Religious Beliefs in Early New England* (New York: Knopf, 1989).

and Baptists, colonial residents revealed both their theological sophistication and their less than wholehearted commitment to a religious establishment. Charles Cohen and Charles Hambrick-Stowe, among others, have correctly argued that ministers successfully communicated the essential elements of the orthodox faith to their congregations. Ordinary colonists obviously understood the doctrinal distinctions that made a Baptist less radical than a Quaker. They appreciated, for instance, that Quakers did not participate fully in the "culture of the Word" that David Hall has declared pivotal to popular religion in early New England. In contrast to Hall, I believe that the Quakers cannot be encompassed in the religious culture that orthodox colonists and Baptists – to a great extent – shared.[75] Only in this light does the reaction of the orthodox community to the Quakers become explicable.

Yet nonsectarian colonists did not always agree with their spiritual leaders on the necessity of religious uniformity. The argument in favor of coerced uniformity was predicated on the unflattering assumption that ordinary colonists needed to be protected from any contact with heresy, since they might not be able to withstand temptation. A growing number of colonists, apparently confident of their own ability to maintain their spiritual allegiances, were not convinced of the necessity of utterly avoiding all dissenters. They freely distinguished between brands of heterodoxy, ostracizing Quakers more vigorously than Baptists. Still, not all nonelite residents were as tolerant as many scholars have supposed. Many initially shared in the hostility toward the Quakers expressed in official policy, and some continued to feel such animosity for many years. Those who were most committed to the local church were also apparently most determined to shun the Quakers; the same cannot be said about the Baptists. In the border region separating these three faiths, the nuances of popular attitudes become clearly visible.

After 1660, three distinctive outlets for popular religious expression existed within Massachusetts. The work that follows explores two of these spiritual options and places them within the context of the larger society that helped to shape their dissent.

---

[75] Hall, *Worlds of Wonder*, ch. 1; for the phrase, see p. 68. For a further elaboration of this criticism, see Carla Gardina Pestana, review of *Worlds of Wonder* in *NEQ* 63 (1990): 163–4.

PART I

Beginnings

1

The Quaker movement in northeastern Massachusetts

A Quaker movement emerged in western Salem in 1657–8. Inspired by the message of English radicals, dozens of Salem residents along with a handful of people from other towns joined together to organize an alternative religious community within the confines of New England's leading orthodox colony. If the encouragement of visiting Quakers helped to give meaning to this concerted act of defiance, the participation of loved ones and friends in rural Salem provided support in the face of vehement community and governmental opposition. Converts to the new sect displayed an unprecedented disaffection from the colony's religious establishment, despite the fact that they had been living quietly under it for years. The events in Salem took orthodox observers by surprise.

The colony's mechanisms for dealing with dissent were pushed to the limit during the conflict that ensued but failed to achieve the accustomed results. The dramatic confrontation between English Quaker witnesses and colonial authorities has occupied center stage in accounts of the sect's introduction to New England. However, the creation of an indigenous sectarian enclave was at the heart of the matter for the traveling Quakers who sought to plant the seed of truth in New England. As Bay colony magistrates sent Quaker missionaries to their deaths, all concerned were engaged in a struggle for the allegiances of the populace. A vocal minority identified openly with the martyrs.

On 26 June 1658, thirty people gathered at the house of Nicholas and Hannah Phelps in the less densely populated region of western Salem called the "woods."[1] Among them were two strangers, William Brend and William Leddra, who were traveling through the colony to spread the Lord's message. These men had found a receptive audience in the Salem area, including many people who had been meeting together to share their newfound understanding of the truth for some time. Brend, "a man of years" who had left his family in London, and Leddra, a native of Cornwall living in Barbados, had felt a call to minister to

---

[1] The outline of this incident can be garnered from the court records relating to it; see *EQC* 2:103–5. Also Joseph Besse, *A Collection of the Sufferings of the People called Quakers*, 2 vols. (London, 1753), 2:185–6.

the seed of the faithful in New England. These traveling witnesses, who had come at great personal risk to deliver their message, probably spoke to the townspeople about the changes being brought about in their own time. Indeed, the coming of the end of the world seemed a feasible explanation for what Brend, Leddra, and many others had experienced.

Most of the gathered artisans, housewives, farmers, and maidens would come to share their novel belief that the light of truth and love shone within each of them, providing divine guidance for human actions. Lawrence and Cassandra Southwick, an elderly couple, had been among the first to embrace this view, forsaking Salem Church after nearly twenty years as members to attend these private meetings.[2] A handful of others were already equally committed to this new faith and had been attending meetings in the Southwicks' home during the preceding months.

While the Scriptures were familiar to everyone present, no biblical passage was read. Rather, each person waited in silence until called by God to speak. Perhaps the silence was broken by the voice of the Southwicks' twenty-six-year-old son, Josiah, who shared their sense that God's message would come to those who waited on him. Actually, it did not matter who spoke at the meeting, or even if no one did. Even Josiah's younger sister, Provided, who had never spoken publicly before, was free to address her older friends and neighbors; for as the observer of a similar assembly in England recorded, "sometimes girls are vocal in their covenant, while leading men are silent."[3] Regardless of who felt called to witness to the truth, they believed that the words came from the same source.

Participating in this outpouring of the spirit caused such excitement that some people, overcome with emotion, might begin to tremble and shake. The experience of gathering to wait in silence for a sense of the divine will, to hear strangers and neighbors share their testimonies to this truth, and to express the promptings of one's own inner light was an overwhelmingly powerful event. For people accustomed to looking elsewhere for guidance – to their betters in the community, to laws and customs, to the word of God as recorded in the Scriptures and explained by a trained professional – looking inward instead was profoundly exciting. Sharing their new understanding of the truth with other colonists in these unstructured gatherings was an experience without precedent in early Massachusetts, where soul searching was conducted in the privacy of one's closet and public relations of spiritual experiences occurred in formal examinations before the community's visible saints.

The thirty participants in this event were not alone in attaching great signif-

----

[2] They had, however, apparently long since ceased to have their children baptized; see Worrall, *Quakers in the Colonial Northeast*, 203n.

[3] Francis Higginson, *The Irreligion of the Northern Quakers* (London, 1653), reprinted in *Early Quaker Writings, 1650–1700*, ed. Hugh Barbour and Arthur O. Robert (Grand Rapids, Mich.: Eerdmans, 1973), 71.

icance to it. Recognizing the gathering as a radical departure from established practice, the alarmed authorities forcibly brought the meeting to a close. The magistrates, "informed of a disorderly meeting of certaine suspected persons att the house of one Nicholas Phelps of Salem," dispatched the constable, Nathaniel Felton, accompanied by maltster Edmund Batter and tailor John Smith, to the woods.[4] During the ensuing fracas, three men and four women were apprehended. The two visitors, Brend and Leddra, escaped but were captured a short while later in the neighboring town of Newbury.[5] The mistress of the house, Hannah Phelps, contributed to the uproar by verbally abusing Smith, whose young wife – Margaret Thompson Smith – was in attendance. Although Goodman Smith would have the satisfaction of seeing Phelps admonished in court for her carriage toward him on that Sabbath day, his efforts failed to alter his own wife's sympathies.

Three days later, on 29 June, the Essex County Court met in Salem and began to take action against this burgeoning movement. The two strangers were examined and "owneing themselves to be such [professed Quakers] were sent to the Howse of Correccon [House of Correction] according to Lawe." There, refusing to work for their bread, they would go without; the jailer would eventually put the intransigent Brend into leg irons and whip him severely.[6] When the local offenders were brought into court after this sentence had been passed on their friends, many of the men stood with their hats upon their heads. This symbolic statement of contempt for the temporal authority of the magistrates was standard practice among English radicals. The court, cognizant of the meaning these men sought to convey, ordered the court officer forcibly to bare their heads. The magistrates then proceeded, dealing with each offender according to the nature of the transgression and the degree of his or her apparent involvement in the Quaker movement. Nicholas Phelps was fined for having the meeting in his home as well as for absenting himself from mandatory public worship services and for attending a meeting of Quakers. Lawrence, Cassandra, and Josiah Southwick, Samuel Shattock, Joshua Buffum, and Samuel Gaskill were all imprisoned for "obstinately owning themselves to be such as are called Quakers."[7] The others were fined or admonished.

Continuing the sentencing of the lesser malefactors into the next month, the court found upon reconvening that a few new offenses had to be tried as well. Nicholas Phelps was "fined for defending a Quaker's writing and sent to the house of correction at Ipswich for an indefinite time for confessing himself a Quaker." Seventeen-year-old Provided Southwick, whose parents, elder brother, and future husband were all in prison, had been "calling the Court persecu-

---

[4] *EQC* 2:104.   [5] Ibid., 103; Besse, *Sufferings*, 2:185–6.
[6] *EQC* 2:103; George Bishop, *New England Judged by the Spirit of the Lord* (London, 1661, 1667; abridged ed., 1703), 64–6.
[7] *EQC* 2:105.

tors"; she was ordered to the stocks for one hour.[8] The Salem magistrates attempted to prevent a small but growing number of the town's residents from joining that illegal and disturbing new sect known as the Quakers. They would not succeed.

The group that met at the Phelps house on that Sabbath day in June included many of the early Salem Quakers, the men and women who were responsible for the establishment of the sect in that region. The six people imprisoned immediately after this meeting were staunch and vocal supporters of this innovative faith. Most notably, the three senior Southwicks and Samuel Shattock had already been imprisoned for demonstrating their affinity for the new movement during the preceding year. Shattock had tried to defend a visiting Quaker from the wrath of an orthodox colonist.[9] All six would remain unreconciled to the colony's established faith until their deaths.

In addition to the committed colonists present, these early, illegal assemblies also undoubtedly attracted a number of kindly disposed or simply curious individuals. When exposed to the excitement that surrounded this rebellion against the established order, they felt drawn to investigate the matter for themselves. While many of these people liked what they found in the informal, emotionally charged gatherings, others were either unimpressed by the Quaker faith or cowed by the legal and social sanctions against these "vile heretics" into returning to the established church. Three of the men present at the Phelpses' proved uncommitted to the sect, and at least two of them would return to the orthodox fold during the next few years.[10] Except for three more people, who apparently left the colony entirely, however, the remaining participants in this June meeting embraced the new faith permanently. One decade later, almost fifty colonists were active in the Salem meeting.

The dramatic events on the Phelps farm and at the quarterly court session three days later came at the end of a two-year period of mounting tensions over the introduction of this new sect into New England. The first Quaker witnesses had arrived in the colony in July 1656, and they were followed by a veritable "invasion" of missionaries bent on converting colonists. The authorities, responding swiftly and vehemently, began passing a series of progressively harsher punishments designed to halt the spread of this heresy. Imprisonment, whippings, mutilations, and, finally, banishment on pain of death awaited the "publishers of truth" who came to Massachusetts.[11]

The repression succeeded in containing the "contagion of Quakerism," ex-

---

[8] Ibid., 107.

[9] That is, Lawrence, Cassandra, and Josiah. *EQC* 2:53, 55, 104; Besse, *Sufferings*, 2:183–4.

[10] On Thomas Brackett, see Perley, *History of Salem*, 2:252–3, 224; on Robert Adams, see *NEHGR* 9 (1855): 126. The third man, John Hill, although affiliated with Quaker families through both his marriages, never actively supported the sect.

[11] *RMB* 4, pt. 1:277–8, 308–24, 345–7.

cept in the only port town of any importance north of Boston, Salem. With little more than a thousand people in 1656, Salem had already spawned three new towns out of its extensive original land grants by that time; another, Beverly, would be established in the following decade.[12] The townsfolk worshiped together in Salem's only church, under the pastoral care of the aging Edward Norris. The town's earlier penchant for religious radicalism had not been much in evidence recently. Within a year of the arrival of the first witnesses, however, a group of previously unremarkable residents would reinvigorate the town's radical traditions by embracing the sect.

The first convincements in Salem may have occurred as early as the winter of 1656–7. In February 1656/7, rumors that a meeting was being held in the town were inspiring English Quakers in Barbados to risk the journey to the inhospitable Bay colony in order to encourage the newly "convinced" there. The Salem selectmen may have become aware of the problem in June, for they prohibited entertaining strangers without permission at that time.[13] When Englishmen Christopher Holder and John Copeland came to Salem later in the year, some residents demonstrated support for the new sect they represented. The Southwick couple received the two witnesses into their home despite the selectmen's order. When Edmund Batter prevented Holder from addressing the Salem congregation by stuffing his mouth with a glove and a handkerchief and dragging him by the hair out of the meetinghouse, Samuel Shattock came to the young man's defense.[14] The Southwicks and Shattock were already strongly sympathetic to Quakerism at this early date. And this incident apparently inspired an increased commitment to the teachings of the sect, for contemporary English Quakers believed that the Salem meeting was founded in reaction to this incident.[15]

News about the movement and perhaps Quaker publications probably reached the area first, convincing some Salem residents of the truth of the sect's message. While privately communicated news of Quakerism – through letters or by word of mouth – cannot be documented, many townsfolk still had family and

[12] Population estimates by Joseph B. Felt (*Annals of Salem*, 2 vols. [Salem, 1854], 2:410) set the figures for 1654 and 1665 at 1,068 and 1,446, respectively. The founding of a separate parish in Salem village, a region in the northern section, was over a decade in the future, and the witchcraft controversy that would begin in the village was still a generation away at this time; Paul Boyer and Stephen Nissenbaum, *Salem Possessed: The Social Origins of Witchcraft* (Cambridge, Mass.: Harvard University Press, 1974), 39–43.

[13] H. Fell to M. F[ell] from Barbados, [19 February] 1656, in Swarthmore Manuscript Collection, LSF (transcription), 2:114. Perley believed that the order anticipated the arrival of Quaker missionaries in the town; *History of Salem*, 2:244.

[14] Bishop, *New England Judged*, 50–3; Perley, *History of Salem*, 2:246.

[15] Bishop, *New England Judged*, 52–5; Bishop does not clarify the exact timing of this development, although presumably it did not occur until after Cassandra's release from prison in December 1657.

friends in England from whom they might hear of developments there.[16] By
1657, pamphlets were reaching the region. William Marston, who worked as a
boatman between Hampton and Salem, was fined in that year for possessing
two Quaker tracts, probably William Dewsberry's *The Mighty Day of the Lord*
and John Lilburne's *Resurrection*, along with an unidentified paper. Marston's
association with the town of Salem had begun much earlier, and by the end of
the 1650s he was worshiping with the Quakers there.[17] The following year,
"Quaker writings" were discovered circulating among the convinced in Salem.[18]

Although the details are sketchy, local involvement in this movement increased from the convincements rumored in February 1656/7 to the full-blown
Quaker meeting that had come to the attention of the authorities by the spring
of the following year. In response, the General Court passed the first law specifically addressing the problem of indigenous Quakerism in May 1658, intend-
ing "that Quakers and such accursed hereticques arising amongst ourselves
may be dealt withall to theire deserts, and that theire pestilent errors and prac-
tizes may speedily be prevented."[19] With this mandate from the high court, the
Salem authorities compiled a list of twelve persons who met at the Southwick
home on the first Sabbath in June.[20] The larger meeting at the Phelpses' three
weeks later was part of a series of gatherings held by self-proclaimed adherents
to the beliefs of the "people called Quakers" and attended by a small but growing number of others, most of whom would eventually embrace these views.

With the first convincements having occurred over a year before, the failure
of the Salem authorities to respond more quickly to this nascent movement is
somewhat surprising. Perhaps they were hoping that local sympathizers would
leave the area of their own volition, as other radicals had done in the past. A
leading English Quaker believed that an effort had been made to persuade the
Southwick family to do just that.[21] Earlier in the year, Dedham magistrates had
detained, questioned, and arrested Josiah Southwick, John Burton, and John
Small, who had been journeying south to explore the possibility of resettling
their familes in Rhode Island. Edward and Priscilla Harnett sold their house
and barn that winter and left Salem completely.[22] That the radicals appeared
ready to follow the time-honored tradition of departing without having formal

---

[16] David Cressy, *Coming Over: Migration and Communication between England and New England in
the Seventeenth Century* (Cambridge University Press, 1987), ch. 9.

[17] *RMB* 4, pt. 1:314; Besse, *Sufferings*, 2:189; Perley, *History of Salem*, 2:255–6, 218; *EQC* 2:194;
Savage, *Genealogical Dictionary*, 3:161. Quaker tracts were reported in Middlesex County in
1657 also; see Felt, *Ecclesiastical History*, 2:165.

[18] Richard P. Hallowell, *The Quaker Invasion of Massachusetts* (Boston, 1887), 173; *EQC* 2:107.
Quaker books were also available in New Haven by 1658; see *New Haven Records*, 242, 244, 246.

[19] *RMB* 4, pt. 1:321.

[20] *EQC* 2:104.

[21] Francis Howgill, *The Popish Inquisition newly erected in New-England* (London, 1659), 26–7.

[22] Bishop, *New England Judged*, 56–8; John Whiting, *Truth and Innocency Defended Against Falsehood
and Envy* (London, 1702), 18; Perley, *History of Salem*, 2:246–7.

charges brought against them might have temporarily stayed the magistrate's hand. In any case, the only legal recourse available until the passage of the May law had been citations for absences from public worship, which half a dozen of those present at the Phelpses' had received recently.

With the latest anti-Quaker law passed in May and the crackdown on Salem Quakers in June, the confrontation between the authorities and local adherents to the sect was under way. The three most committed adult members of the leading Quaker family in Salem, the Southwick couple and their son, Josiah, remained in prison. The other four professed Quakers were released during the summer. In September, Buffum, Shattock, and Phelps were once again imprisoned, "for persisting still in their cause as Quakers."[23] Concerned over the influx of strangers who witnessed against Massachusetts Bay's "civill and religious polities" and over the conversion of some colonists to the sect, a group of Boston merchants petitioned the General Court in October to enact more severe laws against these "professed Enemies to ye christian magistrate, and open Seducers of ye People." The court agreed, passing a law ordering the banishment on pain of death of the most persistent Quakers and commissioning Boston minister John Norton to write a tract stating the case against the sect. Declaring itself unable to "convince or reform" the six residents then imprisoned, the court ordered the aged couple and four young men out of the colony.[24]

The authorities were obviously hoping that the Quaker movement would be severely handicapped by the removal of Salem's most obnoxious converts. Indeed, Lawrence and Cassandra would never return. They traveled to southern New England, where they were taken in by a wealthy Quaker, Nathaniel Sylvester; the pair died in his home on Shelter Island in 1660.[25] The other four honored the sentences of banishment until these were rendered obsolete by a royal decree one year after the death of the elder Southwicks. Yet whatever the immediate effect the banishments had on those who remained, the overwhelming majority held to their convictions despite this loss.

In the Bay colony, the authorities continued to bring pressure to bear on resident Quakers in an attempt to harass the sect out of existence. Fines against them continued to be levied, fines that the sectaries usually refused to pay. On occasion, sympathetic members of the orthodox community came forward to pay fines for their relations or friends. Usually, however, a whipping or the seizure of goods followed instead. The authorities were frustrated by the Quak-

[23] *EQC* 2:118.

[24] Petition for Severer Laws Against the Quakers, October 1658, in Hallowell, *Quaker Invasion*, 153–6; *RMB* 4, pt. 1:345–7, 348, 349; John Norton, *The Heart of New England Rent* (Cambridge, 1659).

[25] A tradition in Quaker historiography has the Southwicks dying of depravation, literal exiles in a wilderness. However, Sylvester was certainly able to give them adequate shelter (as the name of his island implies), and they survived for two years.

ers' tactic of noncooperation, because forced banishment or imprisonment of the numerous offenders was infeasible given the limited resources of the colonial government. The colony simply did not have – and had not previously needed – mechanisms for dealing with widespread apostasy.[26] In a desperate effort to force Quaker compliance, the General Court empowered the treasurers of the county courts to sell Daniel and Provided Southwick into servitude to satisfy their fines. The pair had been "pretending they have no estate [and] resolving not to worke," so the court hoped to make an example of them with this threat.[27] No county treasurer attempted to take advantage of the court's offer, so Daniel and Provided remained, and the Quakers continued uncooperative.

This standoff between local Quakers and colonial officials fueled the escalation of the conflict between visiting sectaries and the authorities. Quaker missionaries were determined to witness against the colony's harsh laws and to support the resolve of the newly convinced. Many of them risked severe punishments – having their tongues bored or their ears cropped – to do so. Salem was on the itinerant preacher's route, which also included Plymouth and Rhode Island. Visitors who avoided detection on their journey north into the colony or left prison only to ignore a sentence of banishment often made their way to the coastal town. Increasingly aware of the difficulty with crushing the heresy once it had taken hold, the colonial authorities were equally determined to prevent its further spread. In autumn 1659, three visitors tested the government's resolve to contain the sect by flouting the sentences of banishment previously passed against them.

All three witnesses defiantly converged on Boston, two of them from Salem. Having recently been ordered by the court to depart from the jurisdiction, William Robinson and Marmaduke Stephenson had headed north instead. They had held meetings in Salem before continuing on to the "eastern parts" – New Hampshire and Maine – where other Quaker communities were coming into being. Upon their return, the two men decided to enter Boston, knowing that they risked death in doing so.[28] A group of Quakers accompanied Stephenson and Robinson on their journey to the colony's capital, demonstrating their solidarity in the cause espoused by the witnesses. With an attention to symbolism typical of the early Quakers, one Quaker woman brought a winding

[26] Jonathan Chu, noting the failure to punish local Quakers as severely as visitors, has concluded that the authorities were more tolerant of resident converts; see *Neighbors, Friends, or Madmen*, 61. Not only was a broader range of penalties available for use on residents (who had goods that could be distrained), but a limit on what could reasonably be done to them helped to stay the magistrates' hand. For instance, driving thirty local Quakers from their homes would have thrown them – impoverished and, in some cases, separated from their families – on to another English jurisdiction.

[27] *RMB* 4, pt. 1:366.

[28] The events that led to the deaths of Robinson and Stephenson are repeatedly described in the literature; see, e.g., Jones, *Quakers in the American Colonies*, 79–86.

sheet in which she planned to bury the martyrs. She would be thwarted, for the authorities had the party arrested and imprisoned upon their arrival in Boston.[29] In prison, this group was joined by Rhode Island Quaker Mary Dyer, a former Boston resident who had been banished as a follower of Anne Hutchinson over twenty years before. Dyer had temporarily left the colony in accordance with her most recent banishment but returned with the intention of defying the law.

The court proceeded with plans for the executions, but displayed concern that their course might fan the flames of controversy rather than stamp them out. The sentence of death was pronounced against Robinson, Stephenson, and Dyer on 18 October 1659.[30] At the same session, the court reprieved Dyer. In doing so, the magistrates ostensibly responded to the intercession of her son, but they also may have been worried that the execution of a matronly woman known to some residents would not engender support for their policies.[31] In anticipation of trouble, they also made extensive military preparations. They did not clarify the nature of the difficulties they sought to avoid: perhaps efforts by the incarcerated to spread their heretical views, popular opposition to the executions, or even an attack on the town by other Quakers – who were not yet known for their pacifism and whose rhetoric was sufficiently aggressive to spark suspicion.[32] The Boston selectmen were required to organize a special night watch that would pay particular attention to the prison. The court also ordered that a fence be erected around the building. Captain James Oliver was to accompany Marshal General Edward Michelson and the three prisoners to the place of execution with sixty-four fully armed soldiers and to arrange a thirty-six-man armed patrol of the town during the proceedings. In the meantime, the magistrates ordered the dissemination of two documents justifying the decision chosen from a number that had been composed at their request. One was selected for publication as a broadside, the other to be circulated to the clerks of each town in manuscript form. Both presented Quakerism as "destructive to fundamental trueths of religion" and the magistrates' support for the campaign against it as reasonable and necessary for the protection of the common good. The unpublished document dealt at length with the issue of persecution, la-

---

[29] Bishop, *New England Judged*, 89; Besse, *Sufferings*, 2:205.

[30] For the measures taken by the court at this time, see *RMB* 4, pt. 1:384–90, 383. For the law providing for banishment on pain of death, see ibid., 345–7.

[31] Ibid., 383–4; William Dyer, *Mary Dyer, Quaker: Two Letters of William Dyer of Rhode Island, 1659–1660* (Cambridge, Mass.: Harvard University Press, 1903). The records do not make clear whether the prisoners were present when the sentence was rescinded; apparently assuming that they were not, scholars have described the events at the site of the execution as if Dyer believed she were to be killed.

[32] On Quaker pacifism, which they did not actively embrace until after the Restoration, see Reay, *Quakers and the English Revolution*, 41–3. In 1661, the authorities would express fears of a literal Quaker invasion; see Henry Cadbury, "The Oldest Yearly Meeting," *The Friend* (24 April 1953), 373–4.

boring to prove that Quakers comported themselves "contrary to the expresse directions of Jesus Christ, & the approoved examples of his saints."[33]

The precautions taken by the authorities were justified, for the condemned men did attempt to appeal to the throngs of people who gathered in Boston to witness the hangings. On the morning scheduled for the event, before the lecture that usually preceded a public execution, Robinson addressed a large crowd from an upper-story window of the prison. Alerted to the danger, Captain Oliver arrived with his company to disperse the people. Failing this, he entered the building to move the prisoners, "hauling some of us very uncivilly downstairs" to be held in a windowless room. Only then did the crowd disperse. Many of them went to attend the lecture, where – one of the incarcerated Quakers assumed – "the priest . . . sharpened and hardened [his hearers] for the service."[34]

After the lecture, the spectators and the condemned Quakers proceeded to the place of execution. The ritual traditionally associated with executions in the colony had to be altered on this occasion, since the prisoners were not penitent and could not be expected to confess their errors with their last breaths. Indeed, these self-styled martyrs threatened to turn the imagery of public execution on its head by presenting themselves as the Lord's faithful servants who went to their deaths joyously.[35] The dying words of the two men, as well as the heckling of the spectators, was drowned out by the beating of drums. Mary Dyer was forced to stand with a halter around her neck as life was forced out of her companions; afterward, she had to be dragged off the scaffolding. The bodies of her friends were unceremoniously deposited into an unmarked grave.

Scholars have generally supposed that the populace was opposed to the harsh measures taken on that day and on the two subsequent occasions when the colony's government executed Quakers.[36] The court's concern to justify its proceedings in statements disseminated through the colony could be interpreted to indicate that the magistrates feared popular opposition. Had the populace been averse to the extreme measures adopted by the court, the executions could have been protested, if not prevented. However, that no formal expression of support for the condemned was forthcoming undermines the prevailing view that most colonists were unsupportive of the policy. Later, Salem Quaker Thomas Maule would boldly declare that the rulers had "the silent consent of

---

[33] Both documents were entered into the court records; see *RMB* 4, pt. 1:384–90; for quotes, see 386, 390.

[34] These events were described by Daniel Goold of Rhode Island, another of the jailed Quakers, in a tract published many years later in response to a then recent effort to justify the policy; see [Daniel Goold], *A Brief Narration of the Sufferings of the People called Quakers, who were put to death at Boston in New England* [Philadelphia, 1700], 8, 9, 1–2.

[35] Hall, *Worlds of Wonder*, 178–84, describes the rituals surrounding executions in New England.

[36] David Hall has recently declared this view "tempting"; ibid., 291, n. 66; also see 242.

the greatest part of the inhabitants."[37] In the only petition bearing on the subject, Bostonians asked that harsher penalties be developed; the government responded with the banishment law that provided for the execution of those who defied it. Keeping colonists away from the prisoners with a fence and an armed guard was probably only intended to protect the unwary from being contaminated by heretical Quaker beliefs. In any case, if the magistrates took these precautions in anticipation of an attempt to liberate the condemned, the events in the prison yard proved that their fears were inflated. The Quakers themselves apparently believed that the crowd that attended the hangings was largely hostile, despite their care at recording the few convincements that occurred in reaction to the martyrdom of Robinson and Stephenson.[38]

At most, a few of the spectators seem to have been Quaker sympathizers. John Davenport, for one, thought that the throng contained some non-Quakers sympathetic to the plight of the criminals. When a bridge collapsed under people who were returning to Boston, he suggested that the injuries were a divine punishment "against the Quakers and theyre abettors." The Quakers were equally certain that a woman who later died of wounds received in the mishap had been especially intent upon "reviling" the martyrs.[39] Although some ordinary people, like some leaders, came to believe that the colony had gone too far in killing these intransigent sectaries, there is no indication that even a sizable minority held this view as the act was being committed. Only with time to contemplate the executions and to witness the policy's failure to stem the tide of Quaker missionaries would some colonists conclude that the measure had been ill advised.[40] As late as the end of the century, at least a few Quakers were certain that most inhabitants of the region had not repented the murders.[41]

The executions of Robinson and Stephenson must have rocked the Salem Quaker community, and news of the incident spread far beyond the colony. Yet

---

[37] Thomas Maule, *Truth Held Forth and Maintained* ([New York], 1695), 196. For comparison, consider the response to attempts to banish Baptists a decade later, discussed in the next chapter.

[38] Although he blamed the "priest" for encouraging it, Daniel Goold believed that the populace went to the executions with hardened hearts; see *Brief Narration*, 9. The convincement of John Chamberlain occurred in reaction to the executions; see Bishop, *New England Judged*, 136–7.

[39] John Davenport to John Winthrop, Jr., 6 December 1659, *CMHS*, 4th ser., vol. 7 (1865): 507–8; Besse, *Sufferings*, 2:205.

[40] The earliest firm evidence that some residents opposed the policy is contained in Samuel Shattock's 1661 letter mentioning an unspecified number of the "moderate sort" who were glad when he arrived in Boston to deliver the king's order to cease executing Quakers; see *CMHS*, 4th ser., vol. 9 (1871): 160–2. The year before, traveling witness John Nicholson had suspected that the people of Boston were relieved when he and his wife departed rather than remaining to risk execution; see his letter to Margaret Fell, 10 July 1660, Swarthmore Collection, LSF, 4:929.

[41] George Keith, *The Presbyterian and Independent Churches of New England Brought to the Test* (Philadelphia, 1689), 202. Also see Maule, *Truth Held Forth*, 176.

a surprisingly large percentage of those first involved in the movement remained active. Only one man who had previously participated curtailed his activities at this time. Of course, some colonial Quakers were gone, banished from
the colony. At best, they faced the seemingly permanent imprisonment that
greeted aged Boston Quaker Nicholas Upshall when he returned that fall. A
few more may have fled or at least gone into hiding to escape punishment.
Hannah Phelps could not be found to receive a summons that was dispatched
for her in 1660. Always outspoken, she had been reported for announcing that
all "priests were deceivers of the people" and that Salem's new minister "Mr.
Higginson sent his wolves abroad and his blood hounds amongst the sheep and
lambs."[42]

As the persecution of Salem's Quakers increased, most sectaries, unlike Phelps,
remained to receive – and some even seemed to seek out – punishments. The
authorities learned, apparently from William Robinson's confiscated journal,
that Edward Wharton had accompanied Robinson and Stephenson through
northern New England. Three days after the execution, he was apprehended
and imprisoned. Eventually, the court banished him. In the next months, a
number of other local Quakers joined him in Boston jail: William King and
Goodwives Smith and Trask, after they had interrupted Salem church services
in February; the newly convinced Bostonian, John Chamberlain, for absences
in June; Margaret Smith's once unsympathetic husband, John, for haranguing
Salem's new minister at his ordination in August.[43] Official efforts to squelch
the sect appeared to be having the opposite effect, as their experience as a
beleaguered community only served to strengthen the local Quakers' sense that
they were struggling to do the Lord's work in a sinful world.[44]

The case of John Smith is illustrative of the failure of colonial policies to
crush the sect. Smith had been willing to assist the constable in breaking up
the Quaker meeting at the Phelps home in 1658. In the fall of 1659, he still
enjoyed a reputation as a non-Quaker. His wife Margaret was released to his
custody at that time on the strength of his orthodoxy. In the following months,
Smith came out decisively in favor of the sect. During the summer, after his
wife had been back in prison for about six months, Smith wrote to Governor
Endecott to chastise him for his role in the persecution. In this remarkable
letter, Smith addressed his former neighbor using the familiar "thee," as only
a Quaker would. The next month, Smith attended the ordination of John Higginson. As he later described it, he felt "moved of the Lord to declare against
them." During the service, he shouted, "What you are going about to set up,

---

[42] The lone man was Thomas Brackett. Perley, *History of Salem*, 2:252–3; John Smith to Joshua
      Buffum, 4 November 1660, in *EIHC* 50 (1914): 245; *EQC* 2:314.
[43] D. Goold, *Brief Narrativ* ., 6; Smith to Buffum, 245–6; "The Examination of Quakers," 7 March
      1659/60, in Hallowell, *Quaker Invasion*, 159–60.
[44] Bishop makes this point repeatedly; see, e.g., *New England Judged*, 78.

our God is pulling down." For this transgression, Smith was sent to Boston to join his wife. United once again in faith, as well as in fact, the Smiths remained in prison together for nearly a year until the following June.[45]

While persecution may have encouraged someone like Smith to join this new faith, the intensity of the confrontation also seems to have heightened the radicalism of the convinced. Certain that the end of the world was at hand and determined to concentrate on living by the light of truth, a number of Salem Quakers advocated celibacy during this period. When visiting English Quaker John Nicholson was incarcerated along with various local adherents to the sect in 1660, they reportedly snubbed him because of his wife's pregnancy. In the irate letter relating this information to Margaret Fell, Nicholson did not name the celibate Quakers, but birth records indicate that he was referring to the prisoners Margaret Smith and Mary Trask as well as, possibly, William King. The celibates claimed to have been supported in this form of witness by none other than the elder Southwick couple and the two martyrs, Marmaduke Stephenson and William Robinson. Since all four of these pivotal figures were dead by the time the conversation reported by Nicholson occurred, he could denounce but not disprove these claims.[46]

As their exchange with Nicholson suggests, imprisonment did not undermine the commitment of the colony's sectaries. With the exception of Trask, who enjoyed a few months at home with her husband and young children, and of King, who was banished, all the imprisoned Salem Quakers and a number of visitors remained in jail until June 1661. In prison, they learned of the executions of two more "publishers of the truth," the irrepressible Mary Dyer and their old friend William Leddra. If the brutal message of these executions did not sway them, neither did the comparatively magnanimous gesture made toward William King. King, returning in defiance of a sentence of banishment and facing the possibility of execution himself, recanted his Quakerism in March. The authorities pardoned King and restored his civil rights, obviously hoping

---

[45] *RMB* 4, pt. 1:433; John Smith to John Endecott, in Besse, *Sufferings*, 2:208–11; Smith to Buffum, 246; Thomas Hutchinson, *The History of the Colony of Massachusetts Bay, 1628–1691*, 2d ed. (London, 1760 [i.e., 1765]), 203.

[46] Joseph Nicholson to Margaret Fell, 1660, Swarthmore Collection, LSF, 4:922–3. Margaret Smith bore no children from 1657 until 1664 and Mary Trask from 1656 to 1669. Apparently the Kings were naturally infertile, since their quarter-century marriage failed to produce a single recorded birth; celibacy practiced by the Kings cannot therefore be demonstrated by a gap in births. Births to Katherine Shafflin King's sister, Sarah Shafflin Stone, occurred at a slightly long interval (forty-two months) at this time, which may indicate that she or her husband Robert advocated the practice briefly. The remaining Salem Quakers had children at the usual intervals, except when the banishment of one spouse disrupted the pattern. No evidence exists to support Nicholson's assertion that celibacy "went for doctrine among them aboute Salem till Jane [his pregnant wife and a traveling witness] came" to the region. Most information on births among Quakers can be found in the biographical notes in Perley, *History of Salem*.

to persuade other sectaries to return to the orthodox fold. This indication that they were prepared to be lenient also failed to dissuade Salem's Quakers.[47]

The patience of the jailed sectaries was finally rewarded. From prison, they witnessed the turning of the tide in the official battle against Quakerism. Two months after the fourth execution, aware that its policy was not producing the desired result of reducing the number of Quakers in the colony and suspecting that it was not likely to meet with the approbation of the newly restored monarchy, the General Court passed the Cart and Whip Act.[48] Henceforth, foreign Quakers would no longer be mutilated, incarcerated, or killed. Rather, they would be transported out of the colony, pausing to be tied to a cart and whipped through the streets of three towns along the way. Local Quakers would fare better as well. In June, the government failed to prosecute Edward Wharton when he followed William King's lead and slipped back into Salem although banished. During the same month, the court ordered the release of the imprisoned Quakers. The authorities drove the nonresident sectaries from the colony under the new act, but permitted Salem converts to return to their homes. After three years of banishment, Samuel Shattock returned triumphant in November, carrying a letter from the king that guaranteed an end to the most severe punishments. After this date, the magistrates would order Quakers whipped as vagabonds or fined and disfranchised for absences, but they no longer punished them specifically for the crime of Quakerism. The banished men were able to return to their families once more.[49]

After four tumultuous years of rapid growth and ferocious persecution, a sizable Quaker meeting existed in Salem. More than fifty people participated regularly during the first decade and a half.[50] Most of them resided in Salem, especially in the western section known as the Farms. The convinced included both men and women, probably in roughly equal numbers. Many of them were, like the Southwick clan that played such an important role in the opening phase of the struggle with the authorities, bound together by family ties. Those bonds

[47] RMB 4, pt. 1:419; Bishop, New England Judged, 317. On King, see Smith to Buffum, 246; Perley, History of Salem, 2:267; RMB 4, pt. 2:8.

[48] Mr. John Leverett to Governor Endecott and the General Court, 13 September 1660, The Hutchinson Papers, 2:41; Daniel Neal believed that public opinion at home and abroad brought about the end of persecution apart from word such as that sent by Leverett; History of New England to 1700, 2 vols. (London, 1720), 1:315. RMB 4, pt. 1:419.

[49] RMB 4, pt. 2:2–4, 19–20, 23–4, 87–8; Besse, Sufferings, 2:221–2; Jones, Quakers in the American Colonies, 96n.; CMHS, 4th ser., vol. 9 (1871): 159.

[50] The following prosopography has been extrapolated largely from biographical notes in Perley, History of Salem; ECPR; and, to a lesser extent, EQC and Savage, Genealogical Dictionary. One's status as a Quaker was determined by the following criteria: either professing oneself a Quaker, undergoing punishment for Quaker crimes (such as attending meetings and refusing "hat honor"), frequent citations for absences in the company of other known Quakers, or mention as a convert in Quaker pamphlets, letters, or meeting records. Although less reliable for the period after the 1660s, the list compiled by Jonathan Chu using many of the same sources is helpful for this period; see Neighbors, Friends, or Madmen, 169–71.

were strengthened by a newfound commitment to this radical religious sect; participation in it set them decisively apart from their uninvolved neighbors and kin. Despite the shocking recantation of one of the least committed members of the Southwick clan in the early 1670s, most participants in this nascent Quaker community remained true to their new understanding of the truth.[51]

The concerted effort to rid the colony of Quakers came to an end in 1661, five years after the first English Quakers arrived in Boston. The obvious failure of colonial policy and the English government's condemnation of it effectively forced the authorities to give up their goal of a religiously unified colony. With no choice but to accept the presence of the convinced in Salem, the colony's leaders struggled to keep the enclave of Quakers from expanding further. Their task was made somewhat easier by a sharp decline in the traveling witnesses coming into the colony. Events in Restoration England apparently drew Quakers home to deal with the challenges there, while Massachusetts lost much of its appeal as a forum for witnessing once the persecution subsided. As one former missionary explained it, Quaker witnessing ceased because God had given up on New England.[52] Still, the struggle between the Salem Quakers and the local authorities continued for the remainder of the decade, albeit at a somewhat lower pitch. The sectaries actively criticized the religious establishment in general and the colony's persecution of the sect in particular. In symbolic statements or in direct confrontations, they carried on the battle against the New England way that had been started by visitors in the previous decade.

Resident Quakers employed forms of symbolic protests then in use among English radicals and developed others to suit their circumstances. Drawing upon a long-standing English radical tradition,[53] Josiah Southwick indicated his "contempt of authority by keeping on his hat after he was required to pull it off." Two New England Quaker women utilized a far more extreme form of witnessing when they went "naked for a sign" during the 1660s, in imitation of the Old Testament prophet Isaiah. Young Quaker Deborah Buffum Wilson, in the company of her mother and half sister, walked naked through the streets of Salem in the fall of 1662. Shortly thereafter, Lydia Wardell, a recently married Hampton Quaker, "came part naked into [Newbury] meeting house on a lords day, a littl before meeting began."[54] Since no visiting Quaker had employed this form of witness in the colony – which had been in use in England during

---

[51] John Southwick, eldest son of Lawrence and Cassandra, recanted in the early 1670s after the death of his more committed wife. The town reclaimed him with a vengeance, elected him constable in 1672; when he died part way through his term, they replaced him with his kinsman Francis Nurse. See "Town Records of Salem," *EIHC*, 49 (1913): 140, 148–9.

[52] Christopher Holder, *The Faith and Testimony of the Martyrs* [London?, 1670], 8.

[53] Denying "hat honor" predated the Quaker movement in the colony. Three Rhode Island Baptist missionaries refused to remove their hats when forced to attend Lynn's church meeting in 1651; see Edwin S. Gaustad, Introduction to *Baptist Piety: The Last Will and Testimony of Obadiah Holmes* (Grand Rapids, Mich.: Christian University Press, 1978), 24.

[54] *EQC* 3:17, 64.

the 1650s and was usually intended to convey the spiritual nakedness of the unconvinced – these young women must have adopted the practice after hearing about it from others. In contrast to England, however, women but not men utilized this form of protest in the colony.[55]

Occasionally, Quakers developed fairly elaborate strategies to communicate their objections to the establishment.[56] In the ongoing battle over the distraint of goods and property to cover the cost of unpaid fines, John Smith demonstrated his stubbornness. When the Salem magistrates had his salt marsh seized and sold, Smith hired two younger Quakers to harvest the hay and thatch that grew on the land. Edmund Batter, a virulent anti-Quaker who had purchased the plot from the county, was forced to sue the harvesters for theft in order to receive the value of the meadow's produce. Batter invariably won these cases.[57] But with the help of Joshua Buffum, Robert Wilson, John Burton, Jr., and others, Smith made his views on fines, confiscations, and Mr. Batter clear.

These acts challenged the authority of the court, denied the legitimacy of punishments meted out to dissenters, or made general, if vague, statements against colonial society. Verbal criticisms, however, had the advantage of directness and precision. While going naked for a sign was the act of the exceptional sectarian woman, Quaker men favored direct, verbal confrontations. In doing so, they reaffirmed magistrate Richard Bellingham's assessment that "their Religion is to speake rebellion and sedition in the presence and to the face of authority."[58] The colonial religious establishment was often a target for such attacks. Long-time Salem resident John Burton brought his criticism directly into the local tavern and to the gathered magistrates in 1661:

> Coming into the court in an uncivil manner, Burton reproached the court by saying they were robbers and destroyers of the widows and fatherless, that their priests divined for money and their worship was not the worship of God, interrupting and affronting the court, and upon being commanded silence, he commanded them silence and continued speaking until the court was fain to commit him to the stocks.[59]

With similar aplomb, Philip Verrin, Jr., delivered his challenge to the colonial elite personally. He "was ordered to be set by the heels in the stocks for dis-

---

55 Richard Bauman discussed the practice; *Let Your Words Be Few: Symbolism of Speaking and Silence among Seventeenth-Century Quakers* (Cambridge University Press, 1983), 84–94.

56 As another example, Gertrude Pope pleaded not guilty in 1667 to absences from the public worship of God. Since she had been attending Quaker meetings exclusively for nearly a decade and had been excommunicated from Salem Church five years before, Pope was apparently trying to suggest that Quaker meetings constituted the public worship of God. Needless to say, she was found guilty and fined. See *EQC* 3:434.

57 Ibid., 2:460, 275–6; 4:52–3. Batter may have been especially hostile toward Quakers because he wanted to disassociate himself from a sect that some of his kin had joined; these family ties are discussed in Chapter 6.

58 Quoted in Howgill, *Popish Inquisition*, 65.   59 *EQC* 2:337.

owning [in open court] the country's power . . . to force anyone to come to public worship." Finally, at the close of the first decade of Quakerism in Salem, the constable whipped newly arrived Thomas Maule for voicing a standard Quaker complaint against orthodox ministers and one that Hannah Phelps would have agreed with: John Higginson preached lies.[60]

Besides attacking the religious establishment generally, the sectaries also protested the executions of their fellow Quakers in Boston. The first person to witness against the executions before the county court was Hampton Quaker Eliakim Wardell. His wife having recently gone naked into Newbury meeting-house, Wardell

> charged the worshipful Mr. Bradstreet as he sat upon the bench, in the face of the county, with acting maliciously, as in the sentence of Wardell's wife at Ipswich, and further instancing the deaths of their four friends as he called them with other reproachful speeches.

Samuel Shattock had something to add to the second of Wardell's themes: He was sentenced for "charging the court and the country, in the face of the court with being guilty of innocent blood."[61]

Nathaniel Hadlock offered a more sweeping indictment, voicing objections to both the town's minister and the colony's anti-Quaker policies. A recent arrival in Salem, he

> confessed to attending three Quaker meetings & to refusing to aid [the] constable. [He] said he profitted more by going to the Quakers meetings than he did hearing John Higgeson, and that the Governor was as guilty in shedding [the] innocent blood of the Quakers as Susanna Cravet [who was convicted of infanticide] was in murdering her child.

Admonished, fined, and whipped, Hadlock was required to post bond for good behavior.[62]

The most dramatic of these incidents occurred five years later, on the tenth anniversary of the first Quaker presentments in Essex County Quarterly Court:

> Edward Wharton, coming into the court in an irreverant manner and [in] contempt of authority with his hat on, and refusing to take it off, he having no business with the court, boldly charged the gov't. in open court with unrighteousness. Afterwards coming into court again, he charged the gov't. in open court with cruelty & the shedding of innocent blood, which upon his trial he owned, and it being demanded whether he did not [act] wickedly in so speaking, he replied "God forbid I shoulde owne that to be wicked which God requires of me." He was sentenced for his high offence to pay a fine of 50 li. and to lie in prison until the fine be paid.

---

[60] Ibid., 3:111.   [61] Ibid., 100, 110.

[62] Ibid., 4:74–5. The court was able to extract a confession from Hadlock around this time, but he may have continued to be affiliated with the Quakers. Heyrman, "Specters of Subversion," 41.

Wharton had already begun a career as an itinerant Quaker witness, having traveled through northern New England and down to Boston on that errand. His coming into court despite the fact that he had no business there was reminiscent of banished English Quaker Wenlock Christianson's dramatic entry into the meeting of the General Court during the sentencing of William Leddra in 1661. Without a sentence of death hanging over his own head, Wharton's act probably did not meet with the stunned silence that greeted Christianson, but the court was clearly disturbed by his audacity.[63]

In protesting the executions of the four Quaker martyrs, Wardell, Shattock, and Wharton attacked the establishment at a particularly vulnerable point. Between precarious political relations with the English monarch and some local grumblings against the policy, colonial authorities felt none too comfortable with having to defend publicly the more extreme measures taken against the Quakers. The confrontations over this issue were highly charged, both for the magistrates who were forced to support publicly what had been done and for the Quakers who had known the martyrs.

One of the more extreme instances of Salem Quaker defiance, Wharton's act was also among the last cited in the local court.[64] The sporadic barrage of challenges against the dominant religious and political system launched by Quakers for a decade after the founding of the Salem meeting subsided after 1668. To the extent that such dramatic forms of witness were fueled by hopes for the immediate end of the world, the local Quaker community must have despaired finally of the imminence of the millennium. By the late 1660s, the radical cause had been defeated in England, and the situation in Massachusetts had begun to stabilize: Convincements had slowed, as had missionary visits. In addition, the Salem meeting was becoming aware of disagreements dividing its coreligionists elsewhere. Concern over this news, if not arguments within the local community about where to stand on the same issues, probably distracted Salem Quakers from their battle with the establishment.[65]

To the extent that government harassment – usually in the form of presentments for absences – had provided a forum for delivering these harangues, the reduction in legal prosecutions of Quakers also helped to defuse hostilities. The policy of repeatedly fining Quakers – the major penalty available for use against resident radicals – was not fully satisfactory, because it would ultimately impoverish familes who would then require assistance from the town. In addition

---

[63] *EQC* 4:41; Besse, *Sufferings*, 2:231–2, 221–2.

[64] One later instance – an attempt by Josiah Southwick, Margaret Thompson Smith, and Mary Southwick Trask to disrupt worship services in 1676 – was recorded, but little evidence about it survives; *EQC* 6:191–2.

[65] One of the few visitors to the region, Samuel Hooten, reported that "friends were much scattered and shattered in their mindes one against another, in so much that their first love was cooled, by ye disorderly spirit that had beene amongst them." See his Something Concerning my travell, 204.

to creating financial liabilities, the policy had political dangers as well. The royal commissioners who visited the colony in 1664–5 reaffirmed the monarch's disapproval of its anti-Quaker policies, which had first been expressed in the missive delivered by Shattock in 1661. Fearful that the charter would be revoked, the authorities quietly reduced the fines levied against resident Quakers and the number of court appearances required of them while the royal commissioners were in New England.[66] Grudgingly, the government gave up the battle. Although Quaker objections to the establishment remained, the conditions necessary to maintain this highly emotional, confrontational stance no longer existed.

After one decade, Quakerism was available as an alternative to the established order, in Salem at least. Successful in this, if not in achieving some of the sect's grander goals for the reformation of the world, the Quakers gradually abandoned their practice of directly confronting the establishment. Always concerned with living by the light of truth, their attentions would soon become focused on maintaining what they had erected and passing it on to their children. With this, the first period of Quakerism in Salem came to an end.

[66] The royal commissioners arrived in Boston in March 1664 and conducted their investigation in New England and New York through the fall of 1665. As a result of their unfavorable report about the Bay colony, the king ordered the government to send agents to England in April 1666 to answer charges; Transactions of the Commissioners in New England, received 14 December 1665, *Calendar of State Papers, Colonial Series*, vol. 5: *America and West Indies, 1661–1668*, ed. W. Noel Sainsbury (London: Her Majesty's Stationery Office, 1880), 345; Richard S. Dunn, *Puritans and Yankees: The Winthrop Dynasty of New England, 1630–1717* (Princeton, N.J.: Princeton University Press, 1962), ch. 7. At the September session of the Essex County Court, the Quakers' fines were reduced; Chu, *Neighbors, Friends, or Madmen*, 127.

2

A *"pretended church"* in *Charlestown and Boston*

Even as the spirited confrontation between the Salem Quakers and the defenders of orthodoxy was slackening, a second sect was struggling to gain a foothold in Massachusetts Bay. A small group of baptized believers gathered a church in Charlestown in 1665. With this act, Anabaptist agitation in the colony – which had traditionally been diffused and sporadic – became focused and sustained. In a continuation of this tradition and in marked contrast to the localistic nature of the Quaker movement, Baptist converts lived scattered throughout many colonial towns. As had been the case in the years before 1665, those who favored the Baptist faith remained intimately engaged in issues of importance to the orthodox faith.

The position of this new church was not as precarious as that of the Quaker meeting had initially been. The presence of Quakers in the colony as well as the monarch's well-known opposition to severe persecution forestalled a similarly vicious effort to suppress the Baptist church. In addition, this second movement had greater credibility than Quakerism, because of both the people who joined and the views they advocated. Despite the relative advantages enjoyed by the Baptists and the recent failure of efforts to crush the Quaker movement, the authorities labored to prevent the creation and growth of a Baptist church in the colony. By the early 1670s, their efforts had failed.

At about two o'clock on the afternoon of 7 March 1668/9, nineteen people met in the Charlestown home of wheelwright and farmer Thomas Goold to worship the Lord.[1] Some came across the Charles River from Boston, others traveled down from the town of Woburn ten miles to the north and west, and the remainder were Goold's neighbors from the community. Although this little group had come together many times in the past, this day in March was a special occasion. Brothers Goold and William Turner were reunited with their companions after many months in Boston prison, giving cause for rejoicing on this Sabbath day. The faithful crowded together in the main room of the Goold house for the service, which probably lasted a few hours.

Consciously patterned on the primitive Christian church, their worship fol-

[1] This meeting was reported to the magistrates, MCC, 7 April 1669.

44

lowed a fairly simple format.[2] Goold or one of the other men who had been blessed with a special gift would read and preach on a passage from the Scriptures. The discourse was a loosely organized explication of the passage, peppered with biblical allusions and homespun analogies. Then, believing that "when the church is mett together they may all prophesie one by one that all may learne and all may be comforted,"[3] the baptized believers had an opportunity to exhort the gathering. Apparently, any church member who felt called to teach or comfort their gathered friends could speak at this point.[4] Next, a second scriptural passage might be explored by Goold or some other, perhaps the promising young shoemaker, John Russell, Jr. Had this particular Sabbath been appointed as a day when the Lord's Supper was to be shared, the seven church members in attendance would have come forward to partake of it. As it had not, everyone simply joined together in prayer, bringing the meeting to a close.

As the Woburn housewright John Johnson was exercising the gift of lay prophecy, Charlestown constables Richard Lowden and John Knight entered the room. Unlike their counterparts in Salem a decade before, Lowden and Knight stood quietly watching, allowing the service to continue. After Johnson had finished, Goold read Canticles I:2, "Let him kiss me with kisses of his mouth, for your love is better than wine." Goold preached on this appropriately joyous, even sensual, Old Testament passage, then ended the meeting with a prayer. Having waited for the conclusion of the service, the constables took down each person's name, ascertained the time their meeting had begun, and departed.

The constables' visit to Goold's farm that Sabbath day was part of a concerted but ill-fated campaign to destroy a "pretended church" established in Charlestown three years earlier and organized around Particular Baptist principles. The constables' list, submitted at the next session of the Middlesex county court, enumerated nineteen law breakers.[5] Of those named, Goold, Turner, Mary Newell, and Edward Drinker had been among the original nine church members. All three men had suffered imprisonment for their activities. Thomas's wife, Mary [ ] Howard Goold, would not join the church that her husband had helped found until about 1670. Johnson, who had been caught in the act of exhorting the gathering, was a recent convert, as was his fellow townsman, Russell. Benjamin Sweetser, Charlestown lastmaker, had been rebaptized quite recently after expressing his support for the group in a petition he had circulated the previous fall.[6] The other eleven people who gathered that day at

---

[2] The Baptists, like orthodox colonists but unlike Quakers, were biblical primitivists; see Bozeman, *To Live Ancient Lives.*
[3] Baptist Record Book, September 1665.   [4] But see note 8.
[5] *RMB* 4, pt. 2:373; MCC, 7 April 1669.
[6] Baptist Record Book, 28 May 1665; Petition to Massachusetts General Court on behalf of Thomas Goold, William Turner, and John Farnum, November 1668, MAE, 10:221; *RMB* 4, pt. 2:413.

Goold's were not baptized believers, although some would later join the church. Thus, the meeting included the truly dedicated as well as the merely interested. The former enjoyed a sense of their own election and felt an antipathy to the practices of the established churches, while the latter were less certain about one or both of these issues. This March gathering was the largest reported to date.

While the converts looked to Goodman Goold for guidance and he alone may have administered the Lord's Supper,[7] leadership was fairly fluid. Any of the baptized men might minister to the little flock, especially as imprisonment or distance sometimes kept their elder Goold from being present. In the three years since its founding, the tiny church had suffered from the imprisonment of four of its most able and dedicated members, which inadvertently promoted this flexibility still further. The emphasis on lay prophecy that set their church apart from the others in the Bay colony encouraged the participation of every member. This practice helped the group to discover who among them was particularly gifted. Any of the eleven active male church members might take a leading role in their meetings, while the three female members may have been able to speak informally at the time set aside for exhortation by the laity.[8]

Although the constables had come and gone without incident, their presence was unwelcome. After months in prison, Goold and Turner had been released temporarily, in order to see to their personal affairs. On that Sabbath day, they were outlaws, having been due back in prison two days before. If they had entertained hopes of remaining at liberty unmolested, the arrival of Lowden and Knight dashed them. Acting for the first time in five months on a warrant issued the year before, the constables had come out to the west Charlestown farm to catch Goold, Turner, and the rest in the act of "schismaticalie meeting on the Sabbath day."[9] This renewed vigilance indicated that the authorities did not intend to let the matter drop. As the meeting broke up late that afternoon and the participants traveled back to their scattered homes and communities, they were uncertain when or where they would be able to meet again.

The circumstances that took constables Lowden and Knight away from the

---

[7] John Eliot to Richard Baxter, 26 June 1669, Baxter Letters, vol. 3, nos. 131–2, Dr. Williams's Library, London, states that Goold administered this ordinance. Whether the church did without during Goold's imprisonment or made other arrangements is unclear.

[8] In sanctioning lay prophecy for all members, the church may not have intended this to extend to women. Member William Turner objected that the established church denied brethren this right; "Baptist Debate," ed. McLoughlin and Davidson, 116. English Particular Baptist churches tended to exclude women; see Murray Tolmie, *The Triumphs of the Saints: The Separate Churches of London, 1616–1649* (Cambridge University Press, 1977), 14. Lyle Koehler believes that only the Rhode Island churches allowed women to preach, although on what authority he does not indicate; *A Search for Power: The "Weaker Sex" in Seventeenth-Century Massachusetts* (Chicago: University of Illinois Press, 1980), 243.

[9] Felt, *Ecclesiastical History*, 2:433; MCC, 14 November 1668.

public worship of God in Charlestown meetinghouse and out to Goold's farm on that Sabbath afternoon were long in the making. The Particular Baptist church that met in the Goolds' main chamber that day, although not quite three years old, developed out of a series of events that began some thirteen years earlier. Only from 1663 until the church's founding in 1665 had antipedobaptist meetings been regularly held in the colony. For eight years prior to that, most of those who would join the church were not publicly associated with such views. From 1655 until 1663, the only future church member taking a principled, public position against the baptism of infants had been Thomas Goold.

Initially, Goold was hardly distinguishable from dozens of other colonists who had "scrupled" the practice of infant baptism, one of the thornier issues in the Christian faith. In 1655, after much soul searching, he refused to bring his newborn daughter, Elizabeth, forward to be baptized. According to her father, this child was born after "God was pleased at last to make it clear to me by the rule of the gospel, that children were not capable nor fit subjects for such an ordinance."[10] For two years after this, while the church followed the usual procedure of discussing his "error" with him, Goold continued in full communion. Only in late 1657 or early 1658 did the church admonish him.[11] Too forward about his doubts, Goold had lost the privilege of having his children baptized, a punishment that ironically removed the occasion for confrontation. This turn of events created a stalemate that would continue for another five years. As long as Goodman Goold attended public worship and did not disrupt any baptisms that he happened to witness, his differences with the established church need have gone no further. Other Bay colony churches apparently included members who had rejected infant baptism but who had not embraced believer's baptism.[12] The standoff might have continued indefinitely.

While Goold's objections to the practice of baptizing infants was relatively unthreatening because he was alone in making them, even during these early years some people signaled their support for Goold's position. According to Goold's own account, some Charlestown Church members were sympathetic to his concerns. In addition, Goold's friends indicated their support for him by participating in a private religious gathering in his home in 1655, just as his troubles with the church were beginning. Apparently to celebrate the fact that Mary Goold had survived the birth of their daughter, Goold arranged "to keep a day of Thanksgiving to God for his mercy shown to my wife." Although the colonists who gathered to take part may not have been conscious of it, this

---

[10] Thomas Goold's narration, in Wood, *History*, 42–43. For other colonists who acted on similar doubts, see Gura, *Glimpse of Sion's Glory*, 105–6.

[11] Church votes [henceforth, Charlestown Church votes], *Records of the First Church in Charlestown*, ed. Hunnewell, 1.

[12] See the Case of John Farnum, Boston Second Church Records, Bk 3, 1683, on deposit at MHS; and, for examples in England during the 1640s, Tolmie, *Triumph of the Saints*, 53–4.

celebration drew upon an English Baptist tradition, which provided an opportunity to commemorate a birth in lieu of a baptism.[13] Unfortunately, except for two men whose names were recorded, the composition of the group (and its relationship to the future church's membership) cannot be recovered.[14]

Goold's objections may have initially received additional support from Harvard president Henry Dunster. A resident in the neighboring town of Cambridge, Dunster had withheld his own child from baptism in 1653. On 30 July 1654, he had interrupted public meeting to object to the practice, "though desired by the elder to forebeare, and not to interrupt an ordinance of Christ."[15] The following year, Dunster was apparently present at the gathering in Goold's home.[16] After Charlestown Church had formally admonished Goold, thereby denying him the ordinance of the Lord's Supper, he avoided church services there by attending public worship at "Cambridge meeting which was" – he later explained – "as near my house as the other [meetinghouse]." Convenience may not have been the only factor influencing his choice: The minister at Cambridge, Jonathan Mitchell, temporarily entertained scruples of his own about the practice of baptizing infants, having been led to doubt the ordinance by Dunster, whose views Mitchell was attempting to reform.[17] Knowledge of this incident may have made Cambridge Church more appealing to Goold than Charlestown Church.

In 1663, the area of open disagreement between Goold and the church expanded, and Goold's dissent began to converge with criticisms made by others. In that year, he was rebuked by Charlestown Church for "persisting in his schismatical withdrawing from the church . . . and now for denying his relation

[13] T. Goold's narration, 43. Some (especially General) Baptists developed a formal dedication service for children, which was denounced by others as "dry Baptism." See T. L. Underwood, "Child Dedication Services among British Baptists in the Seventeenth Century," *Baptist Quarterly* 23 (1969–70): 165–9; Michael J. Walker, "The Relation of Infants to Church, Baptism and Gospel in Seventeenth Century Baptist Theology," ibid., 21 (1965–6): 242–62.

[14] Mr. Dunstan and Thomas Wilder (neither of whom joined the Baptist church) were in attendance; T. Goold's narration, 43–4.

[15] Pulsifer Transcript, 1:74–6.

[16] The evidence for this comes from T. Goold's narration, 43, which refers to a "Mr. Dunstan," whom most scholars have assumed was Dunster. William McLoughlin questions this assumption because Dunster was apparently already living in Scituate at this time (*New England Dissent*, 52n.). His removal in 1655 makes the grand jury presentment against him in 1657 for failure to have a child baptized problematic; see MCC, 22 May 1657. His biographer believes he traveled back and forth frequently during this period to see to his affairs and did attend the meeting at Goold's; Chaplin, *Life of Henry Dunster*, 157–64, 200–4.

Gura, however, makes more of this incident than the records warrant. Goold said that Dunstan helped him to draft a reply to a request for a meeting, but Gura summarizes the document as stating that Dunster advised Goold as he "compiled and publicly defended his baptist beliefs"; *Glimpse of Sion's Glory*, 123.

[17] T. Goold's narration, 43, 48; Pulsifer Transcript, 1:132–3; Charlestown Church votes, ed. Hunnewell, 1; MCC, 21 June 1659; Cotton Mather, *Magnalia Christi Americana* (1702; Hartford, Conn., 1820), 2:79.

to this church, as a brother of it, also for denying the churches power over him." The brethren may have decided, at this point, to press the issue with Goold because, as active proponents of the decision to extend baptism to the grandchildren of visible saints, they may have considered his objections answered by the synod's decision of 1662.[18] In addition, the brethren may have only recently heard that Goold was blaming them for his departure from communion. By denying him his rights as a member, Goold reasoned, they had forced him to seek spiritual fellowship elsewhere. This argument would later be one of the basic premises Goold used to justify the gathering of a new church.

Not only was Goold's position gradually becoming more extreme, his dissent was intermeshing with the radical sentiments of other colonists. At the same time as Goold's case came before the church, two other rebels closely linked with him were disciplined. Thomas Osborn, "leavened with the principles of Anabaptisme," had not only failed to attend public worship but had argued that "it be no sin to neglect the publick ordinances of God on the Lord's day." His wife had gone further: Sarah's Anabaptism was, according to the Charlestown saints, supplemented with a dose of "Quakerisme."[19] Furthermore, she was accused of "denying our churches to be true churches." By the end of the year, Goold and Thomas Osborn were participating in private meetings in Goold's home with a number of others.[20] The "contagion of heresy" was spreading, as any orthodox observer might have predicted.

For eighteen months, these illegal meetings went largely undisturbed, a lapse in colonial law enforcement due in part to the recent experience with indigenous Quakerism and in part to the nature of this new threat. The campaign against Quakerism had proved a failure at home and a political liability abroad. Popular grumblings against the Quaker executions encouraged restraint in the treatment of other dissenters at the same time that they may have swelled the new sect's ranks.[21] Relations with the monarch were also a cause for great concern; in 1664, he dispatched royal commissioners to Boston to prepare a report on the colony's unauthorized activities. At a time when the king and some colonists were dismayed by the excesses of the anti-Quaker crusade, the authorities probably hoped to avoid a confrontation in which this issue would be articulated. A convincing argument could be made in favor of a moderate response to the events in Charlestown based on difficult political lessons learned from the Quaker crisis.

The religious issues raised by the sect were problematic as well. Although the colonial establishment never wavered from the position that certain infants

---

[18] Charlestown Church votes, ed. Hunnewell, 2; Pope, *Half-Way Covenant*, 136–7.
[19] Charlestown Church votes, ed. Hunnewell, 2.
[20] T. Goold's narration, 48; Pulsifer Transcript, 1:297.
[21] Hooten, Something Concerning my travell, 204–5; Charlestown Church votes, ed. Hunnewell, 5.

were acceptable candidates for baptism, some colonists felt that the issue was not "fundamental, plain and clear, but circumstantial, more dark and doubtful, wherein saints are wont to differ."[22] One colonist declared that the confusion over the Anabaptists' heterodoxy was a ploy of the sectaries, whom he likened to wolves in sheep's clothing. Not all lay people were as confident on this score as Roger Clap, however.[23] That a colonist with the stature and intellectual training of Henry Dunster had succumbed to the Baptist faith undoubtedly gave others pause. The sense that infant baptism was a debatable point had been inadvertently encouraged by the halfway covenant and the disagreements that ensued from it. Those who opposed the reform may have been inclined to view doubts about the baptizing of infants with sympathy; certainly, their stance was associated with Anabaptism in the minds of the reform's supporters.[24] That the halfway covenant had served as a catalyst for the founding of the Baptist church served to strengthen this connection. As the new church was being gathered, Boston's First Church was battling over the issue, on the verge of the most serious schism in the Bay colony to date. Even those who hoped to crush the Anabaptist movement knew the confrontation was better postponed. Increase Mather, for one, resented what he saw as the sectaries' clever timing, later observing, "I need not say how New England was circumstanced that hour."[25]

After meeting for eighteen months, nine people gathered a church in the spring of 1665. Quite possibly they intentionally did so while the special commission was in Massachusetts investigating the colony's adherence to royal policies.[26] Four Charlestown men, Goold, Osborn, Turner, and John George, "entered into fellowship and communion" and were baptized by immersion. Next they joined with three men and two women "who hath walked in that order in Old England" and therefore had received believer's baptism already.[27] Although in their faith and practice the Baptists can be described as an indigenous offshoot of New England Puritanism, the Baptist church initially included more English than colonial converts.[28] With the gathering of their church,

[22] Petition on Behalf of Goold.
[23] Memoir of Roger Clap (Boston, 1731), 35.
[24] [Richard Mather], A Defense of the Answer and Argument of the Synod met at Boston in the year 1662 (Cambridge, 1664), 13; Mitchell, An Answer to the Apologetical Preface, 5–6, 27; E. Brooks Holifield, The Covenant Sealed: The Development of Puritan Sacramental Theology in Old and New England, 1570–1720 (New Haven, Conn.: Yale University Press, 1974), 181–2.
[25] The Divine Right of Infant-Baptisme asserted and proved from Scriptures and Antiquity (Boston, 1680), 26.
[26] McLoughlin, Introduction to "Baptist Debate," ed. McLoughlin and Davidson, 94.
[27] Baptist Record Book, 28 May 1665. Robert A. Baker and Paul J. Craven, Jr., believe that two of them, Richard and Mary Goodall, had been baptized in England before 1638 when they came to New England; see Adventure in Faith: The First 300 Years of First Baptist Church, Charlestown, South Carolina (Nashville, Tenn.: Broadman, 1982), 51.
[28] McLoughlin, New England Dissent, 5–7. This trend would, however, be reversed within a few years.

these colonists created an alternative religious institution that they would spend the next decade defending against the authorities.

In addition to these church members, the congregation included others who did not feel the call to baptism at this time. Mary Goold worshiped with the group from the first but did not undergo baptism until the little church was five years old. By this time, her children from her first marriage may have already begun attending meetings as well, although they would never seek baptism.[29] At least one of the religious rebels who had been frequenting a tiny Quaker meeting in the area eventually worshiped with – but did not join – the Anabaptists, an unusual shift in northeastern Massachusetts.[30] Others from the neighborhood may have attended out of curiosity or due to the distance to the meetinghouse.[31] Perhaps some nonmembers in Boston attended the fortnightly lectures held in the home of Boston potter Edward Drinker, while abstaining from the baptismal rite.[32]

The Baptist movement coalesced into a church in 1665 because a modest number of colonists were sufficiently dismayed over the situation in the established churches to find the Baptist alternative attractive. The recent decision to extend baptism may have been the most important single issue leading colonists to join. Thomas Osborn articulated another widely held objection to the standing order: "allowing none but such as had human learning to be in the ministry." Baptists had been criticizing this aspect of the standing order at least since 1651, when Rhode Islander John Clarke offered to debate the issue with Bay colony leaders.[33] Many years later, describing the founding of the Baptist church, Cotton Mather concluded that this penchant for "promiscuous prophesie"[34] was the major point at issue:

> These men having privately exercised their gifts in meetings with applause, began to think themselves wronged that their light was put under a bushel and finding no remedy in our churches, they threw on a cloak of Anabaptism, and so gained the thing that they aimed at in a disguise.[35]

[29] T. Goold's narration, 48; Baptist Record Book, 1669–71; MCC, 7 April 1669.

[30] Only two colonists were involved in both sects. During the early period, Benamuel Bowers, who participated in the 1668 debate, was an overseer of Thomas Goold's will; Mary Goold, Petition to the Council, 22 January 1676/7, Massachusetts Archives Photostat Collection, 39:478, MHS. On his Quakerism, see Henry J. Cadbury, "Early Quakers at Cambridge," *Publications of the Cambridge Historical Society* 24 (1938): 79–81.

[31] Samuel Willard suggested that the relative convenience of Goold's meeting led some unwary colonists to expose themselves to the heresy; *Ne Sutor Ultra Crepidam* (Boston, 1681), 22.

[32] "Rev. Samuel Danforth's Records of the First Church in Roxbury, Mass.," *NEHGR* 34 (1880): 164.

[33] Charlestown Church votes, ed. Hunnewell, 5; John Clarke, *Ill Newes from New-England* (London, 1652), 62. Also see "Baptist Debate," ed. McLoughlin and Davidson, 117; Humphrey Churchwood quoted in Backus, *History*, 1:402–3n; and Increase Mather on John Farnum in his diary, 18 August 1665, Mather Family Papers, typescript copy, AAS.

[34] Thomas Shepard, Preface to George Phillips, *Reply to a Confutation of some Grounds for Infants Baptisme* (London, 1645), n.p., as quoted by Holifield, *Era of Persuasion*, 123.

[35] Mather, *Magnalia*, 2:460.

The bias in Mather's depiction aside, decreasing opportunities for lay preaching in the established churches distressed some colonists who subsequently sought communion with the Baptists. Female members – who were a minority in the church – may have been attracted by the opportunity to participate in governance, since they were apparently allowed a vote in church affairs.[36] Finally, the colony's "severe dealings with those of a contrary judgement" contributed to dissatisfaction with the orthodox system and thus to the growth of the new church.[37] The Baptist faith appealed to a small number of colonists drawn from various towns. By 1671, twenty-one new members had been added; a decade after its founding, admissions reached forty-three.[38]

The range of criticisms of the established order voiced by early converts to the movement can be appreciated through a detailed examination of the well-documented case of Boston joiner John Farnum.[39] A founding member and deacon of Second (or Old North) Church of Boston, Farnum joined with the Baptists in 1666 after battling with the Second Church for eight months.[40] His sympathies had been with the new church from the first, for he spoke out against the Charlestown Church's proceedings against Goold in the summer of 1665. From September of that year until April of the next, the Second Church treated with Farnum for lying, denouncing the Charlestown Church, schismatic behavior, holding communion with excommunicated persons, and "contimacy and hardness of heart." Farnum's case is not only instructive, revealing the range of issues raised by the first converts, his apostasy also helped to shape the official response to the "Anabaptist heresy."

By March 1666, any observer could see that Farnum hoped to reshape Boston's Old North Church along the lines of the newly gathered antipedobaptist church. At a meeting on 30 March, he presented his demands, concessions that were to be made in exchange for his continued communion with the Boston church. First, the church was to set up the ordinance of lay prophecy – an ordinance that the Baptists, with whom he had begun to worship, acknowledged in their church covenant. In addition, Farnum believed a college education an invalid criterion for selecting a church's minister.[41] Not only did Farnum want

---

[36] During the first decade, men outnumbered women twenty-seven to twenty. Jonathan Mitchell stated that the Anabaptists allowed all to participate in elections; *Nehemiah on the Wall in Troublesome times* (Cambridge, 1671), 28–9. Leon McBeth states that women voted in most early Baptist churches; *Women in Baptist Life* (Nashville, Tenn.: Broadman, 1979), 38–9.

[37] Hooten, Something Concerning my travell, 204.

[38] Baptist Record Book, 1665–71.

[39] Unless otherwise noted, the information regarding Farnum has been drawn from the material on the case of John Farnum in the Second Church Records, 3:19–24, 43, on deposit at MHS. Increase Mather refers to frequent conversations with or about him between August 1665 and April 1666 in his diary.

[40] McLoughlin, "Participants on the Baptist Side," Preface to "Baptist Debate," ed. McLoughlin and Davidson, 106; Savage, *Genealogical Dictionary*, 2:142; Thwing Index of Boston Inhabitants, MHS; Baptist Record Book, 1666.

[41] Baptist Record Book, 28 May 1665. Farnum objected to the General Court's opposition to the

the Boston church to refrain from baptizing infants, he also demanded that all members undergo adult baptisms. Last, Farnum singled out the church's newly ordained teacher, Increase Mather, for denunciation. Mather's great personal promise as well as his ties of blood and marriage to two of the colony's most respected first-generation ministers had catapulted him into a coveted Boston pulpit two years earlier, at the age of twenty-five. In the highly unlikely event that the brethren should acquiesce to his other stipulations, Farnum intended to continue to meet with the antipedobaptists unless the church agreed to "put away their teacher & not owne him for a officer." After Mather had spoken in response to Farnum's demands, the older man "made a Legg [i.e., genuflected] to him in a way of scorn & derision before the church." With this "popish" gesture, Farnum expressed his view that Mather held – or, at least, sought – too much authority in the church.[42] Mather, who would shortly emerge as the colony's most influential minister, apparently represented orthodoxy in a particularly profound (and offensive) way to the disgruntled Farnum.

In a final dramatic confrontation, Farnum expressed his severe dissatisfaction with the church. After witnessing Farnum's indictment of Mather, the brethren had agreed to excommunicate him if he had not repented within the month. Finding the ritual humiliation of the proceedings unpalatable, Farnum initially resisted participating. After the worship services, Farnum sat up in the highest gallery and at first refused to come down, saying, "You may speake to me here if you have anything to say to me. I can hear you well enough." Eventually persuaded to join his fellow members on the floor of the meetinghouse, Farnum denied his guilt and accused them of casting him out for conscience's sake. Despite the continued efforts of the brethren, Farnum refused to concede, instead laughing and smiling, until Mather commented "what a said [sad] spectacle" to see a man laughing as he turned to Satan. "At last he turned about & smiled saying 'ye place is too hot for me' (by which words he caused varied youths to burst forth into an open laughter in ye midst of a worke so awfull & dreadfull)." Then, as Farnum once again walked out of a church meeting, John Mayo cast him out. Farnum, glad to have thrown his lot in with "Goold's company," later referred to this as the best day "that ever dawned upon him."[43]

Second Church's calling of layman Michael Powell to serve as its minister due to his lack of education over a decade earlier; see Increase Mather, Diary, 15 August 1665.

[42] On 15 August 1665, Mather (Diary) explained his own accountability for Farnum's apostasy in a way that may have especially irked the older man. During and for a time after the Farnum incident, Mather fielded suggestions that he "ruled the N[orth] Church & that nothing could be done [except] what mr Mather would." See ibid., 11 December 1665, 19 June 1667.

[43] "Baptist Debate," ed. McLoughlin and Davidson, 123. Farnum would, however, reverse his position and return to the Second Church in 1695. Mather apparently responded to the incident by composing an essay defending the principle that magistrates can suppress dissent; although never published, "Power of the Magistrates" – which survives only in fragmentary form – may have circulated widely in manuscript. See Mather, Diary, August–November 1665; also Michael G. Hall, *The Last American Puritan: The Life of Increase Mather, 1639–1723* (Middletown, Conn.: Wesleyan University Press, 1988), 77.

The apostasy of John Farnum was the most sensational event in the early history of the Baptist church in Massachusetts. The demands that he articulated highlighted the issues at stake in the founding of the pretended church in Charlestown. With the impeccable credentials of a church member and deacon, Farnum's involvement in a sectarian movement shocked the orthodox community. Throughout New England, people recounted the story of his irreverent "carriage" toward the Second Church. Godly colonists far from Boston knew of Farnum's openly expressed hostility toward Mather. For instance, before the decade was out, John Eliot had related the incident in a letter to English minister Richard Baxter. Years later, Kittery minister Timothy Woodbridge informed a convert to the Boston Baptist Church that fellow member Farnum "was a grevious, censorious man; and would not let Mr. Mader alone till he had cast him out of his church."[44] Repeated in order to discredit the sect, Farnum's story indicated the range of objections within the nascent Baptist community to the colony's religious establishment.

Even before Farnum's battle with the Boston church had drawn to a close, the religious and civil authorities launched their campaign against the sect. Concerned both to destroy the new church and to advertise their hostility to antipedobaptists at a time when English dissenters were in need of a haven from repressive Restoration policies,[45] the authorities marshaled the forces available to them to deal with "heretics." First, the church at Charlestown excommunicated Goold and the Osborns. After preliminary prosecutions in the lower courts, five of the seven male church members were summoned before the Court of Assistants in September 1665. In anticipation of this confrontation, they prepared a statement of their beliefs, complete with citations to scores of biblical passages.[46] This effort "to let [the] world know there faith & order [was] proved from the word of God" was in vain. The assistants found them guilty of "schismaticall rending from the communion of the churches heere, & setting up a publicke meeting in opposition to the ordinances of Christ here publicly exercised. . . . [They were] solemnly charged not to persist in such their pernitious practices." The next month the General Court had its say. The magistrates chastised "Goold and company" for their "great evill in attempting, wth so high a hand, to polute & prophane Gods holy ordinances." They admonished the schismatics to "desist from such their meeting & irregular prac-

---

[44] Eliot to Baxter, 26th June 1669; Churchwood, quoted in Backus, *History,* 1:402–3n.; Sybil Noyes, Charles Thornton Libbey, and Walter Goodwin Davis, *Genealogical Dictionary of Maine and New Hampshire* (1928–39; reprint, Baltimore: Genealogical Publishing, 1972), 769.

[45] While crushing the church was frequently cited as a goal, leading colonists were aware of the need to discourage English dissenters from migrating too. See, e.g., Thomas Cobbett to Increase Mather, *CMHS,* 4th ser., vol. 8 (1868): 291.

[46] This practice was apparently typical of colonial Baptists but not English Baptists of the same era; William Henry Brackney, *The Baptists* (Westport, Conn.: Greenwood, 1988), 45.

tices." Declaring their sect "no orderly church," the Court disfranchised the freemen among them and provided for their imprisonment if they continued to meet.[47]

Not until the following spring, after the commissioners had departed, did the magistrates move to imprison any of the miscreants. They fined and jailed Goold, Osborn, and a third church member, John George, in early 1666. Five days after the first prison sentences were handed down, the Second Church of Boston excommunicated John Farnum. The law allowing for the imprisonment of Baptist church members would be invoked sporadically over the next five years in an effort "to reduce those that had gone out of God's way to Anabaptism."[48] Farnum would shortly be among the prisoners.

In the face of this effort to end what the General Court labeled its "irregular practices," the church began occasionally holding its meetings on Noddles Island in Boston Harbor. Owned during these years by men who sympathized with the church's plight, this island served as a sanctuary to the beleaguered group.[49] At times, at least Thomas Goold resided there to avoid arrest.[50] The strategy worked as long as the offenders remained on the privately owned island, since the authorities were apparently unwilling to trespass upon it to reincarcerate them.

The men who harbored the illegal church on Noddles Island were only the most active of a sizable group who defended the apostates. According to Farnum's and other accounts, a number of people opposed the excommunication of Goold from Charlestown Church.[51] The participation of Farnum, a former church deacon, in the movement marked an especially serious break in the orthodox ranks. The same year that Farnum left the Second Church, the General Court split over how to punish the Anabaptists, with a majority of the deputies voting against a resolution threatening banishment.[52] Then, in March 1668, when the authorities once again put Goold on trial, they could only rein-

---

[47] Charlestown Church votes, ed. Hunnewell, 6; *RMB* 4, pt. 2:290–1; Baptist Record Book, September 1665.

[48] Felt, *Ecclesiastical History*, 2:371–2; Thomas Goold et al., Petition to the Court, 1666, SCC; Bond for Appeal, 28 April 1666, MAE, 10:214. Quote from John Allin, "Baptist Debate," ed. McLoughlin and Davidson, 108.

[49] Quote from *RMB* 4, pt. 2:290. Edward R. Snow, *The Islands of Boston Harbor* (Andover, Mass., 1935), 239–40. In a will dated 17 July 1666, Henry Shrimpton left a legacy to the "Society of Christians, who now meet at Noddles Island"; Felt, *Ecclesiastical History*, 2:372. Sir Thomas Temple and Samuel Shrimpton owned the island in succession; both would sign a 1668 petition in favor of tolerating the church.

[50] On 30 November 1670, Edward Drinker reported that "Brother Goold is not yet taken, because he lives on Noddle's Island, and they only wait to take him at town (but he comes not over)"; Drinker to John Clarke and his church, in Backus, *History*, 1:316.

[51] Mary Goold reported that a number of people walked out on the excommunication, [Mary Goold's account], in Backus, *History*, 1:306. John Farnum went so far as to assert that the majority did not support the move; case of John Farnum.

[52] McLoughlin, Introduction to "Baptist Debate," ed. McLoughlin and Davidson, 94.

carcerate him after sending his jurors out a second time to bring in a conviction.[53]

Support by various colonists for the church's cause finally led the governor and his assistants to take the unprecedented step of hosting a formal disputation between the proponents of believer's baptism and the colony's secular and religious leaders. Widespread, publicly expressed sympathy for dissenters was a new phenomenon in the Bay colony. At the very least, the debate might rally public opinion behind an effective campaign of repression against the sect. To this end, the authorities summoned the leading dissenters to appear before a dozen magistrates and ministers at the meetinghouse of Boston's First Church on 14 April 1668.[54] Hoping to use the debate to bring an end to the movement, the magistrates took the offensive. At the outset, Governor Richard Bellingham refused to concede to Goold's request for assurances that they would not be prosecuted for what they said.[55] Participants on the orthodox side preferred not to defend the fundamentals of their church order, especially infant baptism. With the colony's churches embroiled in a controversy over the decision to baptize the grandchildren of church members, a public airing of the radical opposition to all such baptisms seemed ill advised. Apparently to avoid fanning the flames in Boston ignited by the halfway covenant, the civil authorities gave ministers from that town no role in the debate.[56]

In all, seven members of the illegal church, two other men who worshiped with them, and John Crandall, the Westerly (Rhode Island) Baptist Church minister, spoke in defense of a wide variety of radical beliefs and practices.[57] They questioned the established church order, the magistrates' authority over dissenters, and the orthodox interpretations of Scriptures. At the outset, William Turner refused to concede that the established churches were legitimate "Churches of Christ." Goold challenged the purity of the colony's churches, justifying his departure from communion with the Charlestown Church by observing "come out from among them, saith the Lord." A number of the Anabaptists advocated lay preaching, illegal in Massachusetts for over a decade. John Trumble, a Charlestown ship captain who worshiped with the sect, made an anti-intellectual jibe at ministerial scholasticism. The group took a strong stand in defense of their right to gather a church unmolested by the civil authorities. They repeatedly attacked the use of carnal punishments for spiritual

---

[53] Backus, *History*, 1:374–5.

[54] A sizable part of the exchange was transcribed and is available in "Baptist Debate," ed. McLoughlin and Davidson, 108–33.

[55] Ibid., 109–10.

[56] John Davenport had been called but not yet ordained as the new minister of First Church; John Mayo and Increase Mather were serving as pastor and teacher over Second Church; and the schism in the First Church that would lead to the gathering of Third Church was just getting under way.

[57] McLoughlin, "Participants on the Baptist's Side," 106–7.

offenses, rejecting the principle upon which such punishments were predicated
– that the civil state ought to police certain aspects of the religious lives of
inhabitants. One of them praised the complete religious toleration practiced in
the Dutch Republic.[58]

For two days, nine ministers and three magistrates wrestled with these "few
plowmen and tailors" who, according to orthodox diarist John Hull, behaved
themselves "exceedingly obstinately, absurdly and ignorantly." Another antagonistic observer described them as "vociferous, bold . . . but in Scriptures &
reason exceedingly weak."[59] Increase Mather, calling upon unnamed adherents
of the sect to bolster his own analysis of the event, asserted that "the Anabaptists concerned did so speak and act, as that some wiser than themselves of
their own persuasion were troubled and ashamed of them."[60] With little regard
for the contempt of their opponents and revealing no significant internal divisions of the sort Mather hinted at, they left the debate not at all "reduced."
Indeed, the three imprisoned men shortly "professed themselves bound to continue in these ways, and . . . ready to seal it with their blood." For a variety of
reasons, many people must have agreed with Mary Goold, who later wrote that
"the two days were spent to little purpose."[61]

Since the disputation had failed to reform the views of the "obstinate and
turbulent Anabaptists," the defenders of orthodoxy moved to remove them from
the colony. At its next session, the General Court voted to banish the three
imprisoned men. In an act of defiance that was reminiscent of the visiting Quakers
a decade earlier, they refused to comply with the court order. The magistrates
reimprisoned them. In October, the General Court, in what was to prove to be
its last effort to rally the populace against the converts, arranged to have the
May sentence banishing the three men published. The order confidently stated
that the sect worshiped in the colony only "to the great grief and offense of the
godly orthodox."[62]

Its publication did not, however, have the desired effect. Instead, sixty-six
self-styled "sober and serious Christians" petitioned the Court to take pity on
the "poor prisoners who . . . are reputedly godly, and of a blameless conversation."[63] Among the petitioners were merchants, artisans, and farmers, many of
them orthodox church members and some of them civil leaders. Not surprisingly, a few vigorous opponents of the halfway covenant joined the campaign.
Charlestown Church member Solomon Phipps continued the support he had
earlier shown for Goold by signing the petition. After a decade, the scattered

[58] For these specific instances, see "Baptist Debate," ed. McLoughlin and Davidson, 111, 113,
116, 131, 132.
[59] "John Hull's Diary of Public Occurrences," *Transactions and Collections of the American Antiquarian Society* 3 (1857): 226–7; Eliot to Baxter, 26 June 1669.
[60] *Divine Right of Infant-Baptisme,* 25.
[61] [Mary Goold's account], 1:307; "Hull's Diary," 227.
[62] *RMB* 4, pt. 2:373–5, 404.   [63] Petition on behalf of Goold.

opposition to the persecution had finally found public expression in this "so scandalous & reproachfull a petition."[64] The magistrates – agreeing that "such a rough thing as a New England Baptist is not to be handled over tenderly"[65] – forced the petitioners to back down. Yet their victory was hollow, for they realized that public support for suppressing the movement was not forthcoming. The General Court summoned a handful of the most prominent and seemingly orthodox petitioners, questioned them, and accepted their apologies. Hearing from these men that the petition had been circulated from house to house in Boston and Charlestown by Joshua Atwater and Benjamin Sweetser, the court summoned, admonished, and fined these men. The colony's magistrates would never again actively pursue the plan to eject the dissenters.

In the wake of these unsuccessful efforts to suppress the antipedobaptist movement, the confrontation between the establishment and the members of the new church reached a stalemate. The authorities, while less energetic in their pursuit, were nevertheless unwilling to accept the Baptists' presence. The Charlestown constables apparently discontinued their weekly Sabbath day visits to the Goolds' farm to record the names of those who worshiped there. Yet the court seemed prepared to hold Goold and Turner in Boston jail indefinitely. When they were briefly freed to attend to personal business, the two men refused to return to the prison as agreed. The meeting that constables Lowden and Knight monitored took place in the context of this standoff. As Mary Goold described the situation, "My husband hath beene at home a little while, but Mr. Danforth hath sent out his warrants and I am expecting every houre he's going to prison."[66] Goold succeeded in avoiding reincarceration, eventually withdrawing to Noddles Island to do so. Other leading church members would not be so fortunate.[67] In any event, the sectaries refused to back down.

The struggle to establish the church on a firm footing faced one final challenge from the standing order in the years that followed, as the authorities responded vigorously to the apostasy of yet another deacon. John Russell, Sr., was probably the most substantial Massachusetts sectarian convert during this period. Following his son and namesake into the church, Russell became a member around 1670 and quickly assumed a leading role in the beleaguered congregation. His conversion represented a boon to the little church. As one member described the situation,

> The Lord has given us another elder, one John Russell, senior, a gracious
> wise and holy man that lives at Woburn, where we have five brethren near
> that can meet with him; and they meet together first days when they cannot

[64] E. Brooks Holifield, "On Toleration in Massachusetts," *Church History* 38 (1969): 192–3; T. Goold's narration, 49; *RMB* 4, pt. 2:413.
[65] Samuel Willard, quoted by Chaplin, *Life of Henry Dunster*, 188.
[66] Mary Goold to John Winthrop, Jr., 23 March 1669, *CMHS*, 3d ser., vol. 10 (1849): 72.
[67] Edward Drinker, Petition to the General Court, 27 October 1670, MAE, 10:228; and to John Clarke, ibid., 316.

come to us on Noddles Island, and I hear there are some more there looking that way with them.[68]

This windfall for the dissenters was greeted by the establishment with approbation, dashing – as it did – hopes to contain the sect. The grand jury indicted
Russell for his Baptist activities, and he was tried and convicted by both the
county court and the Court of Assistants. In a related attempt to break up the
movement in the Woburn area, the authorities fined numerous other Anabaptists at the same time. The harassment of Russell and the others proved ineffective.[69]

That Russell and his companions emerged from Woburn Church to adopt
radical views was, in a sense, unsurprising, for that church had always tended
toward extreme positions on issues of church polity. The first minister had been
ordained by two lay members to avoid participating in a "presbytery."[70] Many
members had signed a 1653 petition asking for the repeal of a law against lay
prophecy. The church staunchly opposed the halfway covenant, clinging to the
older practice of more restricted baptisms. Finally, Woburn Church seems to
have been unique in having seriously considered continuing to hold communion with its members who had undergone rebaptism. Ministers from other
churches asked to consider this proposition concluded in the negative. Furthermore, they repeatedly labeled the Anabaptists' apostasy and, by implication,
Woburn Church's inquiry "scandalous."[71] Although the church records have
been lost, Russell, as a founding member of the town and a deacon of the
church, presumably played an active role in these developments. Indeed, he
may have written the 1653 memorial in favor of lay preaching. As early as 1666,
he and his son had begun turning their backs on infant baptism.[72] The elder
Russell signed the 1668 petition in defense of the beleaguered sectaries before
joining with them himself.

The campaign against the Baptists declined in intensity for the last time in
the wake of the aborted attempt to crush Anabaptist sentiment in Woburn. Six
years of arguments and punishments had had no appreciable impact on the
"pretended church." If the scandalous way John Farnum had left Boston's

---

[68] Ibid., 317.
[69] MCC, 5 April 1671, 3 October 1671; Pulsifer Transcript, 3:4, 13–14, 35. One temporary
recantation, that of John Johnson, occurred around this time; but it actually predated the wave
of prosecutions; see ibid., 3:13; MCC, 15 June 1675.
[70] Foster, "Progress of New England Institutions," 29.
[71] Francis H. Russell, "A Cobbler at his Bench: John Russell of Woburn, Massachusetts," *NEHGR*
133 (1979): 125, 128–30; Christopher M. Jedrey, *The World of John Cleaveland: Family and
Community in Eighteenth-Century New England* (New York: Norton, 1979), 2–4; Woburn Petition, 30 August 1653, *CMHS*, 3d ser., vol. 1 (1825): 38–45; [Samuel Willard], "Questions and
Answers on Baptism from Council at Woburn, Massachusetts [1672?]," Prince Papers, MHS.
The law against lay preaching was replaced with one against heretical preaching, partly because
of the Woburn Memorial; *RMB* 4, pt. 1:122, 151, 332.
[72] Russell, "Cobbler at His Bench," 125; MCC, 5 June 1667.

Second Church had encouraged the proponents of intolerance to attack the sect with renewed vigor, Russell's respectability ultimately worked the opposite effect. The specter of the highly regarded, aged, and ailing Russell in Boston jail did nothing to further the case against the sect.[73] No colonist was incarcerated for belonging to the antipedobaptist church after Russell's release in June 1671. Over the next decade, grand juries in Middlesex County occasionally charged members who resided there with relatively minor offenses, usually absences from orthodox religious services.[74] These presentments, which generally resulted in the fining of the offender, occurred sporadically and invariably involved groups of three or more dissenters.[75] While this fairly mild harassment continued at the local level for some time (much as it had in the Quaker case), the colonial government abandoned the effort to suppress the church.

In 1674, emboldened by the decline in persecution and the continued public sympathy for their plight, the church began worshiping in private homes in Boston. The timing of this decision may have been dictated by the reelection of John Leverett as governor. In his first term, Leverett had proved friendly to the interests of Baptists at least, if not to Quakers.[76] Having gathered their church while the royal commissioners were present, the Baptists again gauged the orthodox community's readiness to act against them in timing their move into Boston.[77] After almost a decade, the church of baptized believers emerged from hiding. By the late 1670s, the Baptists would be fighting for the right to have a meetinghouse in the town. Although those who favored intolerance would reassert their position in response to this bold act, this battle was another that the church would ultimately win.

In 1674, Boston merchant John Hull made a disapproving entry in his diary regarding the recent successes enjoyed by the sectarians:

> This summer the Anabaptists yt were wont to meet at Nodle's Iland meete at Boston on ye Lord's Day one Mr. Simond Lind letteth one of them an house. . . . Some Quakers are also Come & Seated in Boston. Some of the Magistrates will not permit any punishment to be inflicted on heriticks as such.[78]

After dealing with heretics constantly in their midst for almost two decades, the magistrates had discovered the limits to what they could hope to accomplish.

---

[73] John Russell, Sr., Petition to the General Court, October 1672, MAE, 10:231. William Hamlet to [?], 14 June 1672, Backus, *History*, 1:320.

[74] That harassment continued in Middlesex County may be explained by the large number of members residing there or by the particularly vigorous opposition to "heresy" among that county's magistrates, especially Thomas Danforth.

[75] See, e.g., MCC, 15 June 1675.   [76] Holifield, "On Toleration," 197.

[77] Ibid. Holifield suggests that the Baptists immediately began meeting in Boston upon Leverett's election in 1673, but they apparently waited to observe his performance as governor for a year and, more importantly, to see if he would be reelected.

[78] "Hull's Diary," 238; quote revised according to the original manuscript held at the AAS.

While members of the orthodox elite would continue to bemoan the presence of radical sects in the colony for years, the Quakers and Baptists were there to stay. One after the other, they had made a start in the most vehemently intolerant of the English colonies. Their success demonstrated the limits of the orthodox community's powers of suppression in the face of determined efforts to dissent and to remain in the colony. While their heterodoxy found encouragement in the transatlantic radical community, both movements were firmly entrenched in the colony. The Baptists engaged orthodoxy in a debate over such issues as church purity and the baptism of children; the Quakers dismissed the issues as inconsequential even as they drew upon existing communal bonds in establishing their meeting. Subsequently, both sects would struggle to maintain their respective alternatives to the established order.

PART II

Development

3

Sectarian communities

By coming together to organize alternative faiths in Massachusetts, the Quakers and the Baptists created unique communities that transcended the institutions around which life in the Bay colony ordinarily revolved. As scholars customarily emphasize, communal life in early New England typically centered on the town and its church. Sectaries defied the familiar patterns of association in turning their backs on these pervasive local institutions to identify with a sect.

Despite occupying a similar legal position in the colony and despite having been treated as similar by many historians, the Quakers and Baptists erected quite dissimilar spiritual communities bound together by equally divergent beliefs. In carving out enclaves within the colony, the Quakers reshaped an existing community, while the Baptists brought together people who had previously been without ties. Far from chance occurrences, these differences reflected the contrasting relationship of each faith to the colony's religious establishment. Rates of participation by men and women in these two sects may indicate gendered attitudes about what constituted a satisfying spiritual life. The distinctive beliefs of the sects – especially their respective views of the process of salvation – were integrally related to the character of their communities. Throughout the colonial period, the interplay between the doctrines and social characteristics of these movements shaped the day-to-day reality of sectarianism.

Initially, the Baptist community was scattered and the Quaker community was concentrated in one region partly because the Baptist faith, unlike that of the Quakers, arose in dialogue with the colonial establishment. Commitment to believers' baptism was born out of a rejection of orthodox positions on a constellation of interrelated religious issues – the efficacy of infant baptism, the relation of the church to society, the role of the laity in the church. The colony's ministers, by repeatedly using the sect as a foil in theological and polemical treatises, demonstrated an awareness that Anabaptists settled on different answers to many of the ministers' own questions.[1] They appreciated how easily the unguided lay person might fall into the error of Anabaptism. Edward Ran-

---

[1] Thomas Cobbet defended federal theology with reference to Anabaptists, *Just Vindication*, preface, n.p., 93, 119. Also see Mitchell, *Answer to the Apologetical Preface*, 5–7, 27, 37.

dolph made much of this phenomenon in order to discredit the Bay colony, caustically observing that Anabaptists naturally arose under Independent rule.[2] Since Massachusetts converts arrived at their views through a detailed reexamination of the established faith, they overwhelmingly favored the more closely akin Calvinism of the Particular – rather than the General – Baptist position.[3]

Because the orthodox faith could serve as a jumping-off point for conversion to antipedobaptist principles, such conversions could – and did – occur in the privacy of one's closet. The experience of one early convert who later returned to England had apparently been typical; Thomas Patient wrote of his New England conversion, "all [of] which time I was not acquainted with any that opposed Christening children, and conversed only with such as were for that practice."[4] Many of the first converts to the Baptist church followed a similar course. Like Thomas Goold and John Russell, they worked through theological issues that were salient in the established churches, only to arrive at antipedobaptist conclusions. Because the decision to become a Baptist often resulted from extended private contemplation and rereading of Scripture, the Bay colony convert tended to be mature rather than youthful.[5]

Since the lone colonist could take up the Baptist faith with ease, the first converts were drawn from numerous towns and included a sizable number of unrelated individuals. This trend was in keeping with the history of diffused Anabaptist agitation in the colony. The forty-eight men and women who joined the church in the first decade resided in six different towns: Charlestown – where meetings were initially held – and Boston – where a meetinghouse would later be built – as well as Woburn, Billerica, Newbury, and Salem.[6] An early critic of the church found the scattered nature of its membership noteworthy.[7]

[2] Edward Randolph, An Account of the Colonys and Provinces of New England in general, More particularly of the Massachusetts, in *Historical Collections Relating to the American Colonial Churches*, ed. William Stevens Perry (Hartford, Conn., 1873), 3:51.
[3] The pivotal distinction between the two branches of the English Baptist movement was that General Baptists preached the possibility of general redemption, while Particular Baptists held – as did the established churches in New England – limited atonement. McLoughlin cautions against overemphasizing the differences between the two during the colonial period; *New England Dissent*, 281.
[4] Epistle, *The Doctrine of Baptism* (London, 1654), n.p.
[5] Among the first converts, most were apparently middle-aged, in their forties or fifties, with well-established families. Only seven of the forty-eight original members can be classified as young adults in 1670. Early Baptist families were reconstructed with the help of a variety of sources, including MCPR; SCPR; *Probate Records of the Essex County Court, Massachusetts*, ed. George Francis Dow, 3 vols. (Salem, Mass., 1916–20); MCC; SCC; *EQC*; Wood, *History*; Thomas Bellows Wyman, *The Genealogies and Estates of Charlestown, Massachusetts, 1629–1818* (1879; reprint ed., Somerset, N.H.: New England History Press, 1982); and Savage, *Genealogical Dictionary*.
[6] The church's records provide the names of all church members. Place of residence, which was not listed during the early period, has been ascertained from the records listed in note 5.
[7] Willard, *Ne Sutor Ultra Crepidam*, 24.

As a corollary to the geographic dispersion of members, nearly one-third of the first forty-eight members had no close relation in the church, while just over a third joined with a spouse but no other relation. Thomas Goold's family stood out as particularly involved in the new sect, with only four converts among his seventeen immediate adult relations. Typically, ties to the Baptist church cut across familial and town lines, binding together a remarkably far-flung group. If the Baptist faith was theologically akin to that of the orthodox establishment, the social experience of these sectarians was unlike anything the Bay colony had previously witnessed.

The inverse was true of the Salem Quakers, who embraced a faith severely at odds with the dominant religious culture of the colony. Although certain aspects of reformation theology – such as the concepts of the priesthood of all believers and of free grace – contributed to the development of Quakerism, in its early form the sect departed so completely from Protestant beliefs and practices as to be unrecognizable as such to the defenders of Massachusetts orthodoxy. Given their conviction that everything could be traced to either God or Satan, leading colonists initially declared that Quakerism was rooted in the diabolical. In keeping with this explanation, they linked the sect to all manner of other heresies. For most of the colonial period, the sect remained alone in its opposition to various tenets essential to Reformed Protestantism.[8]

The Quakers rejected much that even adherents to earlier radical movements in the colony – such as Hutchinsonians and separatists – had had in common with the orthodox community. They believed that an inner light guided them to the truth. This conviction initially emboldened them to repudiate every known form of church organization, the institution of the ministry, and even the preeminent authority of Scripture. Because this light shone within everyone, Quakers further believed that salvation was potentially universal, a departure from the predestinarianism that fundamentally informed the colony's religious culture.[9] This blasphemy frequently earned them the epithet "perfectionist," since they clearly thought too highly of the human potential.[10]

Colonists took up these extreme views, not as the result of a private reexamination of orthodox polity, but as members of a New England community caught up in a transatlantic radical movement. Dissatisfaction with the establishment presumably predisposed some Salem residents to embrace the Quaker

---

[8] Carla Gardina Pestana, "The City Upon a Hill Under Siege: The Puritan Perception of the Quaker Threat to the Massachusetts Bay Colony, 1656–1661," *NEQ* 56 (1983), 336–41. Not until the revolutionary period would other sects with similarly radical views gain a foothold; Stephen A. Marini, *Radical Sects in Revolutionary New England* (Cambridge, Mass.: Harvard University Press, 1982).

[9] Robert Barclay, *An Apology for the True Christian Divinity, as the same is held forth and preached by the People called in Scorn, Quakers*, 6th ed. (Newport, R.I., 1729), 108.

[10] For instance, Roger Williams, *George Fox Digg'd Out of his Burrowes*, ed. J. Lewis Diman (Boston, 1676; reprint, New York: Russell & Russell, 1963), 179.

message. But word of the sect and, especially, the ministrations of traveling witnesses sparked the rapid growth of Quakerism in the late 1650s. Mass "convincements" had accounted for much of the phenomenal growth of the sect in England. By the early 1660s, after only a decade of proselytizing, at least thirty-five to forty thousand people in England had embraced the nascent Quaker faith.[11] Lone conversions did occur in both old and New England.[12] But, as its opponents were quick to point out, the heresy typically spread from one person to another like an infection.[13] Contact with Quakerism was especially important for its transmission in Massachusetts, because the beliefs of the new sect were decidedly at odds with the faith of the majority of colonists. Wherever it spread, early Quakerism almost always included a social as well as a spiritual component.

Given the communal context for Quakerism, Salem convincements tended to run along lines of neighborhood and family.[14] The majority of those initially involved resided in Salem, especially in the section of the Farms directly west of the harbor. Nearly half of the participants in the early movement belonged to three extended families, the Buffums, Shattocks, and Southwicks. Quaker matriarchs headed two of these families, while the third looked to a Quaker couple – Cassandra and Lawrence Southwick – as its senior sectarian members.[15] In addition, a number of smaller extended families joined the meeting. In part because they joined in multigenerational groups, the first Quakers were younger on average than the Baptists.[16] Within or without these large family networks, 75 percent of the first Quakers had spouses who also embraced the sect.[17] The participants with no known relation in the sect during the early period numbered only six out of sixty-seven people. This communal component to the Salem Quaker movement made the adoption of the sect's radical beliefs easier, in that relations and friends supported one another in making this unconventional move. For all the Quakers' radicalism, the sect in Salem

[11] Reay, *Quakers and the English Revolution*, 11.
[12] For example, see Augustine Jones, "Nicholas Upshall," *NEHGR* 34 (1880): 21–31.
[13] Urian Oakes, "Salutatory Oration: Commencement, 1677," *CSMC*, vol. 31 (1935), 406–7; "Hull's Diary," 189, 215; Mather, *Magnalia*, 2:452; Norton, *Heart of New England Rent*, 82, mispaginated.
[14] The criteria for determining a person's Quakerism and the sources used for this prosopography are described in Chapter 1, note 50.
[15] Sixty-seven people attended meetings during the first decade; perhaps ten of them failed to make a long-term commitment to the sect in Salem, usually due to emigration (8). Thirty-one people belonged to these three families.
[16] Twenty-six of them were young adults, either single or newly married, often with young children. Many had parents and siblings in the movement.
[17] Forty-nine people were married to other Quakers. Most of these (34) had been married prior to their convincement. The odd number is accounted for by the spouses of five married people who were not included in this sample because they lived outside of the area or joined the sect after the close of the first decade.

was as thoroughly "tribal" – to use Edmund Morgan's term – as any godly orthodox family.[18]

In both sects, the relationship of the new faith to the colony's establishment helped to shape the social basis of the first sectarian communities. The Baptists, who moved out of the orthodox fold over issues directly pertinent to the New England way, required little contact with other radicals to arrive at their dissenting views. The biblical analogy of the wheat and the tares captured their own sense of themselves as God's faithful, scattered among the reprobate, at the same time as it fairly accurately described their circumstances. The disjuncture between Quakerism and the orthodox faith was far more extreme, and the movement was spread by advocates of this radical new faith. Colonists took up Quakerism after being convinced of the sect's message. In addition, the movement was community oriented, with a solid social foundation in western Salem. The analogy often used for the spread of Quakerism was that of the planting of seeds; some areas of the English world, such as Salem, offered especially fertile fields for their growth.[19] The close-knit Quaker and the far-flung Baptist communities took on their respective shapes in part due to their relationship to the religious traditions of the colony.

Their diametrically opposed views about salvation also contributed toward the creation of these two different social contexts for sectarianism. In their understanding of the process of redemption, the Quakers and Baptists of Massachusetts occupied positions on either side of the established churches. The Baptist church, in agreement with colonial orthodoxy, officially embraced the doctrine of limited atonement and accepted only those candidates for membership who were seemingly among the elect. The establishment, however, drawing upon covenant theology, softened the impact of the predestinarian doctrine somewhat through the practice of infant baptism.[20] Furthermore, the halfway covenant opened the way for the inclusion of some apparently unregenerate adults as provisional – or halfway – members in the church, which the Baptists found unacceptable. The children of saints – whether infant or adult – had no place in the Baptist church until they experienced conversion themselves.

In terms of the conversion experience, the Baptist position required private self-examination and a personal sense of assurance before the more public, but still individual, rite of baptism. Although a person might come to accept Baptist

---

[18] Edmund S. Morgan, *Visible Saints: The History of a Puritan Idea* (New York: New York University Press, 1963), 138.

[19] Bauman, *Let Your Words Be Few*, ch. 5.

[20] Holifield, *Covenant Sealed*, 146–59. Establishment theologians did not abandon the predestinarian position by endorsing infant baptism, for they believed that baptized individuals still needed to experience an effectual calling. They did conceive of the spiritual community as including those baptized as infants, a conception that eventually informed their support for the halfway covenant.

views in discussion with others, actual membership in the church was sought
only after intense personal reflection.[21] The experience that preceded one's
communion with the group was all-important. Baptism publicly expressed the
individual's private relationship with God. In joining the church, new communicants consciously set themselves off from the bulk of humanity, claiming a
special, elevated status.[22]

While full membership in the orthodox churches was predicated on a similar
conversion experience,[23] other features tended to ameliorate the potential for
isolation. The congregation was geographically specific, like an English parish,
and everyone in a given community was expected to attend meetings.[24] The
baptism of the infants who were the grandchildren of visible saints ensured that
identification with the church would continue among subsequent generations.
Eventually, churches expanded baptism further still, including people who did
not technically qualify under the provisions of the halfway covenant. Group
renewals of the church covenant were becoming increasingly common during
the late seventeenth century. Commenting on these developments, E. Brooks
Holifield observes that "it was as if a host of zealous Puritans had suddenly
discovered the usefulness of the visible rites and tangible sacraments that so
frequently had aroused suspicions."[25] Their usefulness lay precisely in that they
ensured that everyone in the community could be involved in the local congregation on at least some level.

The Baptists did not share in any of these practices. Their church was geographically nonspecific; infants were not baptized under any circumstances; no
halfway category of membership existed; and the surviving church records give
no indication that ritualistic covenant renewals were ever conducted. Seen in
this light, the conversion of a lone individual living far from any other sectarian
becomes more understandable. In a sense, this social experience mirrored the
spiritual isolation of every member of the church. The Baptist faith was, in
theory and in practice, exclusive.

For reasons that may be tied to this greater exclusivity, the Baptist church

[21] For example, "The Diary of John Comer," ed. C. Edwin Barrows, *RIHSC* 8 (1893), 24 February 1723, 10 October 1724, 25 January 1725. (The editor apparently modernized these
dates.)

[22] For a lay statement on the special position of the elect, see Ebenezer Byles to Josiah Byles, 1
July 1751, Belknap Collection, MHS.

[23] The future Baptists who joined Thomas Shepard's church (including Henry Dunster, William
Hamlet, and possibly John Trumble) did not relate conversions that were distinctive on this
score; see "Thomas Shepard's Confessions," ed. George Selement and Bruce C. Woolley,
CSMC 58 (1981): 155–64, 125–9, 106–9. (Although there is no record of Trumble joining the
church, he did participate in the 1668 debate on the Baptist side.)

[24] Once population pressures made the formation of new congregations necessary, the parish system retained the geographic specificity of the individual churches until a new town could be
established. Boston, with numerous churches by 1750, was exceptional.

[25] Pope, *Half-Way Covenant;* Miller, *Colony to Province,* 115–18; Holifield, *Covenant Sealed,* 169.

attracted larger numbers of men than women.[26] Women who did join the church were more likely than men to do so with another family member. Unlike Elizabeth Hale Richardson of Newbury, who joined fully nine years before her husband, they tended not to precede their relations into the church.[27] In the established churches, the move in a more inclusive direction – with the halfway covenant and group covenant renewals – was accompanied by a decreasing proportion of male church members. Contemporaries as well as later scholars have suggested that women, especially concerned about their own salvation and that of their children, sought out the comfort that church membership could provide. If women were attracted to the more inclusive church of the late seventeenth century, men may have been put off by the very changes that women found amenable.[28] This argument would seem to be supported by the fact that men were drawn to the Baptist faith, with its stark predestinarian position, its more exclusive spiritual community, and its greater emphasis on individual over communal experiences. At a time when active religious participation was becoming the province of the colony's matrons, some men – such as the Woburn –Billerica father, son, and grandson who became Baptists over a forty-year period without any of their four wives – defied that trend.[29]

If, from the point of view of the establishment, Baptist church membership was too restrictive, the Quakers were far too lax. Quakers believed that any person who followed the inner light was saved. Convincement – a revealing term for conversion to Quakerism – required only the acceptance of this view. Besides faith in the sect's beliefs, no other qualification for membership existed. Whereas for the Baptists the pivotal distinction was between the godly

[26] Women made up the majority of new admissions in only twelve of the fifty-two years for which there are records before 1740. Overall, men outnumbered women two to one over the same period, which may have been a general trend. Robert G. Gardner estimates that for all colonial Baptist churches, men outnumbered women prior to 1700, but that the ratio evened out for the period to 1770. These generalizations are based in part upon the questionable assumption that baptisms of female members were underrecorded; his church-by-church totals show women in the minority through the colonial period, except in Rhode Island, New Jersey, and Pennsylvania; *Baptists of Early America: A Statistical History, 1639–1790* (Atlanta: Georgia Historical Society, 1983), 20–1, 361, 363–429. Patricia U. Bonomi has suggested that men were especially interested in opportunities for an expanded lay role, another factor that may have played a role; see *Under the Cope of Heaven: Religion, Society, and Politics in Colonial America* (New York: Oxford University Press, 1986), 112.

[27] Only 40 women (of 215 unrelated members) had no identifiable familial connection to another church member. Richardson joined the church in 1708, her husband Edward in 1717.

[28] Cotton Mather, *Ornaments for the Daughters of Zion* (Boston, 1692); Benjamin Colman, *The Honour and Happiness of the Vertuous Woman* (Boston, 1716); Laurel Thatcher Ulrich, "Vertuous Women Found: New England Ministerial Literature, 1668–1735," *American Quarterly* 28 (1976): 20–40; Nancy F. Cott, *The Bonds of Womanhood: "Women's Sphere" in New England, 1780–1835* (New Haven, Conn.: Yale University Press, 1977), 126–8, 144.

[29] George Farley joined between 1665 and 1669, his son Caleb in 1677, and his grandson George in 1708; Baptist Record Book.

and the reprobate, the saved and the damned, the Quakers' division between the convinced and those who refused to accept the truth reflected personal choice, rather than foreordained fate. Although to join the Baptist church one had to have been predestined for sainthood, it was possible for anyone to become a Quaker.[30] The Quaker faith was, in theory, inclusive.

In practice as well, the Quakers emphasized the communal. Meetings, during which the convinced gathered to await the spirit, stood at the center of the sectarian experience. That the light within might shine forth from anyone tended to break down boundaries between individuals, highlighting that which was shared. Friends made decisions collectively, arriving at "the sense of the meeting" through repeated discussion and, if necessary, the postponement of any matter upon which the group was unable to agree.[31] Quakerism was the least individualistic spiritual option available in colonial Massachusetts.

With the Quakers on the opposite pole from the Baptists in these matters, women might be expected to have flocked to that sect in greater numbers than they did. Phyllis Mack and Jack Marietta have described the Quakers as having an especially "feminine" religious style. And numerous scholars have emphasized the important role of women in the Quaker movement as well as, in some cases, the preponderance of female converts to the sect.[32] Although women – especially the early Quaker matriarchs – took a leading part in establishing the sect in Salem and they continued to exercise authority in the meeting, women did not numerically dominate Salem Quakerism. As a sect of families, the meeting had, of necessity, a fairly balanced sex ratio. Whatever comfort and community support a woman gained by embracing the Quaker faith, she could also alienate family and friends by associating herself with this heresy – unless she did so in their company. Only some women in western Salem and, later, northern Lynn enjoyed the opportunity to adopt this faith without breaking with their loved ones. These circumstances possibly explain why male and female rates of participation did not follow exactly from the theological divisions between the three faiths in early Massachusetts.

Within the communities they created, sectarian ideas about convincement

---

[30] Richard T. Vann, *The Social Development of English Quakerism, 1655–1755* (Cambridge, Mass.: Harvard University Press, 1969), ch. 4; J. William Frost, *The Quaker Family in Colonial America: A Portrait of the Society of Friends* (New York: St. Martin's, 1973), 13–21.

[31] Arnold Lloyd describes this procedure: *Quaker Social History, 1669–1738* (New York: Longmans, Green, 1950), 22–4; he believes that it was rejected (apparently temporarily) in England as a result of infighting and the excessive power of the London Yearly Meeting.

[32] Phyllis Mack, "Feminine Behavior and Radical Action: Franciscans, Quakers, and the Followers of Gandhi," *Signs* 11 (1985–6): 457–77; Jack D. Marietta, *The Reformation of American Quakerism, 1748–1783* (Philadelphia: University of Pennsylvania Press, 1984), 31. Keith Thomas, "Women and the Civil War Sects," in *Crisis in Europe, 1560–1660: Essays from Past and Present*, ed. Trevor Ashton (London: Routledge & Kegan Paul, 1965), esp. 324–5; Mary Maples Dunn, "Saints and Sisters: Congregational and Quaker Women in the Early Colonial Period," *American Quarterly* 30 (1978): 582–601.

and conversion mirrored the experiences of the respective sects. Quakers witnessed to the possibility of universal convincement within a community of believers linked together by overlapping social and spiritual ties.[33] The experience of the antipedobaptists was just the opposite. Preaching the limited nature of redemption, the Baptists saw themselves as the chosen people of God scattered to live among the reprobate but regathered in communion with other saints. Only the select few drew together around the Lord's Table, leaving spouses, children, neighbors, and friends behind. Both groups literally lived what they believed.

The trends inaugurated in the first years – toward community-bound Quakerism and socially dispersed antipedobaptism – continued to shape both movements for decades. The Quakers remained densely interrelated. Six entended families accounted for fully two-thirds of the more than five hundred people known to have been members of the monthly meeting through 1740.[34] The Southwick,[35] Buffum, and Shattock[36] clans that initially had numerically dominated the movement contributed more than one-third of these later members. In addition, three families from the neighboring section of Lynn joined the meeting in the late seventeenth century.[37] These clans made up almost a third of the meeting members by 1740, and their influence increased as their numbers grew during the second half of the eighteenth century. Most of the remaining meeting members were part of smaller Quaker family groups. With this trend so widespread, one traveling Friend visiting the region in 1742 found an Ipswich couple divided in its allegiances to the sect worthy of comment.[38] A more typical problem in the Salem community was locating a Quaker spouse who was not too "near of kin" according to the sect's testimony against marriage between second and even third cousins.[39]

---

[33] Barry Levy found this to be true of Quakers in northern Wales; see *Quakers and the American Family: British Settlement in the Delaware Valley* (New York: Oxford University Press, 1988), 61–6. The same was apparently true later of the Shakers; Priscilla J. Brewer, *Shaker Communities, Shaker Lives* (Hanover, N.H.: University Press of New England, 1986), 23–4.

[34] A more detailed description can be found in Carla Gardina Pestana, "Sectarianism in Colonial Massachusetts" (Ph.D. diss., University of California at Los Angeles, 1987), 57–64, 231–9.

[35] Descendents of the three youngest children of Lawrence and Cassandra Southwick, along with the closely affiliated Boyce family, accounted for at least forty meeting members to 1740.

[36] Gertrude Shattock Pope's descendents traced their lineage back to the original Shattock Quakers; other Shattocks left the area early to participate in Quaker meetings in New Jersey and possibly elsewhere.

[37] Samuel and Hannah Collins were convinced in the 1680s, and Sarah Hood Bassett and many of her relations joined in the following decade. The Estes family, which initially included two brothers who had been convinced in England and the women they married in New Hampshire, arrived in Lynn in the 1680s or 1690s.

[38] *An Account of the Gospel Labors and Christian Experiences of that Faithful Minister of Christ, John Churchman* (Philadelphia, 1779; reprint ed., 1873), 74–5. Churchman was hopeful that his preaching swayed his host's unsupportive wife.

[39] SMM, March 1729/30. See Frost, *Quaker Family*, 160–1, for a discussion of these regulations.

Only occasionally did individuals or couples with no apparent relation to other members of the meeting appear in the documents kept by the sect. During the first eighty years, fewer than one-tenth of all local Quakers (forty of five hundred) were completely unrelated to other meeting members. Sometimes these people were sectarian immigrants who arrived in the region prepared to participate in the Quaker community there.[40] In a few other instances, colonists were convinced by the sect's message despite their lack of personal connections to the increasingly tribal group.[41]

Still, the overall picture of the Salem Monthly Meeting indicates intense tribalism. Family ties fostered and reinforced sectarian commitment. Coreligionists were further linked as parent and child, as siblings, neighbors, and coheirs. The realities of daily life, of work and worship, involved the same people interacting continually on various levels. The Salem-area Quakers remained a sect of kin throughout the colonial period.

Among the Baptists, familial and sectarian affiliations remained comparatively disjoined during the period before 1740. In contrast to the Quakers in the Salem Monthly Meeting, the members of the Boston Baptist Church were not generally connected by family ties. Throughout its first eighty years, the church's membership continued to be composed mainly of isolated individuals. Fully one-half (215) of the 428 baptized members bore no apparent relationship to any of their coreligionists. The case of Mr. Samuel Hutchinson, whose elevated social status and the fact that he joined the church at age sixty-eight made him somewhat unusual, was not untypical with respect to his family circumstances; no member of his immediate family joined him in the Baptist faith, for they were all communicants with the Charlestown Church.[42] The geographic dispersion of the Baptists, a related tendency that dated from the earliest years, continued. Almost one-half (194) of all members resided outside of Boston – in forty-four different towns – when they were received into the church. Although these individuals occasionally joined in the company of other local converts, some distant communicants were not only the sole dissenters in their families but the only antipedobaptists in their towns as well.[43]

The remaining one-half of all communicants were related to other church members, but generally to just one or two others in truncated nuclear families

---

[40] For obvious reasons, Quaker migration into Massachusetts before 1740 was negligible, accounting for probably only about 5 percent of the Salem meeting membership.

[41] Because of the difficulties in identifying weekly meeting members and in reconstructing families, some individuals or relationships have certainly been missed. The ratio of unrelated individuals may have been slightly higher, but the general trend within the meeting seems clear.

[42] Baptist Record Book, 28 September 1740. On his family, most of whom were "children of the church" rather than full members, see Wyman, *Genealogies and Estates of Charlestown*, 536; and *Records of the First Church in Charlestown*, ed. Hunnewell, 135.

[43] The church records list the towns of residence (other than Boston) of all church communicants joining after 1681.

spanning, at most, two generations.[44] One hundred and thirty people, almost one-third of the total membership from 1665 to 1745, participated in small sectarian family units. Most people (eighty-eight) had only one other family member among their fellow communicants. On the other extreme, the largest of these units – the Bound family of Boston – numbered only five or six Baptists. The Bound couple was unusual in that some of their children eventually became church members. The children of Boston Baptists were far more likely to remain outside of the faith. At most, sectarian couples with one or more children who shared their faith accounted for just twenty-three of the communicants who had relatives in the church. Thirty-three couples who were members raised children who failed to join the church as adults.

For those individuals who joined the Boston church without some or all of their kin, their choice probably served to isolate them from the others in their family who did not participate. John Comer, for instance, found the decision to take up the Baptist faith difficult because his relations could not support him in it.[45] In some cases, other members of the family may have attended church meetings along with those who were full communicants but failed to take the steps necessary to embrace the sect fully.[46] Under such circumstances, the sense of isolation experienced by the lone member would have been ameliorated somewhat. Still, especially when compared with the Quakers, the Baptists did not blend familial and sectarian commitments into an integrated whole. Whether completely alone or in the company of just one or two of their kinfolk, Baptists joined their church as individuals rather than as part of large sectarian families.

Three extended Baptist families, all of which included church leaders, provide the exceptions that prove the rule that Boston Baptist Church members tended not to be interrelated.[47] All three of these families coalesced around

---

[44] The following family connections have been reconstructed from the Baptist Record Book; *BTR;* the Thwing Index to Boston Inhabitants, MHS; ECPR; SCPR; MCPR; published vital records for various towns; and *NEHGR.*

[45] "Diary of John Comer," ed. Barrows, 27.

[46] See, e.g., the case of one Tollison, related by Increase Mather in his Diary, 10 September 1680.

[47] Another exception, that of the Scott family of Springfield, has been excluded from this discussion. Fourteen of the seventeen western Massachusetts residents who entered into communion with the Boston church between 1727 and 1740 were related. The group sought dismissal in 1740 to form its own church, one of a handful of Baptist churches gathered in the decade leading up to the revivals. The interrelatedness of these Baptists anticipated a new trend within the denomination; in the years after 1740, Baptists apparently tended to be drawn from such extended families. While these Baptist converts were more likely to be kin, John L. Brooke has found that they still crossed town boundaries to join churches. See " 'For Honour and Civil Worship to Any Worthy Person': Burial, Baptism, and Community on the Massachusetts Near Frontier, 1730–1790," in *Material Life in America, 1600–1860,* ed. Robert Blair St. George (Boston: Northeastern University Press, 1988), 471, 479. The increasing number of Baptist churches in the late colonial period ensured that church membership would cease to be so scattered.

Baptist patriarchs, in keeping with the significant role that men had had in shaping the church. Two early church members, Salem cooper Isaac Hull[48] and prosperous Boston tailor Ellis Callendar,[49] initially sought membership in the church alone and only later were joined by other family members. As their families' connections to the sect developed, the importance of the role played by Hull and Callendar within the church was also increasing. Eight descendants of Hull and from eighteen to twenty of Callendar eventually joined the church. Second-generation convert Joseph Russell occupied the pivotal position in a somewhat later and slightly different version of these Baptist patriarchies. Although never a church officer himself, Russell was the son and grandson of the John Russells, who had been elders during the early period. In addition, he was married to the granddaughter of Thomas Goold.[50] His wife never joined the church, but Joseph and six of the couple's nine children did. Eventually, these offspring intermarried into other important Boston Baptist families, creating a network of sectarian relations with power in the church far greater than its numbers would suggest.[51]

Although these leading Baptist families – especially the Boston-based Callendar and Russell clans – profoundly influenced the church, their existence did little to change the reality of church life for the majority of Baptists. While in one respect these three clans represented a radical departure from the traditional social circumstances of church members, they also carried on a tradition of male leadership among Baptists, since men forged the initial links that tied these kin groups to the church. Despite the existence of these networks, the fit between sectarian and familial commitments remained less than comfortable for the average church member. Of the 428 people baptized into the church before 1740, just 14 percent were involved in one of these three families. Baptists with numerous relations in the church remained as unusual as Quakers without kin in the meeting.

Over the long run, this difference between the two communities depended in large part upon the decisions that the offspring of sectarians made about their own spirituality. Quaker marriage regulations eventually ensured that the majority of Friends had spouses in the meeting; this practice helped to set them apart from the Baptists, who freely married nonmembers.[52] But to recreate the

---

[48] Hull, who was probably a Baptist at the time of his arrival in Salem in 1663, joined the church soon after it was gathered. By the late 1670s, he was acting as church elder. Most of his immediate family eventually joined, as did one or two of his grandchildren. Pestana, "Sectarianism," 245–7.

[49] Callendar became a church member in 1669 at the age of twenty-seven. He served as church elder from perhaps 1708 until his son, Elisha, became the first ordained minister a decade later. Three generations of his family eventually included church members. Ibid., 248–50.

[50] Mary Skinner Russell's parents – Thomas and Mary Goold Skinner – were Baptists.

[51] Leadership of the church is treated in Chapter 5 and the Great Awakening in Chapter 8.

[52] Quakers could have non-Quaker spouses (usually through marriages that took place prior to convincement, although Friends were occasionally allowed to remain in the meeting despite

complicated familial networks that bound Salem-area Friends together required multigenerational participation within families. Only as long as the children of Quakers followed their parents' example and participated in the meeting themselves would the tribalism of the first generation be replicated. Because
the adult children of relatively few Baptists entered the church, members continued to have spiritual commitments that separated them from their close kin.

The clannishness of Salem Quakerism, once established, was conducive to
bringing Friends' children into the meeting as adults. The young members of
one of the extended Quaker families must have sensed not only that anyone
could follow the light within, but that everyone of any significance did so. In
the terms used by sociologists Peter Berger and Thomas Luckmann, the Quakers had created a "symbolic universe," in which meaning and institutions were
integrated and therefore strengthened.[53] Since both parents and, often, other
relations were likely to be active in the meeting, children of Quakers were provided with a standard of adult religiosity that their counterparts in orthodox and
Baptist households often did not have. Numerous sectarian role models and a
great deal of interaction among the adult Quakers provided concrete examples
of sectarian life for young people. Coming of age in the midst of so much
sectarian activity helped to prepare children to take their place in that community as adults. The orthodox minister who married Thomas Blaney and Desire
Dean in 1720 was well aware of this phenomenon; apparently he thought of
Blaney's Quaker ancestry as he recorded in his diary, "God preserve him from
Quakerism & her from following him therein." His fears proved well founded,
for both Desire and Thomas became active in the Quaker meeting eventually.[54]
Thomas was unusual only in having been disassociated from the sect for a time
in his early adulthood. Most children of Quakers cut a more direct path into
the meeting.

In addition, some of the sect's practices fostered a consciousness that the
Quakers represented a distinct group. Because Quaker beliefs departed radically from those of the larger community and because those beliefs led the sect
to adopt a series of unusual practices – such as the use of plain language and a
refusal to participate in the militia – Quakers stood out.[55] In adopting these

marrying out, generally after acknowledging their error). Some Baptists discussed the question
of appropriate marriage partners; see, e.g., Norman H. Maring, *Baptists in New Jersey: A Study
in Transition* (Valley Forge: Judson, 1964), 34. No evidence survives to suggest that the Boston
church did so.

53 Peter L. Berger and Thomas Luckmann, *The Social Construction of Reality: A Treatise in the
Sociology of Knowledge* (Garden City, N.Y.: Doubleday, 1966), 88–96.

54 "Fragment of a Diary kept by Rev. Samuel Fiske of Salem, 1719–1721," *EIHC* 51 (1915): 288.
Desire Blaney attended the Rhode Island Yearly Meeting in 1732; see SQM (women's). Thomas
was apparently the man of that name rated for a special tax on Quakers in 1759; Salem Tax
List, Massachusetts Local Tax Lists Through 1776, comp. Ruth Crandall, Harvard University
Library, Cambridge, Mass., microfilm, reel 8.

55 For an early example of plain language, see Smith to Endecott, 2:208–11; for militia service,

78 Development

testimonies, Salem Friends underscored their outsider status. Growing up in the Quaker meeting, the children of Friends would have been aware of their family's unique religiosity from an early age. This often led to an intense identification with the sect, which in turn encouraged these people to remain within the meeting once they reached adulthood.[56]

Not content to leave the matter solely to these forces, however pervasive they might be, Friends eventually began to work at perpetuating familial involvement through the education of the younger generation. Salem Quakers trailed behind on this reform, as on many others developed by English Friends.[57] To the extent that such reforms were instituted to maintain barriers between the sect and the "world's people," the Salem meeting's greater estrangement from the larger community forestalled the need for such innovations. Pennsylvania and Rhode Island Friends – living in colonies where the sect was more readily accepted – took up the cause of sectarian education earlier than their coreligionists in less tolerant Massachusetts. As a result, some of the impetus for educational reform came from outside the Salem area, most directly from the yearly meeting in Rhode Island to which the Salem Friends belonged.[58]

By the early eighteenth century, however, the monthly meeting had begun to focus some of its energies on educating the next generation about the sect's beliefs and practices. The need for a school for Quaker children was acknowledged in 1715, although no record survives of any arrangements made at that time. Special meetings for youths, which presumably included an educational component, were held sporadically beginning before 1724.[59] The first Quaker

"Walter Phillips Sen. Sufferings," SMM, 5 June 1705 (sufferings appear after minutes for 1700).

As far as other testimonies are concerned, the surviving evidence makes it difficult to determine which of them Massachusetts Quakers followed and how consistently. For instance, Leanna Lee-Whitman has recently concluded that the testimony on the plain style of dress was widely implemented in Pennsylvania only in the nineteenth century; "Silks and Simplicity: A Study of Quaker Dress as Depicted in Portraits, 1718–1855" (Ph.D. diss., University of Pennsylvania, 1987). One of the wealthiest Salem Quakers bought a wig; see Zaccheus Collins, Diary, Essex Institute, Salem, Mass., 3 November 1736. On the question of consistency, see *A Relation of the Labour, Travail and Sufferings of the Faithful Servant . . . Alice Curwen* ([London?], 1680), 19–20, and *Some Cursory Remarks Made by James Birket* (New Haven, Conn.: Yale University Press, 1916), 27–8, for variations in other colonies.

[56] R. Laurence Moore has recently described a somewhat similar process among such nineteenth-century sects as the Church of the Latter Day Saints; *Religious Outsiders and the Making of Americans* (New York: Oxford University Press, 1986). Colonial Massachusetts Quakers did not, however, paradoxically become insiders as a result of embracing their outsiderhood.
[57] The development of sectarian discipline will be discussed in the following chapter.
[58] RIYM, 1708, 1709, 1717; Antient Epistles, Minutes and Advices or Disciplines, ibid., 1708; both in RIHS. Salem records first mention the need for a school in 1715.
[59] SQM (men's), RIHS, April 1708; SMM, August 1715, October 1724, July 1733. Similar meetings in Pennsylvania included an educational component; Sydney B. James, *A People Among Peoples: Quaker Benevolence in Eighteenth-Century America* (Cambridge, Mass.: Harvard University Press, 1963), 69.

work produced on a Boston press – a 1723 reprint of an English pamphlet outlining good family governance and the proper upbringing of the children of Quakers – further indicated growing concern over this issue.[60] With measures such as these, Salem meeting began a concerted effort to pass on its faith to its children.

Barry Levy has argued that a concern for family governance gave shape and meaning to the Quaker movement from the first. In fact, the sect turned its attention to the questions of child nurture and sectarian continuity rather later than Levy's thesis would suggest. Initially, Quakers expected the imminent end of the world and consequently gave little thought to the faith of future generations. Far from being the aberrant event of Levy's account, the celibacy movement among early Salem Quakers was therefore completely consistent with the sect's initial focus on the world to come.[61] Only after the sobering experience of the Restoration did they take up the problems associated with long-term survival. Even then, child nurture held a lower priority than the organization of meetings and the development of general disciplinary procedures.[62] After English Friends had begun to address the problem of sectarian continuity within the family, Quakers elsewhere only gradually turned their attentions to this issue as they became convinced of the need to do so.

When they did decide systematically to educate their children in the Quaker faith, that faith itself bolstered their decision. The sect's belief that salvation was universally available permitted them to approach their children as potential members. Unlike the Baptists, who were not certain their children were fit candidates for membership, the Quakers had no theological cause for discomfort as they encouraged their offspring to follow the light of truth.[63] Quaker

---

[60] Elizabeth Head Jacob, *An Epistle in true Love containing a farewell exhortation to Friends' Families* (London, 1712; Boston, 1723). The publication was financed by the Rhode Island Yearly Meeting, and the Salem Quarterly Meeting received three hundred copies for distribution to its members; RIYM, 1723.

[61] See Levy, *Quakers and the American Family* generally; for the discussion of Salem celibacy, 72. Levy believes that celibacy arose from a misreading of George Fox's views on marriage and sexual relations. Following a tradition in Quaker literature that has been challenged in the last twenty years, his argument assumes that Fox was the wellspring of Quakerism and that his influence was immediately felt by even the newly convinced on the periphery of the English empire. Until Fox – in the company of Margaret Fell – gained control of the movement in the 1660s, he had no noticeable impact on the Quakers in Salem; even then, his influence was both indirect and vigorously contested. The authorities the celibates themselves cited for their practice were other local Quakers and two traveling witnesses; see Nicholson to Fell, 1660.

[62] On the Restoration, see Reay, *Quakers and the English Revolution*, ch. 6. Arnold Lloyd chronicles the organizational process in *Quaker Social History*.

[63] No evidence of child-raising practices exists to support Philip Greven's assertion that these beliefs would lead the Baptists to adopt a particularly harsh attitude toward their children, nor do I intend to imply that I believe such was the case. Greven cites early Quaker writings along with those of Congregationalists and Baptists as examples of the "evangelical temperament" that led to (and arose out of) such practices. In doing so, he disregards the very theological distinc-

tribalism could be maintained among later generations through an inculcation program that relied on the belief that anyone could become a Quaker but that, ironically, concentrated only on the children of the convinced.

In the context of the Salem Quaker community, leaving the sect always constituted an extreme step. To the extent that the Salem Friends created a total sectarian environment, the failure of a family member to join in would have been a wrenching experience for all involved. More so than among the Baptists, whose faith never had such a strong social component, the Quakers felt many daily repercussions from an individual's failure to take part in the group's activities.

Despite – or, possibly, because of – these strong sanctions, the children of some Quakers did rebel. In one extreme case, a first-generation meeting member was sufficiently outraged at his son's failure to join him in his newfound faith that he disinherited him in favor of a Quaker grandson. In later years, a few sons of Quakers married outside of the meeting or even joined the established church.[64] On two occasions, in 1718 and 1728, minister Samuel Fiske noted the fact that a former Quaker had joined Salem Church. That Fiske saw these as noteworthy events gives some indication of their rarity. Not surprisingly, both of these apostates had grown up in Quaker families elsewhere and had left their town of origin before abandoning their parents' faith.[65] The offspring of local Friends occasionally left the area, and perhaps a few of these also took the opportunity presented by emigration to abandon Quakerism. Unlike in Pennsylvania, the Salem meeting did not punish parents whose children failed to become Friends. The general rule, however, was for the children of Quakers to remain in the sect, to marry in the meeting, and to pass their faith on to their own children.

That the same cannot be said of the offspring of Baptist church members underscores the impact of the different beliefs and social circumstances on that sectarian community. Because Baptists wanted to separate the godly wheat from the reprobate tares in accordance with the scriptural analogy, their inclination was to take a somewhat passive stance toward the larger community, including their own children. Having "come out from among them" by gathering a church as close to pure as humanly possible, the Baptists strove to protect that purity by screening candidates for membership. In this respect, the Boston Baptists

---

tions that supposedly fueled the differences he attempts to describe. *The Protestant Temperament: Patterns of Child-Rearing, Religious Experience, and the Self in Early America* (New York: Knopf, 1977), esp. 28–55.

[64] Probate Records of Joseph Boyce (d. 1695), ECPR. The only two men dealt with by the monthly meeting for marrying out during the first eighty years were Edward Webb and Nathaniel Hood (or Whood), SMM, November 1706. The women's monthly meeting records are not extant for this period, so the number of women (if any) disowned for this offense is not known.

[65] *The Records of the First Church in Salem, Massachusetts, 1629–1736*, ed. Richard D. Pierce (Salem, Mass.: Essex Institute, 1974), 317, 325.

conformed to the classic sociological definition of a sect.[66] There is no evidence that the church or its officers took an active role in recruiting potential communicants during the colonial period. Rather, they waited for a candidate to approach the church.[67] Colonists did continue to come forward to seek admission into this exclusive community, sustaining the church with their conversions.

The Baptists' view that the few qualified members should be left to seek out the Lord's people of their own accord influenced their approach to their own children. Certainly communicants encouraged their children to live moral and upright lives and to examine themselves for any signs of election. And, like church member Rachel Proctor, they longed to see their children among the elect so that families could be together in heaven.[68] Beyond that, however, the concerned parent could not go without contradicting his or her own beliefs about salvation and sainthood. Baptists occasionally attempted to make a virtue of this necessity, as in the English treatise popular among Boston Baptists that advocated the independence of children from the spiritual choices made by their parents. Although this freedom could protect children from becoming "Jews, Heathen or Turks" – as John Walton pointed out – it could prevent them from becoming Baptists as well.[69] In spite of Walton's efforts, Baptist parents must have felt anxious about the souls of their children. Along with increasing numbers of parents in the orthodox churches, their personal convictions and concerns could not be directly translated into conversion for their offspring.

The geographic dispersion of the church's membership, itself a result of the emphasis placed on the communicant's personal experience, also undermined the sect's ability to pass its beliefs on to the next generation. Because an individual could come to the Baptist position through private soul searching and Scripture reading, some members (and their families) had no sustained contact

[66] Thomas Goold quoted this passage to the authorities in 1668; "Baptist Debate," ed. McLoughlin and Davidson, 113. As Patricia Bonomi points out, New Lights in the Great Awakening favored the passage; *Under the Cope of Heaven*, 154. For the characteristics of a sect, see Ernst Troeltsch, *The Social Teachings of the Christian Churches*, trans. Olive Wyon, 2 vols. (New York: Macmillan, 1931), esp. 742–3, 336; Max Weber, "The Social Psychology of the World Religions," in *From Max Weber: Essays in Sociology*, trans. and ed. H. H. Gerth and C. Wright Mills (New York: Oxford University Press, 1946), 287–8, 305–6.

[67] For a statement to that effect, see John Langdon Sibley and Clifford K. Shipton, *Sibley's Harvard Graduates*, 17 vols. (Boston: Massachusetts Historical Society, 1883–5, 1933–75), 5:515. Apparently because of the Particular Baptist attitude on this matter, the great Baptist itinerants during the English civil war tended to be General Baptists; Sydney E. Ahlstrom, *A Religious History of the American People* (New Haven, Conn.: Yale University Press, 1972), 172.

[68] Rachel Proctor to [Josiah Byles], November [17___], Belknap Collection, MHS; also see *Baptist Piety: The Last Will and Testimony of Obadiah Holmes*, ed. Edwin S. Gaustad (Grand Rapids, Mich.: Christian University Press, 1978), 101, 102.

[69] John Walton, *A Just Vindication of the True Christian Baptism* (Boston, 1738), 38. The American Antiquarian Society copy had been owned by church deacon Josiah Byles (1682?–1752).

with the community of believers. In such cases, the task of communicating sectarian beliefs to a younger generation fell on the shoulders of a lone individual or on a small group of people. Whatever the young person might have learned by watching a parent participate in a large sectarian community would have been missed.

The leading Boston families of the mid-eighteenth century provided the one notable exception to this divergence between family and sect among the Baptists. By birth and through marriage, these people eventually developed overlapping familial and sectarian commitments. To a certain extent, this exception can be explained in terms of the group's unique circumstances. The social experience of sectarianism was more intense for the offspring of the church's leading men. More than any other group of future Baptists, these people had come of age in a town where their families were identified with the church and, in some circles, were respected for the important roles they played in it. In this sense, these families began to approach the situation enjoyed by the orthodox colonist or by the Salem and Lynn Quakers. Certainly these people had attended services at the meetinghouse by the Mill Pond all of their lives. With the concentration of church members in Boston, children of communicants were also more likely to intermarry. Marital ties between Baptist families served to intensify further the sectarian identification of these individuals.[70]

By embracing a less rigorous attitude toward conversion, this group of Baptists demonstrated once again the close link between ideas about salvation and the social basis of sectarianism. In the 1730s, these leading Baptist families moved away from the church's traditional Reformed emphasis by choosing the theologically liberal Jeremiah Condy as church minister. The "Arminian" message Condy preached was compatible with the trend toward multigenerational conversion, explaining and giving legitimacy to these conversions.[71] The powerful clique formed by these families and the liberal doctrine they upheld would both become sources of contention with other members of the church during the Great Awakening. Even in the exceptional case presented by these families, sectarian beliefs continued to interact with the social reality of sectarianism in profound ways.

This shift in the doctrinal position of the church's leading families offers a classic example of the dilemma inherent in sectarianism. In his path-breaking

---

[70] As in the orthodox churches, Boston Baptist Church communicants were joined at religious services by other worshipers who were not members. The available evidence does not allow for the reconstruction of this marginally involved group, but it is presumable that the children of those members who resided in or near Boston were likely to attend.

[71] Although the term "Arminian" was used then and has been used since to describe this theological shift toward an emphasis on good works, no one openly advocated the sixteenth-century Dutch theologian's view that salvation was universal until the revolutionary era. On the spread of theological liberalism, see, e.g., James W. Jones, *The Shattered Synthesis: New England Puritanism before the Great Awakening* (New Haven, Conn.: Yale University Press, 1973), esp. 131–98.

The Social Teachings of the Christian Churches, sociologist Ernst Troeltsch described two ideal types of Christian organizations – the sect and the church. Sects, such as the early Baptists, are always in danger of disintegrating for lack of new members worthy to join with God's chosen people. Churches, in contrast, are not similarly troubled with a shortage of acceptable members, since they welcome anyone regardless of spiritual qualifications; but they are susceptible to charges of impurity and worldliness for the same reason. Given the precariousness of their position, sects might move in the direction of the more conservative and inclusive "church-type" to overcome their difficulties. When some Boston Baptists embraced a doctrine that minimized the need for membership qualifications and encouraged their children to convert, they were participating in the shift from sect to church that sociologists have described. Robert Pope has argued that the established churches had been responding to a similar problem when they adopted the halfway covenant during the previous century.[72]

The sect and church typologies do not fully explain the Salem Quakers' case, however. The Quakers were able to avoid the problem of sectarian disintegration for at least a century in eastern Massachusetts because their belief in universal redemption allowed them to recruit new members without abandoning their fundamental principles. Membership in the Salem Monthly Meeting continued to expand largely through the participation of subsequent generations of Quaker families. The Quakers avoided the dilemma that confronted the Baptist church because their peculiar social and religious practices set them apart and, with the help of their educational program, increased their numbers. In Troeltsch's terms, Quakerism in colonial Massachusetts functioned as a sect but held more inclusive "churchlike" beliefs.[73]

Viewed in the context of colonial New England society, the two sects can be seen following one of the two, somewhat contradictory trends that were shaping that society and emphasizing it at the expense of the other. Scholars have long seen early New England as pulled between corporate communalism and na-

[72] Troeltsch, *Social Teachings of the Christian Churches*. The idea that sects evolve into churches was first systematically developed by H. Richard Niebuhr, *Social Sources of Denominationalism* (New York: Holt, 1929), 17–21, 5, 6; also see Liston Pope, *Millhands and Preachers: A Study of Gastonia* (New Haven, Conn.: Yale University Press, 1942), esp. 122–4. Michael Hill, *A Sociology of Religion* (London: Heinemann, 1973), chs. 3, 4, reviews the literature on sect and church. Pope, *Half-Way Covenant*, 261–2.

[73] Troeltsch discussed Quakerism briefly, placing it in the context of mysticism, which he viewed as a less fully articulated third tendency within Christianity; see *Social Teachings of the Christian Churches*, 780–4. Other sociologists have tried to account for the persistence of sectarian features in the Society of Friends; see J. Milton Yinger (who limited his qualifications to twentieth-century Quakerism), *Religion in the Struggle for Power: A Study in the Sociology of Religion* (Durham, N.C.: Duke University Press, 1946), esp. 23; and Elizabeth Isichei, "From Sect to Denomination among English Quakers," in *Patterns of Sectarianism: Organization and Ideology in Social and Religious Movements*, ed. Brian Wilson (London: Heinemann, 1967), 161–81.

scent individualism. The insular New England town and the evolving covenant theology emphasized the centrality of the community both socially and religiously, but the stark individualism of the Reformed Protestant emphasis on election and the changing realities of colonial life pulled in the other direction. The belief system and the daily life of orthodox colonists held elements of both an individualistic and a communalistic ethos.[74] Men and women were possibly inclined to favor one or the other of these trends, as the preferences they expressed in making their spiritual commitments suggest.[75]

Quakers and Baptists similarly endorsed one tendency within the culture more than the other. The stress laid by the Quakers on the community of believers encouraged sectarian continuity within the family so that sect and family converged. With a faith in the possibility of universal redemption, the more "feminine" Quakerism achieved on a smaller scale the overlapping social and religious allegiances that the orthodox were striving for in town and congregation. To the Baptists' way of thinking, at least for the first half-century of the church's history, this convergence was achieved at too great a cost. They preferred to accept a disparity between sectarian and familial affiliation in the interest of maintaining a pure church. The Baptists' initial position was difficult to maintain. Generations of Baptists, attracted to this especially "masculine" faith, upheld the church's tradition. Rather than confront the damnation of their loved ones and the possible dissolution of their church, however, a few of the leading members in Boston apparently chose not to maintain the traditional stance. The Quakers' position created no such dilemma, the convergence of sect and family ultimately strengthening both institutions.

[74] For an effort at synthesizing and reinterpreting much of this material, see Michael Zuckerman's "The Fabrication of Identity in Early America," *WMQ*, 3d ser., 34 (1977): 183–214.

[75] A rigid conception of gender differences – women as emotional, spiritual, home and family oriented; men as rational, political, public – was taking hold over the course of the colonial period, according to Ruth H. Bloch, "Untangling the Roots of Modern Sex Roles: A Survey of Four Centuries of Change," *Signs* 4 (1978): 237–52. To some extent, these distinctions follow the communal/female versus individual/male division dealt with here. Linda K. Kerber, *Women of the Republic: Intellect and Ideology in Revolutionary America* (Chapel Hill: University of North Carolina Press, 1980), uses the terms "traditional" and "modern" (p. 7) when discussing the implications of this division for female political activity in the revolutionary era.

4

Organizational maturation

By the end of the seventeenth century, both the Baptist church and the Quaker meeting had become fairly structured and had laid the groundwork for further organizational development. The marked contrast between the religious institutions of the eighteenth century and the precariously established communities of the mid-seventeenth century suggests that both sects gradually became staid and respectable, giving up various radical qualities. In broad outline, their histories conform to sociological models of sectarian development as each took on the characteristics of a church and became more routinized with time.

The Baptists and the Quakers arrived at the more churchlike form of the later colonial period by very different paths, however, and achieved dissimilar results. The Baptist church evolved its institutional trappings gradually, drawing upon biblical models it had consistently venerated. In contrast, the Quaker meeting accepted organizational reforms only after tremendous upheaval within the meeting and concerted pressure from outside it. The structure the Quakers eventually erected forestalled some of the compromises usually associated with sectarian evolution. In such basic areas as sectarian discipline, the Baptists and Quakers developed distinctive traditions.

By the turn of the century, the Baptists and Quakers had adopted many of the same basic organizational forms. Both had abandoned the earlier practice of meeting in private homes, taking the symbolically significant step of building their own meetinghouses. As in other areas, the Baptists embraced this symbol of legitimacy first. They erected a meetinghouse on the bank of the Mill Pond in the North End of Boston in 1679 on property owned by two members, Phillip Squire and Ellis Callendar. Despite a fight with the authorities over its right to use the building for unauthorized religious meetings, the church was soon able to meet there regularly.[1] The Quakers built their meetinghouses later and did not have to contend with the opposition that had temporarily hampered the

---

[1] Baptist Record Book, 1679–80; "Increase Mather's Diary," *PMHS*, 2d ser., vol. 13 (1900): 408; Edward Drinker et al., Petition to the General Court, 24 February 1680, MAE, 11:30. The meetinghouse was enlarged in 1737, which has often been mistaken for the erection of an entirely new structure; a second edifice was not built until 1771; see Annie Haven Thwing, *The Crooked and Narrow Streets of the Town of Boston, 1630–1822* (Boston, 1925), 67.

Baptists' efforts. By 1700, the Salem Monthly Meeting owned buildings in Salem, Boston, and, possibly, Lynn.[2]

The regularly scheduled meetings for worship and for business that were held in these meetinghouses constituted additional departures from earlier practices. Like the established churches, both sects eventually gathered for worship on the Sabbath and on a weekday. The Baptists held a morning and an afternoon service on Sunday as early as 1679. They also eventually established a weekday meeting, although when is not certain. The Quakers originally met only once on Sundays but may have begun gathering two times during the eighteenth century. By 1677, they were also meeting on Thursday.[3] Worshiping at regular times in a specified place provided a radically different experience from that of the first sectaries, who had gathered when and where they could.

More than a prearranged schedule for worship services, the institution of regular business meetings denoted a new stability and a degree of organizational sophistication. Initially, neither sect had distinguished between types of meetings, addressing practical questions that occasionally arose informally. Eventually the work of assisting members in need, disciplining errant members, and making decisions about other issues reached such a volume that separate meetings were needed to handle them.[4] The Salem Quakers held monthly meetings for business beginning in the 1670s and segregated these into men's and women's meetings during the following decade. Eventually, the business meeting rotated between the sites of the three weekly meetings. The Baptists set aside every fourth Monday for a business meeting in 1682.[5]

The business transacted at these meetings was carefully recorded; such record keeping marked another reform that bespoke an increased organizational complexity. More than any other reform, record keeping suggested a concern for continuity and a sense of establishing a tradition. The Baptists had set down the names of church members from the outset, and these lists became more detailed after the first decade. Around the same time, the church began to keep an account of church business.[6] The Salem Quakers began keeping

---

[2] Perley, *History of Salem*, 2:273; SMM, May 1714; RIYM, 1694, 1708. Although the meeting records do not mention financing a structure in Lynn, a wedding took place in the Lynn meetinghouse (presumably a public structure and not a private residence) in 1700; Salem Monthly Meeting Marriage Certificates, 13 May 1700, New England Yearly Meeting Archive, RIHS. Alonzo Lewis and James R. Newhall believed that the structure built later in the eighteenth century replaced an earlier one; *History of Lynn* (Boston, 1865), 320.

[3] Baptist Record Book, 28 July 1679, 1 October 1739. After Jeremiah Condy's ordination in 1738, the church agreed on a lecture day; they were probably innovating but may have been reviving an earlier practice. SMM, July 1677, December 1709.

[4] Instances of destitution mentioned in the church and meeting records are few. There is some evidence, particularly for the Quakers, that permanent poor relief funds were established; RIYM, 1697; SMM, August 1706, May 1731; Baptist Record Book, 6 December 1742.

[5] SMM, July 1677, February 1688/9, May 1707; Baptist Record Book, February 1681/2.

[6] The church records for 1696 through 1708 are no longer extant, however.

sporadic records of business in the 1670s. Meeting minutes were systematically recorded from 1689, at which time the early records were recopied into a new book.[7] By keeping increasingly detailed accounts of their transactions, both sects indicated their growing consciousness of themselves as ongoing organizations and as part of history.

In keeping records, in scheduling regular meetings for worship and for business, and in building meetinghouses, the Baptists and the Quakers were adopting the forms of an organized religious community. Both instituted these reforms at roughly the same time, suggesting a parallel movement toward more highly structured organizations. With these developing institutional apparatuses the sects responded to the challenge of long-term survival, laying the groundwork for the continuation of sectarian life beyond the first generation. They apparently relinquished some of their early radicalism, ensuring themselves a more certain if staid future. These changes are consistent with observations made by various sociologists, from Max Weber – who was interested in the general process of institutionalization – to the scholars of sectarian development – who have argued that sects are inclined to become more churchlike over time.[8] In the context of colonial Massachusetts, this gradual transformation from sect to church would, according to this interpretation, carry the Quakers and Baptists closer to the established churches. The institutionalization of sectarianism could ultimately undermine the distinctiveness of the two sects.

This conclusion has much to recommend it in the case of the Baptists, for the reforms they gradually instituted sprang from the same sources that had long been guiding the colony's orthodox churches. The Baptists initiated changes in their practices gradually, as opportunities and needs arose. Many changes – such as holding regularly scheduled meetings or building a meetinghouse – were instituted as soon as church members believed that they could make them without harassment from the authorities. Other reforms – especially the minute recording of church business – were made once members came to appreciate the needs of later generations of members. The Baptist church became more churchlike incrementally. In taking on many of the features of any other church in the colony, the Baptists drew upon the same source as the orthodox colonists, the Scriptures. Baptists, having been motivated to break with the establishment over contrasting readings of the Bible, relied "almost exclusively on primitivist grounds" in defending the very existence of their churches.[9] In addition to

---

[7] SMM, July 1689, May 1720, August 1725, January 1726/7. Possibly in the process of switching to a new book, the records for 1690 through 1700 were lost.

[8] Weber repeatedly dealt with how charismatic movements eventually become routinized; for a brief discussion of this issue, see S. N. Eisenstadt, Introduction to *Max Weber: On Charisma and Institution Building* (Chicago: University of Chicago Press, 1968), xvi–xxii. On sectarian development, see the works cited in Chapter 3, note 72.

[9] Holifield, *Era of Persuasion*, 119–20. Sidney Mead has suggested that the importance of biblical authority was increased by New World conditions; "Denominationalism: The Shape of Protes

fueling disagreements, the sect's biblicism also fostered areas of agreement with the established churches.[10] Because the establishment was similarly concerned to erect pure churches based on scriptural example, the Baptists found many aspects of orthodoxy acceptable. As the church perceived the need to introduce new procedures, it settled on many that were already in place in the colony's other churches. While the Baptist church fulfilled its own changing needs, it almost inadvertently grew more like the established churches in the colony.

The Baptist church revealed its reliance on scriptural guidelines most fully in its disciplinary procedures. Of the various types of business that the church handled, disciplinary matters came up most frequently. The church recorded twenty-one actions from 1679 to 1740.[11] Offenses thought to necessitate intervention included such moral transgressions as excessive drinking or sex before marriage as well as – more rarely – disagreements among members and doctrinal errors.[12] Disciplining members, one of its most solemn tasks, received the church's thoughtful attention; special care was taken to follow proper procedure on this matter. The Baptist church, like the established churches in the colony, had a graduated system of discipline that moved from persuasion to coercion and that closely followed biblical precepts.[13]

The Baptists first attempted to persuade privately; only when that failed did they bring the problem into the more public arena of a church meeting. When confronted with a member who was thought to have breached its standards for Christian comportment, the church would appoint a committee to approach

tantism in America," in *The Lively Experiment: The Shaping of Christianity in America* (New York: Harper & Row, 1963), 113–15.

10   For instance, the Baptists gathered their church with the customary seven members. For the established churches following this practice, see Cotton Mather, *Ratio Disciplinae Fratrum Nov Anglorum* (Boston, 1726), 2; and J. M. Bumsted, "Orthodoxy in Massachusetts: The Ecclesiastical History of Freetown, 1683–1776," *NEQ* 43 (1970), 280.

11   The cases in the Baptist Record Book were distributed over time as follows: 1679, 1683, 1687, 1688, 1692 (2), 1695 (2), 1696, 1709, 1714, 1715, 1728 (2), 1733, 1734 (2), 1735, 1737 (3); (for the four cases that dragged out over a number of years, only the year in which they were resolved has been given). At least one additional case went unrecorded during the period prior to the introduction of systematic record keeping. According to the Middlesex County Court records, John Russell, Sr., cast out fellow Woburn Baptist John Johnson before 1672. His excommunication was apparently only temporary, for he was again affiliated with the sect by 1675. MCC, 3 October 1671, 15 June 1675.

12   The first of these was most common; see, e.g., Baptist Record Book, 4 December 1687; March 1694/5; 1696; 13 February 1714/15; 16 July 1728; 4 May 1733; 7 January, 1 February, 1 March 1733/4. On only two occasions did differences between members demand formal action, and Ephraim Craft was involved in both incidents. See 3 August 1733, 16 January 1736/7. For unacceptable doctrine, see 5 November 1708, 6 June 1709, 26 December 1715.

13   Thomas Hooker (*A Survey of the Summe of Church Discipline* [London, 1648], pt. 3, ch. 3) and later Cotton Mather (*Ratio Disciplinae*, 141–57) laid out the procedures utilized in the established churches. For Baptist agreement on these procedures (but disagreement over whether their use against Baptists had been justified), see "Baptist Debate," ed. McLoughlin and Davidson, 119–21.

that individual. Dozens of such committees were formed over the years, beginning in 1677. Consisting of two and occasionally more male members, they were disbanded after their specific task was completed.[14] If the person under scrutiny was deemed guilty and the committee sent to the errant member proved unable to persuade him or her to repent, the church then summoned the miscreant. Occasionally, such a summons was the first official reference to a given case to appear in the records. Presumably, an informal visit by one or more members had already taken place without being recorded in the church minutes. Once the offender responded to a summons, the church as a whole would attempt to bring him or her to repentance.[15]

If the church failed to reclaim the disobedient person, one of two punishments could be imposed. A wayward member might be denied access to the Lord's Supper. Because this re-creation of the biblical meal was meant to reunite the godly in a symbolic act of community, a saint who was at odds with the rest of Christ's followers could not very well take part. As long as the offending member remained intransigent, he or she had to refrain from participating with the other baptized believers.[16] Before 1740, six suspensions from the Lord's Table were listed in the church records.[17] Although not consistently recorded, suspension was generally accompanied by a formal admonition. The admonition might be renewed later, if the sinner remained unreconciled to the church.[18]

Finally, the church could excommunicate the stubbornly unrepentant member. The church resorted to this tactic only eight times during its first thirty years of existence and avoided using it entirely for three decades after 1708.[19]

---

[14] Baptist Record Book, 1677. Committees in the established churches were also apparently comprised only of men; Mather, *Ratio Disciplinae*, 144, 148.

[15] For instance, early church member John Farnum was visited by brethren in 1683, although they had not been sent by the church (or the order was not recorded); Baptist Record Book, under "A Record Concerning John Farnum."

[16] Just as in the established churches, the Baptists seem to have occasionally used suspension while an individual's conduct was being investigated, as in the case of Sarah Tozer; Baptist Record Book, 4 May 1733. Emil Oberholzer, Jr., *Delinquent Saints: Disciplinary Action in the Early Congregational Churches of Massachusetts* (New York: Columbia University Press, 1959), 36, 279 n.48.

[17] Baptist Record Book, 24 March 1688, 13 February 1714/15, 16 July 1728, 4 May 1733, 1 February 1733/4.

[18] See Baptist Record Book, 20 August 1683, 27 May 1687, 1 March 1733/4. Assuming that the act of suspension included admonishment, the clerk may have noted the entire procedure simply as a suspension. Oberholzer found similar entries in the records for the established churches; see *Delinquent Saints*, 36, 279 n.48. Also see Mather, *Ratio Disciplinae*, 144–48.

[19] Baptist Record Book, 19 February 1678/9, 13 October 1683, 4 December 1687, 14 July 1692, 24 July 1692, 5 January 1695/6. The temporary "casting out" of John Johnson, previously discussed, constituted one additional case. For the years from 1698 to 1708, no records are extant. In 1715 (26 December), a member was granted liberty from the church because of theological differences, but the records suggest an amiable parting rather than an excommunication.

Excommunication usually occurred after a period of suspension from the Lord's Supper, although with an extremely egregious offense or intransigent individual, the church might skip the lesser punishment. In all cases, casting a member out was reserved for a last resort, because the Baptists preferred reclaiming wayward members over expelling them.[20] At any time during the disciplinary process, the peccant individual could offer proof of repentance and be fully readmitted to the community.

The ultimately unsuccessful disciplinary action against Edward Drinker demonstrates how long a case might drag out. The brethren finally excommunicated Drinker, the last living founding member of the church, in 1696 when he was seventy-four years old. For fifteen years or more before this, he had been in and out of favor with the church. He was admonished and removed from the office of deacon twice, reinstated once, suspended from communion for eight years, and finally excommunicated. The details of Drinker's offense went unrecorded, but at times he was denying himself to be a member of the Boston church and refusing to meet with its representatives altogether.[21] His thirty years as a Baptist probably gave the church pause when it came to excommunicating him, but the care that was taken on his case was not unusual.

This detailed, graduated disciplinary system mirrored that used in the established churches. In fact, the few early Baptists who had been members of orthodox churches before joining the sect were quite familiar with these procedures, having been subjected to them for embracing Anabaptism. John Farnum managed to be cast out of both the Second Church of Boston and the Boston Baptist Church during a twenty-year period. In each case, he gave offense by joining with the rival religious society. The two churches proceeded against him through a similar series of steps, carefully recording his disrespectful carriage toward them.[22] Even as he acted upon his own erratic inclinations toward the spiritual options available to Bostonians after the mid-seventeenth century, Farnum's case highlighted the similarities between the town's orthodox and sectarian churches on the question of discipline.

The only real difference between the two on this issue lay in the fate of the excommunicant. Former Baptists had no further contact with the church unless they repented and formally sought readmission.[23] The colonist cast out of one of the established churches lost the ecclesiastical privileges of a saint but was

---

[20] John Farnum, who returned to Boston's Second Church after almost two decades in the Baptist church, was repeatedly interviewed privately and before the church prior to being cast out; "Record Concerning John Farnum."

[21] Baptist Record Book, 12 December 1680, 11 December 1682, 1685, 27 May 1687, 24 May 1688, 2 September 1695, 5 January 1695/6.

[22] Case of John Farnum; "Record Concerning John Farnum." The Baptists, having been criticized for years for accepting Farnum as a member after the way he had treated the Second Church and especially Increase Mather, kept an account of his dealing with them that was unprecedented in its detail.

[23] Except apparently for John Johnson, discussed in note 11, no one sought readmission.

expected to continue attending worship services and paying toward the minister's salary. The latter system sometimes did not work as intended, for former members could – assuming they were prepared to suffer the consequences – turn their backs on the church entirely.[24] At least in theory, however, the difference between congregationalist and Baptist church discipline pivoted on the distinction between a state-sanctioned church – participation in which was expected to be universal – and a sectarian church that lacked both the power and the will to make such demands. In other respects, their disciplinary systems, sharing a common basis in biblical precedent, were markedly similar. Over time, the Baptist church became increasingly like the established churches.

If the Baptists' case can be described largely in terms of a sect evolving in the direction of a church in order to survive, the Quakers' experience does not fit so neatly into this schema. Far from gradually augmenting their organizational apparatus to meet specific needs, the Quakers initially had to be forced into accepting the reforms that made their meeting somewhat more churchlike. The early Quaker movement in Salem had no component that could guide the sect toward organizational maturity, as did the Baptists. Change, when it came to the Quaker community, was revolutionary rather than evolutionary. Once the Salem Quakers had accepted the need for change, the reforms they adopted would lead to the creation of a more structured sectarian organization, but one that remained quite unlike that erected by the Baptists.

The blueprint for the organization of Quakerism was drawn up in England by two leaders of the sect, George Fox and Margaret Askew Fell (later Fox). With the Restoration, the pair realized that the divergent movement known as Quakerism was in immediate danger of being persecuted out of existence. They hoped that a successful reformation could strengthen the sect and, at the same time, assuage the authorities' fears about its radicalism. With these goals in mind, they developed a formal meeting structure, governing procedures, and guidelines for various aspects of sectarian life. The authority for these changes was the Christ within more than the historic Christ or Scriptures generally.[25] Unlike the Congregationalists and the Baptists, the Quakers built neither their sect nor the case for it primarily upon biblical precedents.[26] Through the efforts of Fox and Fell, the initially unstructured Quaker movement became a relatively stable organization, and the Society of Friends was born.[27]

---

[24] Consequences were fewer in Boston, where a sizable population was served by numerous churches and residents were increasingly free to chose which to attend. In this context, nonattendance was more difficult to police.

[25] On this aspect of Quakerism, see Endy, "Puritanism, Spiritualism and Quakerism," esp. 289–94.

[26] Holifield, *Era of Persuasion*, 120–1. See also Bozeman, *To Live Ancient Lives*, 366–8. Quakers did assert occasionally that they had returned to the purity and simplicity of early Christianity, but they made no effort to substantiate this claim with specific citations or comparisons.

[27] Hill, *World Turned Upside Down*, 231–58, 373–4, 378; and idem, *The Experience of Defeat: Milton*

Although the Society of Friends would be the least structured religious organization in England for a century or more, the very act of institutionalization flew in the face of the spirit of the early movement. Many Quakers eventually saw the wisdom of the program, which had been designed to retain various early beliefs and practices. The reformers themselves disclaimed any desire to make any fundamental changes in the sect. Despite this, Fox and Fell spent many years quelling occasional overt opposition and urging the lackadaisical to implement their program. Because of the initial diversity of the movement, some Quakers' conception of it precluded cooperation with "Foxonian" reforms; others simply refused to give up the liberties of the interregnum era despite compelling reasons to do so.[28] Only in 1671 did Fox find time to tour the colonies, where he began systematically pressuring the meetings there into conformity.[29]

Nowhere was the resistance within the sect sustained longer than in the Salem community.[30] Reports that Salem and Boston Quakers opposed the reform effort appear in the correspondence of traveling Quakers and in their journals from 1663 to 1672.[31] As late as 1672, John Burnyeat reported one group "that pretended to be against all Forms" and another that was unwilling to commit itself either way. Apparently, even as George Fox was arriving in Rhode Island to further the reformation of American Quakerism, the community in Salem was more inclined than not to oppose his efforts.[32]

The opposition in Salem was wedded to Quakerism as it had initially been introduced into the region and perceived the changes recommended by Fox as contrary to its spirit. An overwhelming number of those who most vigorously fought reform had been participants in the Quaker movement from the first.[33]

---

and Some Contemporaries (New York: Viking, 1984), esp. 130, 53, 168. Vann, *Social Development of English Quakerism,* ch. 6.

28 "Foxonian" appears in [William Mucklowe], *The Spirit of the Hat* (London, 1673), 11. The opposition has been treated in Kenneth L. Carroll, *John Perrot: Early Quaker Schismatic* (London: Friends Historical Society, 1971); Vann, *Social Development of English Quakerism,* 103–4; and William C. Braithwaite, *The Second Period of Quakerism,* ed. Henry J. Cadbury, 2d ed. (Cambridge University Press, 1961), 295–323.

29 On Fox's American visit, see Jones, *Quakers in the American Colonies,* 111–18. Also during the 1670s, Fox issued a number of tracts dealing with the situation in the colonies, especially New England.

30 The Long Island "Ranters" clung more tenaciously (or at least in larger numbers) to their radical stance, but were drummed out of the sect while the Salem Quakers were still fighting among themselves; the Flushing meeting circulated a denunciation of them in 1676, *Antient Epistles.*

31 *The Truth Exalted in the Writing of that Eminent and Faithful Servant of Christ John Burnyeat* (London, 1691), 50–3; Worrall, *Quakers in the Colonial Northeast,* 29–31. These accounts often refer to the opponents of reform as "Perrotians," after an influential English antireformer. Carroll, *John Perrot,* 103–5, 85, 90–1.

32 Burnyeat, *The Truth Exalted,* 52.

33 Of those known to oppose reform, only Jane Lemarcon Blethen (who was described as "a Jarzey Maid" in 1676 and probably arrived in Salem around that time with other French-speaking

Having embraced an inchoate, millennialistic movement that allowed them unprecedented freedom, they were loath to acquiesce to new restrictions. Furthermore, women played a major role in sustaining the opposition to reform,
carrying on a tradition of female commitment to radical Quakerism. Not only
were the antireformers named in the records disproportionately women, but
two older women stood at the middle of an extended family that formed the
core of that faction.[34] In addition to the general appeal a radical stance seems
to have held for some sectarian women, these particular reforms may have been
perceived as especially disadvantageous to them.[35] As women and long-time
participants in the movement, Tamesan Buffum, Gertrude Pope, and Mary
Trask were especially inclined to fight against innovation.

A few years after John Burnyeat's 1672 visit, a faction that supported reform
began to wrest control of the Salem meeting from their opponents, bringing the
struggle over reform into the meeting itself.[36] In contrast to the antireformers,
this group consisted largely of more recent arrivals to the region.[37] In 1675, the
proreformers persuaded Josiah Southwick to compose a testimony "against that
spirit that leads men to keep their heads covered in ye time that god's servants
draw near to him in publick prayer."[38] Hat wearing, which had long been invested with symbolic importance both within the movement and outside of it,
was being used by radicals in Salem to make a statement against reform.[39] As

settlers from the Channel Island of Jersey) and her husband John Blethen (who was apparently
not a Quaker in the early years and who also may not have been a resident of Salem then) had
not been active in the movement initially.

[34] In a 1680 incident discussed later, eight women and four men were deemed disorderly walkers
by the proreformers (SMM, July). Samuel Shattock, who was also part of that faction, was not
dealt with at that time. The men in the movement tended to be related to female participants,
sometimes to more committed radical women. John Maston, an elderly carpenter, was the only
male disorderly walker without family ties to any of the women. John Blethen vacillated and later
capitulated altogether to the reformers' view. His wife, Jane, appears to have been the more
committed of the two.

[35] For other instances of women who were especially radical, see Hill, *World Turned Upside Down*,
250; Carroll, *John Perrot*, 40–1, 50. The Quaker movement originally acknowledged no sexual
distinctions and no hierarchy. The new system of segregated and graduated meetings interjected
both elements into the sect for the first time, moving toward the inegalitarianism that pervaded
English society. On that note, it is interesting that only ten women signed the paper against
Shattock and Buffum and that their signatures appeared in a separate column from those of the
men; SMM, October 1682.

[36] This struggle contributed to the context that led to the trial for blasphemy of one recanted
Quaker; see Carla Gardina Pestana, "The Social World of Salem: William King's 1681 Blasphemy Trial," *American Quarterly* 41 (1989): 308–27.

[37] Of the eleven signatories on the 1682 paper of denial (discussed later) who were members of
the local meeting, six were recent arrivals in the area and five were long-time participants in the
Salem Quaker movement. Josiah Southwick, one of the five, had recently been aligned with the
radicals.

[38] SMM, December 1675.

[39] Early Quaker men refused to doff their hats as a sign of respect to their social superiors; when
magistrate Simon Bradstreet took this as a sign that a man was a Quaker, one Salem convert

Hugh Barbour has pointed out, in England the hat had already been used to challenge George Fox's authority. In Salem, too, hat wearing made a symbolic statement in favor of older Quaker practices.[40] Southwick's capitulation had a symbolic significance of its own, for in writing a testimonial to mark his change of heart, he utilized one of the new procedures for sectarian governance. Appropriately enough, the first recorded meeting for business would be held in his home two years later.[41]

By 1680, the reformers were sufficiently powerful to discipline some of those who still continued intransigent, thereby drawing upon yet another of the newly developed procedures in their struggle to reform Quakerism in Salem. The balance of power had, by this time, shifted in favor of reform, and that faction sought to pressure the remaining "contrary spirited people" into conformity. Because the early Quaker movement in Salem was a source of legitimacy for whomever could lay claim to its heritage, the reformers declared that the radicals had abandoned the light of truth in favor of "a sedussing spirit, that ledd them into many erronous opinions and notions." The meeting judged a dozen sectaries to be "disorderly walkers," as a result of this supposed apostasy.[42]At the time, all twelve remained "very stubborn and obstinate," although some of them would later return to the meeting.[43] Others apparently drifted away, leaving the sect to implement change without them.

Two years later, the reformers moved to purge the meeting of the last radicals participating in it. By this time, the active opposition had dwindled to Samuel Shattock and Joshua Buffum. Confronted with this challenge from two men of great significance to the early movement, the meeting called upon reform-minded Quakers from outside of the community to add weight to their denunciations. In that year, sectarians from well beyond the immediate area joined with a dozen or more local Friends in renouncing the two men.[44] With this, the

reportedly said, "It was a horrible thing to make such cruel laws, to whip, and cut off Ears, and bore through the tongue for not putting off the Hat." Quoted in Besse, *Sufferings*, 2:187. Not only was the hat used by other radicals to express disapproval, some Boston Third Church members wore hats during a sermon to demonstrate their objections to their minister's new wig; James Fenimore Cooper, Jr., "A Participatory Theocracy: Church Government in Colonial Massachusetts, 1629–1760" (Ph.D. diss., University of Connecticut, 1987), 301.

[40] Hugh Barbour, "Young Controversialist," in *The World of William Penn*, 15–36, quoted on 25. Also see [Mucklowe], *Spirit of the Hat*, esp. 23, 25.

[41] SMM, December 1675, July 1677. His sympathy for the radicals' cause found expression one last time, in 1676, when he accompanied Margaret Thompson Smith into Salem Church so she could disrupt worship services there. Although the details of this incident have not survived, renewed hostility to Quakers during King Philip's War presumably sparked it; *EQC* 6:191–2.

[42] SMM, July 1680.

[43] John Blethen and Damaris Buffum would sign James Goodridge's certificate to travel; SMM, September 1689.

[44] As many as twenty people from outside the Salem area signed the paper. Eight were residents of Maine, two of Plymouth colony, one of Gloucester, and one of Cambridge. The identities of the other eight, who were apparently not Salem-area residents, have not been confirmed. This

meeting drove out two of its founding members, men who had endured much in the early years. The statement disowning Shattock and Buffum, the first such "paper of denial" composed by the Salem Quakers, heralded the victory of the reform movement within Salem Quakerism. At this traumatic moment, the meeting turned its back on the most radical aspects of its unique history in order to enter the new Quaker mainstream.

Although little evidence survives to suggest what became of those who were drummed out of the meeting, they may have continued to think of themselves as true Quakers. Given their ties to the early movement, such claims would have had a certain ring of truth. A number of them lived out the remainder of their lives in Salem, without associating themselves with either the reformed Quaker meeting or the established church.[45] No evidence remains to indicate how they responded when they found themselves driven out of the sect they had helped to found. Like those residents of Marblehead whom Christine Heyrman has identified as "village atheists," perhaps they lapsed into an in-choate hostility toward the established faith (and possibly toward organized religion generally).[46] Until this radical remnant of the early movement died out, the Salem residents may have included a small and ever decreasing number of persistent extremists who neither acquiesced to the reforms nor boasted a large enough number to establish a viable splinter sect. Their presence outside the local meeting challenged its efforts to present itself as the uncontested heir of the early movement.

The defeat of these radicals allowed the victorious faction within the meeting to guide it into the Society of Friends. By the early part of the next century, Salem Friends participated in a monthly meeting for business that also included Lynn and Boston Quakers, in a quarterly meeting encompassing Maine and New Hampshire, and in a yearly meeting in Rhode Island with representatives

---

sketch has been constructed using biographical information in Noyes, *Genealogical Dictionary;* Perley, *History of Salem;* Savage, *Genealogical Dictionary; EQC;* and published vital records for various New England towns.

[45] Shattock died at the close of the decade, Buffum in 1705. Perley, *History of Salem,* 2:269; SMM, August 1705. Perhaps because he was a close relation of some of the meeting's members, Buffum's death was recorded in the meeting records. He had not been mentioned therein since 1682, but a son of the same name had been married in the meeting in 1702. Disorderly walkers John Hill died in 1680, John Maston in 1681, and Tamesan Buffum in 1688; Perley, *History of Salem,* 2:203–4, 39; *NEHGR* 27 (1873): 292. Two of the women in that group married non-Quaker men in later years; Mary Trask's second husband, William Nichols, was apparently not a Quaker, although I have found no evidence to confirm Perley's suspicion that she returned to Salem Church; *History of Salem,* 2:252. Lydia Hill married non-Quaker George Locker, who may have been her cousin, during the 1680s; *NEHGR* 7 (1853): 83; David Curtis Dearborn, "Lydia Hill, Wife of William Curtis of Salem, Massachusetts," *American Genealogist* 59 (1983): 71–6.

[46] Heyrman, *Commerce and Culture,* 222–3; despite the use of the term "atheist," unbelief in God or basic Christian tenets – as opposed to hostility to the orthodox establishment – is difficult to document, even in relatively marginal early Marblehead.

from all of New England.[47] Beyond the Rhode Island Yearly Meeting, the London Yearly Meeting functioned as the unofficial international center for the sect.[48] These connections brought Salem-area Quakers into a transatlantic religious network of unprecedented sophistication. Neither the Baptists nor the established churches had such a support system to connect them to their coreligionists elsewhere.[49] Ironically, what had begun as the most spontaneous faith in the colony eventually had the most extensive organizational structure. On the periphery of that network, northeastern Massachusetts Quakers were not as fully integrated as some other colonial meetings. But after the reformers' victory, they were free to assume a place on the outskirts of the transatlantic Quaker community.[50]

In this context, the Salem Quakers took on the forms of a religious organization. The organizational changes that usually accompany the routinization of religious practices were, in their case, introduced from without.[51] In contrast to the Baptists, who had their scriptural guide for institutionalization from the beginning, the Quakers organized around more recently developed principles. And while the Baptists developed policies as the need arose, the Salem Quakers could do so only after the reformation and then only within the parameters of the Society's institutional structure. Most significantly, just as the Quaker movement had initially been imported, the impetus behind reform arose elsewhere and was brought to Salem by others. The very act of institutionalization enhanced their sense of separateness from the larger society. The process that moved the Baptists closer to the establishment kept the Quakers apart.

Just as the Baptists' disciplinary procedures indicated commonalities between them and the established churches, the Quaker system suggested the continuing singularity of that group. The sect had two formal procedures that

---

[47] The first records for the monthly, quarterly, and yearly meetings date from 1677, 1705, and 1683, respectively. The intermediate level of meetings was slow to develop in New England; see Worrall, *Quakers in the Colonial Northeast,* 69–70.

[48] Jones, *Quakers in the American Colonies,* 438, discusses the role of the London Yearly Meeting. Although Pennsylvania dominates our perception of colonial Quakerism, Quakers there seemed to have had little impact on their coreligionists in northern New England. Instead, bonds with England and Rhode Island continued to be the most significant extracolonial connections for Quakers in northeastern Massachusetts.

[49] Because its belief in limited atonement placed it in the theological minority among New England Baptists, the church was excluded from the first Baptist association founded in the colonies; see McLoughlin, *New England Dissent,* 281. The establishment had informal ties to English dissenters; see, e.g., Francis J. Bremer, "Increase Mather's Friends: The Transatlantic Congregational Network of the Seventeenth Century," *Proceedings of the American Antiquarian Society* 99 (1984): 59–96.

[50] Thomas E. Drake, *Patterns of Influence in Anglo-American Quakerism* (London: Friends Historical Society, 1958); and Henry J. Cadbury, "Intercolonial Solidarity of American Quakerism," *Pennsylvania Magazine of History and Biography* 60 (1936), 362–74, deal with this network.

[51] For an application of Weber's concept of routinization to English Quakers, see Bauman, *Let Your Words Be Few,* ch. 9.

were broadly analogous to those used in the colony's churches, including committees to visit errant members and a process called "disowning" to exclude the completely uncooperative.[52] This somewhat attenuated version of the steps taken by the Baptists worked in conjunction with an increasingly refined preventative program. The measures taken by the Quakers to forestall lapses were part of a self-conscious effort to maintain the sect's separation from colonial society.

The preventative system, as instituted in Salem, had three distinct parts – repeated discussions of proper comportment, certification of a member's "clearness" to marry or travel, and the visiting of families of Friends. Periodically, the monthly meeting reviewed and reaffirmed its position on a particular issue – such as war, pride, sleeping in meetings, or neglecting weekday meetings for worship.[53] No disciplinary action followed from these discussions, which served to reinforce standards indirectly by gently chiding any guilty members. A second practice that helped to obviate the need for formal discipline was that of requiring certificates of members who were traveling or planning to marry. The vast majority of members who requested certificates from the men's business meeting were duly granted them.[54] The women's meeting displayed a similar willingness to comply with requests for permission to marry.[55] But for those appointed to verify that a fellow member comported him- or herself as befitted a Quaker, for those who were questioned about the person under scrutiny, and for those being certified, the process reaffirmed standards of acceptable behavior.[56]

While discussions and the process of certification allowed for sporadic reminders of correct deportment, visitors, first appointed in 1708, provided systematic checks on each sectarian family. On the recommendation of the quarterly meeting, a total of twelve visitors were appointed to oversee families in the three towns encompassed by the Salem Monthly Meeting. Ideally, two women and two men visited each household every month, returning a report to their respective monthly meetings. These reports were summarized and passed on to the women's and men's quarterly meetings. Visitors often had to be "cau-

---

[52] The first recorded committee was formed in 1680 to deal with the "disorderly walkers" and included siblings Daniel Southwick and Provided Gaskill, SMM, July 1680. Only six people had to be disowned to 1740; see SMM, October 1682, 1689, July 1717, August 1724, February 1735/6. Other cases dealt with by the meeting occurred in the following years: 1706 (2), 1722, 1723, 1729, 1739.

[53] SMM, June 1700, November 1716, October 1719.

[54] In only two cases were certificates denied, those requested by Jacob Allin and Caleb Buffum, Jr., (SMM, July–September 1689, May 1716).

[55] Although the women's monthly meeting records for this period are not extant, this statement can be made with confidence because if the women declined to give permission, the men's meeting would have noted that a couple who had previously sought its permission no longer required it.

[56] For a general description, see Lloyd, *Quaker Social History*, 49–50, 69, 125.

tioned to more diligence in that service," for the task was time consuming and presumably burdensome. Yet the system both provided specific information about the degree of "love, unity [and] . . . good order" among members and spurred Quakers to behave properly.[57] With all of these preventative measures, the Salem meeting consciously created a sectarian enclave with a strong sense of itself as distinct. No other religious institution in the colony had anything to compare.[58]

Although the emphasis in the Quaker meeting was on prevention rather than discipline, when the Quakers did find it necessary to discipline one of their number, they were slow to resort to punitive measures. The case of Rebecca Trask Potter Boyce suggests that even once a problem did develop, the meeting's preference was to reclaim the errant member. Rebecca ran an unruly, unlicensed tavern. Her husband Joseph patronized his wife's establishment to the point of drinking to excess and neglecting his responsibilities to his family. Neither of them was attending meetings regularly. The women's monthly meeting treated with the couple for some time without success. In February 1722/ 3, they presented a request for assistance to the men's business meeting. The men then took up the case, eventually preparing a statement that enumerated the Boyces' objectionable activities.[59] Rebecca responded by writing a "scandalous, reviling and abusive paper." Despite this insult, they continued to labor with Rebecca for over a year, Joseph having died in the interim. Finally, in April 1724, the meeting renounced her, though it again stated that its "ernst desire is that she may through ye Lords mercy and assistance see repent off and reform from ye said evils and live as becomes a servant of God."[60] Even though the meeting's efforts were ultimately wasted on Boyce, as the Baptist church's had been on Edward Drinker, the intent in both cases had clearly been to reintegrate the miscreant into the community of believers.

Using preventative measures in order to avoid the necessity of discipline was

---

57 Antient Epistles, 1708; SQM (men's), April 1708; SMM, May, October 1708; September 1710. The practice was later referred to by the meeting as "a branch of disciplining," SMM, October 1745.

58 Two scholars have described English Baptists as using preventative measures, but they generally emphasize the indirect effects of undergoing baptism and ascribing to the church covenant; no procedure primarily intended to be preventative was used by the Boston church. See T. Dowley, "Baptists and Discipline in the 17th Century," *Baptist Quarterly* 24 (1971): 157–66; and James R. Lynch, "English Baptist Church Discipline to 1740," *Foundations* 18 (1975): 126–31.

59 The women's monthly meeting records for this period have not survived, so it is unclear exactly why this case was referred; possibly the women did not have full disciplinary powers and sent the case to the men when the Boyces appeared stubborn or, as seems more likely, they could discipline women but not men and referred the case because of Joseph's role in it. Jean R. Soderlund found that among middle-colony Quakers, men's meetings confirmed disownments made by the companion women's meeting; "Women's Authority in Pennsylvania and New Jersey Quaker Meetings, 1680–1760," *WMQ*, 3d ser., 44 (1987): 744. In Salem, however, no other case was referred during the colonial period.

60 SMM, March 1722/3, August 1724.

in keeping with the Quaker concern for continuity within the sect. These procedures were conceived in terms of erecting "a hedge about us,"[61] for they helped to mark the boundaries between Quakers and others. The various badges of Quaker distinctiveness encouraged a sense of community identity and enhanced the differences between members and nonmembers. By vigilantly overseeing sectarian behavior, the meeting safeguarded the standards that served to separate the sect from the larger community. The child of Quakers who grew up in the midst of a densely interrelated and self-evidently different community to take his or her place in the meeting as an adult was but one of the indirect beneficiaries of the meeting's separatist stance and the preventative disciplinary program that helped to foster it.

Not only in its procedures but in its standards for sectarian behavior, the Society of Friends distinguished itself. Quakers ascribed to a number of principled positions that rendered them unique among English Protestants during this period. In identifying offenses it considered worthy of disciplinary action, the monthly meeting went farther than either the Baptists or the established churches. All three treated with people for doctrinal differences,[62] quarreling with coreligionists,[63] and lapses in generally held standards of morality.[64] But for a Quaker to marry a non-Quaker was also forbidden, and two men were chastised for finding spouses outside the meeting in 1706.[65] Excessive tobacco smoking, the keeping of slaves, and marrying "to near of kin" were also discussed by the Salem Quaker community.[66] In addition, Quakers were encouraged to maintain a simple lifestyle and not to become too "worldly." For a few years beginning in 1737, the meeting struggled with the problem of wedding receptions that were too large and went on too long, sending a committee to make sure that they were "carried on orderly & that the guests departed in

[61] The Rhode Island Yearly Meeting used this phrase later, during an especially difficult period for the sect, but it captures the goal of discipline for the colonial period as well; quoted in James, *A People Among Peoples*, 251.

[62] This was even more rare among the Quakers than the Baptists; before 1740, only one disownment resulted from unacceptable doctrine; see SMM, February 1735/6.

[63] As in the Baptist church, the Quakers dealt with two cases of differences between members. Both cases involved the same individual, who was apparently having other personal problems at the same time. For the cases involving Quaker Elijah Collins, see SMM, March 1728/9, November 1739; SQM (men's), April, September 1740; RIYM, 1740.

[64] These problems were most common; the list of unacceptable activities included sex outside of marriage, riotousness, excessive drinking, gossip, and sloth. For examples, see SMM, January 1713/14, March 1722/3, August 1724, April 1713.

[65] SMM, November 1706. The dearth of disciplinary cases dealing with this issue could be interpreted to mean that few married out or that the meeting was lax on enforcement. The latter was the case in a number of other colonial meetings; Soderlund, "Women's Authority," 739, 742–3; Edward Byers, *The Nation of Nantucket: Society and Politics in an Early American Commercial Center, 1660–1820* (Boston: Northeastern University Press, 1987), 118.

[66] SMM, May, November 1716, March 1717/18, October 1719, January 1719/20. None of these offenses were acted upon during this period.

Good Season."[67] By adhering to such unusual standards, the Quakers worked to remain aloof from the "world's people."[68]

Both the Quakers and Baptists moved in the direction of greater organization during the late seventeenth century. In order to ensure sectarian continuity beyond the first generation, they instituted formal procedures for self-governance, including policies for disciplining troublesome members. The act of institutionalization may have been necessary for their survival, as H. Richard Niebuhr has argued, in that the movement that does not eventually crystallize into a more static form will simply dissipate.[69] A concern for the future of Quakerism that was grounded in an awareness of this danger had motivated George Fox and Margaret Fell to reform that movement. In this general sense, both sects did undergo the transformation Niebuhr and others have described.

To the extent that this process was to bring both sects into greater conformity to the world, the situation appears to have been considerably more complicated. With the implementation of organizational changes not based on biblical primitivism, the Quaker meeting erected a polity unique in colonial Massachusetts. The Baptists, drawing upon biblical traditions they shared with colonial orthodoxy, became more churchlike and more like the established churches at the same time. These changes would have profound implications for the future of the Boston Baptist Church, which would find it increasingly difficult to retain a distinct identity. The Quaker meeting, however, instituted changes that were developed by the Society of Friends in England and that had various unusual components that helped it to remain apart. The Quakers intentionally became a "peculiar people," precisely because they wanted to avoid compromise with the world.

This is not to say that the Quakers remained the radical sect that they had been initially. The organized sect of the early eighteenth century departed fundamentally from the inchoate movement of the mid-seventeenth century. Arguably, the Quakers had come farther from their origins than the Baptists had over the same period. The Baptists had always intended to found a church, albeit a church that upheld distinct traditions within the colony. The Quakers, having gathered to await the millennium, had not intended to create anything lasting; later they were forced to confront the future. Except that they were pulled into the organizing efforts of English Quakers, the movement in Salem might have met the classic end of a sect, dying out with the first generation. Instead, some of the Quakers in Salem chose reformation. In doing so, they carried the sect into a new era. Having once aroused the establishment's fears of disorder, they in turn became concerned to maintain " good order and unity" among Friends.[70]

[67] SMM, August 1737, April 1738.   [68] SMM, August 1689.
[69] Niebuhr, *Kingdom of God in America*, esp. 167–9.
[70] On Puritan fears of Quaker disorder, see Pestana, "Puritan Perception of the Quaker Threat." The phrase recurs frequently in the sect's records for the eighteenth century.

Although the Quakers did become more churchlike over time, the impact of this change was softened by their unique circumstances. The Baptists might move closer to the establishment, drawing as they did upon a common source of ultimate authority. The Quakers, because they did not use the Scriptures as their only guide and did not strive to recreate the primitive Christian churches, were unlikely to replicate closely the practices of the colony's churches. Baptists might debate the orthodox establishment about the best way to go about re-creating true churches of Christ; Quakers had no interest in the topic. Their extrabiblical source of inspiration rendered them singular within the context of early New England. In that respect, the sect remained truly radical even after becoming, in some ways, more like a church.

5

Leadership

The development of systematic approaches to sectarian leadership was perhaps the single most important component of the organizational transformation that occurred in the Boston Baptist Church and the Salem Quaker meeting in the years before 1740. This aspect of their organizational development – like all other aspects – was informed by either scriptural models or the reforms designed by the Society of Friends, and the distribution of authority in each sect differed accordingly. With authority in the Baptist church more narrowly focused, the Baptists eventually found it difficult to locate adequately qualified laymen to fill the position of elder. They finally moved beyond this impasse by embracing the distinction, common in the established churches, between laity and clergy. This solution created ties between the Baptists and the establishment that have been applauded by scholars interested in the development of religious toleration; but it also undermined the autonomy of the Baptist church.

The Quakers at first had trouble accepting a formal leadership at all, but they eventually instituted practices that ensured their continuing independence. Once the local meeting had adopted the institutional structure emerging within the Society of Friends, it proceeded to erect the various offices utilized within the society without noteworthy difficulty. The system adopted by the Quakers preserved their distance from the other religious groups in the colony and permitted a flexible approach to filling its various posts. Although leadership in both the Baptist church and the Quaker meeting became more clearly defined over time, the implications of these ostensibly similar transformations for the functioning of either sect could not have been more different. Again, routinization was not a uniform process for the sectarians of colonial New England.

During the years from 1680 to 1720, the Baptist church moved gradually away from its earlier reliance on undistinguished lay leaders until, by the end of the period, it had hired a professional minister. This transformation came about as a result of a crisis of legitimacy. The Baptists felt themselves increasingly unable to provide adequate leadership from their own ranks as the founding generation passed from the scene. The church labored to find leaders who could compare to the founders. The brethren tried various strategies to end the impasse, appointing men of higher social status and greater educational attainments to the post of elder. Over the same period, the holder of that office became exclusively responsible for the duties associated with it. At least by the 1730s, the Baptists recognized a sharp distinction between clerical and lay, one that had not previously existed. What Jon Butler has called "the diffusion of ministerial responsibility" common among seventeenth-century Baptists had ended in the Boston church by this time.[1]

The Baptists initially called a professional minister in order to resolve a leadership crisis that plagued the church around the turn of the century. The difficulty arose with the deaths of the first generation of church members.[2] These people had stature within the church, having borne the brunt of official disapproval in their heroic effort to plant a true "Church of Christ" in the colony. As a result, those who had gathered the church or had joined it during the first years continued to provide its leadership as long as they were able.[3] Once they were gone, the Baptists – not untypically – felt unable to replace them from the ranks of current members. In the aftermath of the heroic age of the church, the Baptists experienced a crisis of confidence, analogous to that which the colonial establishment had fretted over with the passing of its founding generation.[4] In that case, the second-generation leaders worried about their relative abilities, and many of the children of the church founders deemed themselves unworthy to join their parents' churches. The halfway covenant was instituted largely in response to the latter development. Given that the innovation had been introduced by a younger generation that felt inadequate, it had to be justified with reference to the views of the founders.[5]

[1] Jon Butler, "Power, Authority, and the Origins of American Denominational Order: The English Churches in the Delaware Valley, 1680–1730," *Transactions of the American Philosophical Society*, 68, pt. 2 (1978): 48.

[2] Of the original male members, all but two were dead or had long since left the area by 1681. By 25 October 1682, Thomas Osborn had removed to Nantucket from whence he wrote a letter to George Little; *NEHGR* 16 (1862): 25–6. Edward Drinker, who was proving an unsatisfactory deacon, would eventually be excommunicated.

[3] The last first-generation elder named in the records was Isaac Hull. Although he died in 1700, he was apparently unable to minister to the church from his home in Salem during the last years of his life. At first, deacons were assigned to perform his duties in his absence; by 1689 – and perhaps as early as 1684 – other elders had been chosen to serve in his stead. See Baptist Record Book, 21 December 1680, 12 August 1688, 28 December 1689.

[4] Obadiah Holmes similarly feared that no one would emerge from the ranks of his Rhode Island Baptist church to succeed him as pastor after his death; see Gaustad, *Baptist Piety*, 109, 109n., 106. On the establishment, see, e.g., Nathanial Morton, *New England's Memorial* (Cambridge, 1669), 176, 178.

[5] On the ministry, see Robert Middlekauff, *The Mathers: Three Generations of Puritan Intellectuals, 1596–1728* (New York: Oxford University Press, 1971), 98–103. Edmund S. Morgan first suggested that "religious scrupulosity" kept some people from becoming church members; "New England Puritanism: Another Approach," *WMQ*, 3d ser., 18 (1961): 241–2. Increase Mather, *The First Principles of New England, concerning the Subject of Baptisme & communion of churches* (Cambridge, 1675).

In the Baptists' case, the office of the elder became the focal point for the second generation's insecurities. Occupying the first post mentioned in the church records, the elder had done the bulk of the preaching and had typically – but probably not exclusively – administered the ordinances from the first. As early as 1680, when deacons were formally appointed to assist the elder, the church was already coming to expect an officer – rather than any available male member – to see to its various needs.[6] An exceptional layman had to be found for the pivotal position of elder during a time when the church was uncertain about its abilities to carry on in the absence of its patriarchs. This sense of crisis was exacerbated by a string of disappointing developments in the late 1670s. The departure of John Myles – who returned to his Swansea congregation when it was reconstituted in the aftermath of King Philip's War – and the death of John Russell, Jr., brought to an end a heady period during which the church had optimistically planned to divide into two churches, one at Woburn and the other in Boston.[7] Shortly after having a surfeit of leaders, the church found itself bereft of an elder and running short on founding men to fill the post.

In an effort to move beyond this impasse, the Baptists first looked outside their church for an acceptable candidate. The brethren sent out inquiries in hopes of finding someone to minister to them. By searching for a nonmember to serve them, they may have been hoping to recreate their brief experience with John Myles during the preceding decade. In any case, in 1681 the church wrote to London. The London Baptists replied by recommending that the church select one of its own as elder, reminding their Boston brethren that this was the practice in most English Baptist churches. Possibly as part of their efforts to find a new elder, the church heard the preaching of a number of nonresident Baptists, such as John Cooke of Dartsmouth and Richard Brown of Carolina.[8]

---

[6] Baptist Record Book, 13 January 1678/9. In 1680, two men – later referred to as deacons – were appointed to "carry on the work of God in Boston in ye absence of ye Elder Hull"; ibid., 21 December 1680, 11 December 1682. According to the Particular Baptist *Confession of Faith* originally published in 1644, baptism could be performed by any church officer but was not exclusively their responsibility; reprinted in *Baptist Confessions of Faith*, ed. Timothy Lumpkin (Chicago: Judson, 1959), 167. Deacons of the established churches were not to administer the word or "Sacraments," according to the Cambridge Platform; reprinted in Walker, *Creeds and Platforms*, 213.

[7] Myles, who was educated at Oxford, had been a minister in Wales before coming to New England in the early 1660s. He settled in Swansea (in Plymouth Plantation) and eventually participated in the organization of a Baptist church there. See *Dictionary of National Biography*, 1921–2 ed., s.v. "John Myles (1621–1684)"; "Swansea, Massachusetts, Baptist Church Records," ed. Robert Charles Anderson, *NEHGR* 139 (1985): 21–4. On the expansion plans, see Baptist Record Book, 26 January, 10 March 1678/9; 30 June, 28 July 1679. The evidence for how these plans came to be aborted is sketchy; McLoughlin suggests Myles's unexpected departure as the cause (*New England Dissent*, 74–5).

[8] Wood, *History*, 189; John Cotton to Cotton Mather, 19 April 1681, *CMHS*, 4th ser., vol. 8 (1868): 252; Samuel Hubbard, Journal, John D. Rockefeller, Jr., Library, Brown University, Providence, R.I., typescript, 130.

Finally, they located two men – John Emblem and William Milbourne – who seemed able to assume the post.

In choosing Emblem and Milbourne, the church brethren also evinced a new preference for socially prominent leaders, which represented a further departure from earlier practices. Initially, elders were male members who demonstrated a gift for preaching. Because they lacked other credentials, Cotton Mather would later dismiss them as "ministers out of the dregs of the rabble – tailors, cobblers, fools."[9] They continued to farm and pursue their trades as wheelwright, shoemakers, and cooper. They cannot be described as enjoying high social status. At most, they were substantial artisans and farmers, with Thomas Goold probably the most prominent among them.[10] The first deacons named in the records – a potter and a tailor – were indistinguishable from most of the elders in terms of social status.[11] The credentials of these men were spiritual rather than social; presumably, they were adept preachers who led lives that their brethren felt befit one of Christ's saints.

With the selection of Emblem and Milbourne, the church moved away from the practice of choosing members of modest social stature as officers. Although not much is known about either man, both held the title "Mister." Familial connections, economic status, educational attainments, or a combination of the three could have earned them that distinction.[12] At least in part because of their status, they appeared more acceptable candidates than better-known members who lacked titles and worked as artisans in Boston. After these men had ceased to serve, the church demonstrated its continued preference for officers of relatively high social status when it elevated Ellis Callendar to the post. Callendar had been a church deacon. Only after he had become financially successful did the brethren name him as their elder.[13]

[9] "Ministros de extrimitatibus Populi, Sartoribus, Sutoribus, Idiotis"; Mather, *Magnalia*, 2:460. Translation provided by Lucius F. Robinson for the 1853 (Hartford) edition (2:533).

[10] Thomas Goold was a wheelwright, both John Russells were shoemakers, and Isaac Hull was a cooper. Wyman, *Genealogies and Estates of Charlestown*, 428; Savage, *Genealogical Dictionary*, 3:591–2; Perley, *History of Salem*, 2:316. Numerous scholars have followed Nathan Wood (*History*, 31–2) in describing Goold as a wagonmaker, but land deeds give his occupation as wheelwright. Goold's estate was valued at £782 in 1674; see SCPR.

Sidney Mead has described early Baptist leaders as enjoying high social status, using Rhode Islanders Roger Williams and John Clarke as examples; "The Rise of the Evangelical Conception of the Ministry in America, 1607–1850," in *The Ministry in Historical Perspective*, ed. H. Richard Niebuhr and Daniel D. Williams (New York: Harper Bros., 1956), 234. William R. Estep overstates the case in the opposite direction; see "New England Dissent, 1630–1833: A Review Article," *Church History* 41 (1972): 248.

[11] These men were Edward Drinker and Ellis Callendar.

[12] How Milbourne and Emblem earned this distinction is not clear. Neither received a degree from Oxford or Cambridge, according to the published lists of alumni; see *Alumni Cantabrigiensis*, comp. John Venn and J. A. Venn, 4 vols. (Cambridge, 1921–9), and *Alumni Oromienses*, ed. Joseph Foster, 2 vols. (Oxford, 1891–2). Also see Savage, *Genealogical Dictionary*, 2:117; Noyes, *Genealogical Dictionary*, 479.

[13] Callendar rose from tailor to shopkeeper to merchant; see Suffolk County Deeds, Suffolk County

The trend toward socially respectable leadership entered a final phase in 1718 when the Boston Baptists embraced a professional ministry. The difficulty of periodically securing lay elders whom they considered worthy finally led the Boston Baptists to abandon the practice of lay leadership altogether. Aware that the problem had yet to be solved, Ellis Callendar – quite possibly in consultation with other church members – decided to send his son, Elisha, to Harvard College to train for the ministry. Upon graduating in 1713, twenty-one-year-old Elisha joined the church. Five years later, he became the youngest elder in the church's history as well as the first with a university degree.[14] Callendar was apparently the first elder to depend solely on the church for his livelihood,[15] as well as the first to be formally installed in an ordination ceremony.[16] Other ministers, rather than the laity, conducted the ceremony, which emphasized the

Registry of Deeds, Boston, Mass., 3 July 1675, 13 July 1683, 30 August 1718; Savage, *Genealogical Dictionary*, 1:330; Mary Levering Holman, "Callendar Family," NEHGS, typescript, 15. Savage erred in describing Callendar as a cooper.

A gap in the church's records from 1696 until 1708 makes it difficult to recover the history of the eldership during these years. Traditionally, Callendar has been described as assuming the position of elder in 1708, after former member William Screven refused to leave the Georgetown, South Carolina, church, which he had helped found, to take over the Boston church; Wood, *History*, 184–5. If that date is accurate, it is unclear who – if anyone – served as elder during the six years after Emblem died in 1702. Cotton Mather claims that an imposter, Samuel May (a.k.a. Samuel Axel), preached to the Baptists in 1699; see "The Diary of Cotton Mather," *CMHS*, 7th ser., vol. 7 (1911), 313–14, 315–16, 337–8, 351. I have been unable to confirm his sensational tale.

[14] Sibley and Shifton, *Sibley's Harvard Graduates*, 5:512–17; Baptist Record Book, 10 August 1713, 21 May 1718. John Myles, who had an Oxford degree, was never officially named an elder since he retained that post in his scattered Swansea congregation while he preached temporarily in Boston. From Elisha on, the sons of Baptists who went to Harvard during this period invariably joined the church after graduation. McLoughlin has suggested that this was out of courtesy to the establishment; *New England Dissent*, 284–5.

[15] Because little is known about Emblem and Milbourne, this statement cannot be made definitively. During the 1680s and 1690s, however, the little church could not have supported two men. Callendar was presumably paid by voluntary contribution; his successor, Jeremiah Condy, was salaried. John Callendar made an indirect reference to this innovation when he cautioned the church against resenting the latter as a "hireling"; *A Sermon preached at the ordination of Mr. Jeremiah Condy* (Boston, 1739), 9.

Like many ministers of established churches, Callendar did not find his calling especially lucrative. When he died in 1728, his estate was valued at only £195 sterling; Sibley and Shifton, *Sibley's Harvard Graduates*, 5:516. This and all other valuations for eighteenth-century estates have been converted to pounds sterling, using the table "Values of Massachusetts Paper Currency, 1685–1775," compiled by Gary B. Nash, *The Urban Crucible: Social Change, Political Consciousness, and the Origins of the American Revolution* (Cambridge: Mass., 1979), 405–6.

[16] The first ordination mentioned in the Baptist Record Book was that of Callendar. Prior to that, if ordinations were performed, they went unrecorded by the church and commentators on its practices; presumably any that did occur were conducted by the brethren of the church, since more elaborate arrangements were far more likely to receive some mention. According to Charles Hambrick-Stowe, the established churches had shifted away from ordinations run by the laity during the 1670s; see *Practice of Piety*, 128–9. The church may have been participating in the same shift to clerically run ordinations at this time.

fact that Callendar was being accepted into an exclusive profession. The participation of three orthodox ministers, including his distant kinsmen, Increase and
Cotton Mather,[17] in the event indicated their approval of the increased respectability of Baptist church leaders. As befitted one of his vaunted status, Callendar would be referred to as the "reverend Mr. Elisha Callendar."[18] Both Callendar's personal educational attainments and the fact that he was being set
apart from his flock through the act of ordination enhanced the prestige of the
eldership. With Callendar's ordination, the lay eldership in the Baptist church
– experiencing the fate that had already befallen the orthodox churches' more
modest version of the same office – became a thing of the past.[19]

As the eldership was moving through the successive stages that culminated
in Callendar's ministry, the connection between high status and church officeholding was being forged among deacons as well, although to a lesser extent.
The men who served as deacons continued to be artisans, all but one of whom
were Boston residents. Three of the six men who served during the period from
1700 to 1750 were sufficiently successful to have opened their own shops. Elisha's father, Ellis Callendar, was one of them. Josiah Byles left an estate worth
£3,500 sterling, including land in Boston and Connecticut, the contents of his
Boston shop, and numerous debts owed him. Although Shem Drowne turned
his Boston real estate over to his son before his death in 1774 at the age of
ninety-one, he had pursued a fairly successful career as a metalworker, even
investing in property in New Hampshire.[20] Expectations for the social status of
church deacons – although not as high as those for elders, even during the
period prior to professionalization – had risen by the middle of the eighteenth
century.

Family connections as well as social prominence distinguished the church's
ruling elite from its average members. In the first half of the eighteenth century,
all save one of the church officers belonged to one of two Boston Baptist family
networks.[21] The Callendar family included not only elders Ellis and Elisha

[17] Callendar's sister, Abigail, was married to Josiah Byles. The second wife of Josiah's father of
the same name was Elizabeth Mather Greenough, daughter of Increase Mather.

[18] Baptist Record Book, 31 March 1738. Assuming William McLoughlin was accurate in dating
the adoption of the term "Reverend" in the 1770s, the Boston church anticipated other New
England Baptists in this; *New England Dissent*, 742–3.

[19] Many congregations had appointed a lay ruling elder during the first decades in Massachusetts.
The office had been phased out in most churches by about 1680. See Harold Field Worthley,
"The Lay Officers of the Particular (Congregational) Churches of Massachusetts, 1620–1755:
An Investigation of Practice and Theory" (Ph.D. diss., Harvard University, 1970), 753–97; and
I. N. Tarbox, "Ruling Elders in Early New England Churches," *Congregational Quarterly* 54
(1872): 401–16.

[20] Benjamin Sweetser, appointed in 1688, resided in Charlestown. On Byles and Drowne, see
SCPR, 1752, 1774. In addition to Callendar, Byles and Richard Proctor kept shops. Three
deacons were metalworkers – Joseph Hiller, Drowne, and Byles (who also may have made
saddles).

[21] From 1665 until 1750, a minority of officers lacked extensive family ties, including two elders
from the late 1680s – William Milbourne and John Emblem – and three deacons – Edward

Callendar but also deacon Josiah Byles.[22] The more complex set of relationships that had been cemented by marriages between Russells, Hillers, Drownes,
and Condys linked deacons Joseph Hiller and Shem Drowne to Elisha Callendar's replacement as minister, Jeremiah Condy, as well as to numerous other
Boston Baptists.[23] Interrelated, economically successful, and holding almost all
of the church offices, this handful of men wielded an unprecedented degree of
influence in the church.

While authority was concentrated within this tight-knit group, the ministers
among them carried the bulk of the responsibility and prestige. This situation
sharply contrasted with the church's earlier practices, when a group of lay people baptized each other[24] and various church members preached to the gathered saints. One of the most remarkable aspects of the early Baptist church –
the centrality of lay preaching and leadership – was thus minimized. In a classic
instance of sectarian evolution, the Baptists assigned the performance of these
fundamental acts to a professional minister.[25] The most important activities of
the church were exclusively in the hands of one man, and he had to meet
qualifications that not a single member during the church's first fifty years could
have filled.[26] The church's traditional emphasis on exclusivity and patriarchy
became more pronounced as church offices were increasingly divorced from
the laity. No one, apparently, had any qualms about these changes, however.
Callendar's modestly successful ministry seemingly attested to the wisdom of
his father's decision to have him educated. The church experienced a surge in
membership under his leadership.[27] For the first time, the Baptist church en-

Drinker (who served from 1680 to 1685), Benjamin Sweetser (1688 to 1718?), and Richard
Proctor (1718 to 1720). All but one of these men was chosen to serve prior to 1700.

[22] Byles married Ellis's daughter, Abigail, in 1705; see *NEHGR* 69:104.

[23] Joseph Hiller's son married Elizabeth Russell, daughter of Joseph in 1715; Thomas Russell,
Elizabeth's brother, married Elizabeth Condy (sister of Jeremiah) thirteen years later. In 1743,
Jeremiah and Sarah Drowne, a daughter of Shem, wed. These marriages are recorded in *BTR*,
28:52, 146; Sibley and Shifton, *Sibley's Harvard Graduates*, 8 (1951): 26.

[24] No extant account describes this series of baptisms, and scholars speculated about how they
occurred; see, e.g., McLoughlin, *New England Dissent*, 57n. Since a few members had undergone believer's baptism in England and were therefore considered legitimately baptized by the
group, they presumably began the process in Charlestown.

[25] The professionalization of the clergy is generally considered a major feature of this trend; for
one historian's attempt to test the "Troeltsch–Niebuhr thesis" using this criteria, see Ruth B.
Bordin, "The Sect to Denomination Process in America: The Freewill Baptist Experience,"
Church History 34 (1965): 77–94.

[26] The church had the benefit of a university-educated man's preaching during its second decade
when John Myles lived in Boston briefly after Swansea was attacked during King Philip's War.
He retained membership in the Swansea Baptist Church, despite the efforts of the Boston
Baptists to get him to stay. See Baptist Record Book, 26 January, 10 March 1678/9; "John
Myles (1621–1684)."

[27] New members had rarely numbered as many as four a year during the twenty years between
1688 and 1718 for which records exist, but fell below that number only four times during the
next two decades. See admissions in Baptist Record Book.

joyed both social legitimacy and stability. During the 1720s, the Baptist church appeared to have overcome its leadership crisis.

The Quakers systematized leadership as well, but the structure they utilized in doing so was unlike that of the other religious organizations in the colony. Rather than appointing deacons and elders, as the churches did, the Quakers utilized a variety of leadership posts. Women as well as men held these positions, gathering in gender-segregated meetings to conduct the Society's business. Appointees to these offices handled the affairs of the local meeting in such relatively permanent positions as Public Friend (or minister), clerk, and visitor or they served on an occasional basis as the representative to the quarterly or yearly meetings. This system ensured that power not only would continue to be relatively diffused throughout the meeting but would permit an unusual degree of flexibility in the choice and retention of leaders. Even while becoming a more structured sect, the Salem Quakers remained distinctive.

If the Quakers experienced any crisis over leadership, theirs revolved around whether to have leaders at all. Among those reforms opposed by radicals in the Quaker meeting between 1666 and 1682 had been the creation of an approved class of preachers and a graduated system of meetings attended by representatives. Hat wearing – one of the gestures of protest used by the radicals – was often meant to imply disapproval of a particular preacher or, by extension, the idea that some should be singled out to preach.[28] Whether or not this was the message Josiah Southwick and possibly others intended to communicate through the wearing of hats, the creation of formal mechanisms for providing sectarian leadership was one of the major points at issue in the fight over reform. The confrontation ended in victory for those who advocated the systematization of the sect, but not without a major rupture in the Quaker community.

In the process of refashioning the early Quaker movement into an organized sect, the Society of Friends developed the least hierarchic leadership structure of any English religious organization. Local meetings were free to create a leadership clique by elevating a select group to multiple offices. In the major centers of the Society of Friends during the eighteenth century, authority tended to be concentrated in the hands of a group of "weighty Friends" who composed a corporate leadership.[29] Even their power was collectively exercised, and their authority rested ultimately with the local meetings that first elevated them to their positions and then deferred to them. At these centralized meetings – as at all other levels – decision making was consensual, and harmony was highly valued. Decisions had to have near unanimous support at all levels before they

---

[28] For hat wearing used in Pennsylvania to indicate opposition to a specific minister, see Barry John Levy, "The Light in the Valley: The Chester and Welch Tract Quaker Communities and the Delaware Valley, 1681–1750" (Ph.D. diss., University of Pennsylvania, 1976), 50–1.

[29] See Butler, "Power, Authority, and the Origins of American Denominational Order," 18–21, and ch. 3; Worrall, *Quakerism in the Colonial Northeast,* 75–8; Jean R. Soderlund, *Quakers and Slavery: A Divided Spirit* (Princeton, N.J.: Princeton University Press, 1985), ch. 2.

could be successfully implemented.[30] The London meeting served as a center for the sect, passing on its recommendations to the other yearly meetings as well as to its member meetings, but even its customary preeminence accorded it no official power. This diffused structure allowed for wide variations in local practices, especially in outlying meetings like those in northern New England. Although the eighteenth-century sect was, in many ways, quite unlike the movement of the 1650s, authority within the Society of Friends continued to be shared.

The trend toward the creation of a Quaker elite, although less pronounced in Salem, occurred there as it did in other colonial meetings. The Salem Monthly Meeting for men – in which leadership patterns are more fully documentable than in the women's meeting – did rely upon a number of Friends to provide consistent leadership.[31] A two-tiered group apparently held most of the positions of responsibility.[32] From the 1680s to the 1740s, a dozen men performed important duties repeatedly. A few of them served as leaders for only a short period; in all cases but one, their careers in the meeting came to an end when they left the Salem area entirely.[33] The other seven held a variety of posts over long periods. Especially remarkable was Zaccheus Collins (1698–1770), who served as visitor, representative, meeting clerk, and possibly in another position for more than forty years.[34] For the period after 1700, the records are suffi-

---

[30] In some exceptional cases, such as that of slavery, the majority finally agreed to implement a change and to disown those who failed to conform; Soderlund, *Quakers and Slavery*, 87–90.

[31] Because the women's monthly meeting records for the colonial period have not survived, this discussion will focus on the men's meeting. Some information about Salem women gleaned from the quarterly meeting records will be covered later. For comparison to other colonial meetings, see Frederick B. Tolles, *Meeting House and Counting House: The Quaker Merchants of Colonial Philadelphia, 1682–1763* (New York: Norton, 1948), esp. 113–23; Worrall, *Quakers in the Colonial Northeast*, 75–8.

[32] With the exception of Public Friends and overseers, whose names were not systematically recorded, these posts and the men appointed to fill them are given in the meeting minutes; see SMM, SQM (men's). Public Friends and overseers attended a separate meeting beginning in 1710; SMM, September 1710. Men apparently assumed at least the former role without a formal appointment. One of the few references to a Public Friend in the records stated that Caleb Buffum III had begun acting in that capacity against the meeting's will, which implies that others did so and earned its approbation; SMM, December 1722. Although the group cannot be fully reconstructed, those men who repeatedly accepted other major responsibilities were likely to have been part of it.

[33] Edward Shippen (1639?–1712), Walter Newberry (1682–1737), and Thomas Richardson (1680?– 1761) all resided in Boston for a time, serving the meeting in various capacities. Savage, *Genealogical Dictionary*, 4:87; Walter Newberry, Suffolk County Deeds, 1724; Collins, Diary, 19–20 August 1737; *Vital Records of Rhode Island, 1636–1850*, 1st ser.: *Births, Marriages and Deaths*, comp. James N. Arnold, 21 vols. (Providence, R.I.: Narragansett Historical Publ., 1891–1921), 7:69; Selleck, *Quakers in Boston*, 48. Thomas Maule (1645–1724), to be dealt with in more detail, was the only leader to remain in the region without continuing in his early position of prominence.

[34] Collins, a Lynn blacksmith, farmer, and maltster, was first appointed a visitor in Lynn in 1724 at the age of 26. Within a few years, he was attending meetings at all levels and, in January

ciently detailed to reveal a second group of less prominent leaders, five men who were also given duties regularly.[35] The meeting chose them less frequently than the major leaders. In addition, they tended to hold minor posts, such as representative to the quarterly but not to the yearly meeting. While these five men remained active at this level, most of the major leaders passed through a period of similarly modest involvement on their way to greater prominence.[36]

Members completely outside the elite also played an active part in sectarian governance. Not including this two-tiered elite group, more than fifty men attended quarterly meetings over the thirty-four-year period for which complete records are extant. A total of three dozen men from the Salem Monthly Meeting were sent to the yearly meeting in four decades.[37] Many nonelite men also served as visitors after that position was created. And the meeting asked numerous men to verify the "conversation" of one of their number who planned to travel or to check the "clearness" of a man who wanted to marry.[38] By comparison, lay Baptists were neither involved in such large numbers nor given the same degree of responsibility as Quakers. Without one formally sanctioned leader, Quakers shared more generally in governing their sect.

Among the monthly meeting leaders, some were successful economically, although wealth and officeholding were not as highly correlated within the Salem meeting as was the case elsewhere.[39] Of the dozen men who served the meeting for an extended period, the records offer at least a glimpse of the social status of nine of them. Estate inventories and tax rates provide a fairly accurate measure of the relative wealth of eight leading men, revealing that leaders were drawn from all ranks, but especially from the wealthiest. Two of these men had exceedingly modest estates, two were average among Salem Quakers, and four owned fairly substantial wealth.[40] Although specific information on Bostonian

1726/7, was named clerk. The records do not indicate whether he served as an overseer of the meeting or as a Public Friend. Because of an October 1716 decision preventing Public Friends from serving as visitors, Collins was clearly not the former prior to 1736, when he ceased to hold the latter post.

[35] At least one member of this group, Samuel Gaskill, was a Public Friend and traveled in that capacity. SMM, June 1707.

[36] For instance, before becoming more active, Benjamin Bagnall attended three quarterly meetings in six years; Samuel Pope, six in twelve years; and Jonathan Boyce, seven in eighteen years. See SMM and SQM (men's), 1722–7, 1709–26, and 1715–26.

[37] See SMM entries for March, June, August, and October; SQM (men's) entries for April.

[38] Visitors were first appointed in 1708 (SMM, May). The first committee to check conversation was appointed in 1689 to deal with Jacob Allin (August); such committees were regularly formed beginning in 1712 (September, December). A committee to confirm clearness to marry was first created in 1702 (May).

[39] For England and Pennsylvania, respectively, see Vann, *Social Development of English Quakerism*, 98–9, and Soderlund, *Quakers and Slavery*, 35–9. The connection between wealth and leadership status in the Salem meeting was more comparable to the situation among the rural Quakers of Pennsylvania studied by Barry Levy; *Quakers and the American Family*, 141.

[40] On a 1721 Salem tax list, thirty-two Quakers were listed, including Samuel Gaskill, Samuel Pope (with the second and third smallest rates of any Friends), Samuel Osborn, and Jonathan

Benjamin Bagnall is unavailable, he was clearly among the successful: Originally a watchmaker, Bagnall pursued a mercantile career for the last thirty-five years of his life.[41] Despite the cases of Bagnall and Zaccheus Collins – who died the fifth wealthiest man in Lynn in 1770 – the richest meeting members were not necessarily leaders, and the most prominent leaders were not necessarily wealthy.[42]

Far more than wealth, membership in one of the region's major Quaker clans was an essential ingredient in the making of a lasting career as a meeting leader. Among the seven men who provided most guidance to the meeting, only Benjamin Bagnall was not part of an extended Quaker family. With the possible exception of Joseph Thresher, all of the men in the second tier of leaders were related to these families.[43] The importance of family ties was demonstrated in the cases of the few leading men who failed to commit permanently to the Salem meeting. Merchants who had been born outside of Massachusetts and had not married into local clans, they all left the area for more hospitable environments: Edward Shippen went to Philadelphia, Thomas Richardson to Newport, and Walter Newberry to London.[44] Quite possibly, this string of disappointments around the turn of the century taught the meeting to depend more fully on local men whose commitment to the region was assured. Over time, Salem's leadership became increasingly tribal. Whereas kinship ties among eighteenth-century Baptist leaders set them apart from the rest of the church, the fact that Quaker leaders were members of the meeting's clans served to reflect as well as amplify a trend that involved many meeting members.

If the men's meeting created an identifiable elite while continuing to spread

---

Boyce (who occupied the middle position); Joseph Thresher (near the bottom of the top 25%); and Robert Buffum (who paid the highest rate of any Quaker). See Massachusetts Local Tax Lists through 1776, Salem Town and County Tax, 1721. Estate inventories survive for twenty-seven male meeting members who were of an age to assume a leadership role during the period 1700 to 1740; see ECPR. Among the six largest estates inventoried were those of three leaders, Zaccheus Collins (1770), Robert Buffum (1746), and William Bassett (1762). Jonathan Boyce (who, like Robert Buffum, was among those rated in 1721) left an estate of only £152 sterling. However, by this time (1767) he was an octogenarian and had deeded most of his land to his sons; see Essex County Deeds, Essex County Registry of Deeds, Salem, Mass., under his name, especially 24 February 1742.

[41] See his land deeds, 1723–73, Suffolk County Deeds.

[42] Bagnall's death warranted an obituary in *Massachusetts Gazette and Boston Weekly Newsletter* (15 July 1773). On Collins, see ECPR; *The Massachusetts Tax Valuation List of 1771*, ed. Bettye Hobbs Pruitt (Boston: Hall, 1978), 90, 84–94. Jonathan Boyce and Samuel Pope (with modest and small estates, respectively) were among the most active leaders; Robert Buffum and Joseph Thresher were among the richest Quakers, but were in the second tier of leaders.

[43] However, Josiah and Mary Boyce Southwick had a daughter who married a Thresher; Joseph, who was from Falmouth but lived in Salem for many years, may have been her son. See Josiah Southwick's estate (1693), ECPR. The name was sometimes spelled "Thrasher."

[44] On Shippen, see Savage, *Genealogical Dictionary*, 4:87; on Richardson, see RIYM, 1714; Walter Newberry, Invoice of goods shipped to Josias Byles, 2 March 1720/1, Belknap Collection, MHS.

responsibilities fairly widely, the women's meeting apparently utilized the sect's potential for egalitarian sectarian governance more fully. The surviving quarterly meeting records indicate that women were relatively disinclined to single out a small number of their peers for the most important duties.[45] Of twenty-five monthly meeting members chosen to attend the yearly meeting, no one was selected more than three times.[46] The two other monthly meetings encompassed by the Salem Quarterly Meeting did consistently send one woman apiece to the quarterly meeting; both Rose Tibbets of Dover and traveling minister Lydia Norton of Hampton also frequently went on to the yearly meeting.[47] Salem's women Friends sent only Elizabeth Sawyer Collins year in and year out, but she (like her husband) was the quarterly meeting clerk and therefore was required to attend.[48] The lack of a female Quaker elite to complement the men's leadership rendered the women of Salem unusual in comparison to at least some other colonial Quaker meetings.[49]

This egalitarian inclination among Salem women may have been connected to that meeting's tradition of female commitment to radical Quakerism.[50] Women in Salem had been especially active in opposing reforms, including the designation of specific leaders. Once the reform program had been instituted, they took advantage of the relative flexibility of the sect's organizational structure to eschew the creation of an elite. Rather, they governed themselves collectively, more fully in accordance with the traditional values of the sect. Both Jack Marietta and Jean Soderlund have observed that Quaker women in Pennsylvania followed long-standing Quaker practices in that they did not concern themselves with matters beyond the family and the sect. Men, however, limited themselves only belatedly to these concerns when they withdrew from politics

---

[45] The meetings were segregated by sex shortly after records began to be regularly kept, and the women's records had a lower rate of survival. For the period before 1740, only sixteen years of quarterly meeting records are extant, covering the dates 1721–5 and 1729–40. See SQM (women's).

[46] Ibid.

[47] Tibbets went to the yearly meeting for all but two of the years for which records exist between 1722 and 1739; Norton attended eleven of them; ibid. Norton's visits to the Salem/Lynn area as a Public Friend were recorded by Zaccheus Collins in his diary between 1726 and 1737.

[48] Collins's role and that of her husband may have been linked. Another woman who was modestly active, Abigail Boyce, was apparently the wife of male leader Jonathan. For a similar pattern elsewhere, see Soderlund, "Women's Authority," 728.

[49] Women's leadership in Pennsylvania and New Jersey has been studied in this way; see ibid.

[50] The failure to create a leadership cadre could have been dictated in part by each woman's personal maternity cycle, for – as Laurel Thatcher Ulrich has demonstrated – frequent childbearing and the period of breast feeding that followed rendered most married women periodically unable to travel; see *Good Wives: Image and Reality in the Lives of Women in Northern New England, 1650–1750* (New York: Knopf, 1982), 138–42. Because women could travel during one year out of every two- to three-year-long cycle, the meeting could have chosen these women every two or three years and older women continually. That it did not, however, suggests that it was not so inclined.

in the 1750s. Under those circumstances, women represented tradition by default, since the distinction hinged upon whether men – who were alone able to pursue political careers – chose to be involved with the world.[51] In Salem, however, women actively chose to perpetuate tradition. Following their own understanding of Quakerism, they rejected new opportunities to create an inegalitarian system of governance and thereby sustained an older tradition within the sect.

Even in the men's meeting, which did develop these opportunities, the authority of the elite was tempered in a number of ways. The fact that a sizable group of Friends shared the top posts distinguished the meeting from the churches in the colony, in which an ordained minister held the highest office.[52] The position of the Quaker elite depended ultimately upon their being continually selected by their peers. Zaccheus Collins captures this nuance in his diary when he went back over it to number each passage recording his attendance at a yearly meeting. Chosen year after year for the honor, he perceived each trip south as noteworthy.[53] Although the meeting deferred to Collins and others regularly, its members were frequently presented with an opportunity to choose otherwise.

This diffusion of authority helps to explain the meeting's relative lack of concern in locating leaders with great wealth. No single Quaker had to bear the weight of leadership alone, so the expectations for leaders' qualifications did not become inflated in the meeting as they did in the Baptist church. Some wealthy men did achieve prominence in the meeting, for material success could be taken as an indication that a man had the skills required to oversee the governance of the sect. And, presumably, some leaders enhanced their economic position through contacts they made while acting as sectarian leaders.[54] But every one of their duties – with the exception of clerk of the meeting – was shared with men of more modest stature. The major criteria for leadership remained "godly conversation" and, increasingly, membership in a local clan; social status was not as significant as either of these in determining leadership status.[55] The structure of authority in the men's meeting not only allowed for

[51] Marietta, *Reformation*, 30–1; Soderlund, "Women's Authority," 748–9.

[52] Some churches (especially wealthier, urban ones) employed two ministers who divided the duties of pastor and teacher. But the principle of focusing authority in an exalted office filled by uniquely qualified men remained the same.

[53] Collins made such notations every June from 1726 until his diary breaks off in 1769, beginning with "Ye 4th time."

[54] For instance, Zaccheus Collins traded with Quakers in Nantucket; ibid., August 1741. Edward Wharton, a merchant and an early convert to Quakerism in Salem, may have handled business matters on his preaching trips "eastward"; see Worrall, *Quakers in the Colonial Northeast*, 27, for reference to one such trip and *EQC* 7:60–7, for his fairly extensive estate.

[55] With comparatively few people disciplined during the colonial period in Salem, the meeting never faced the opportunity to remove a leader after censuring one of his children. According to Levy, this was done in some Pennsylvania meetings; see *Quakers and the American Family*,

fairly broad participation but also shaped the expectations of those who did lead.

In contrast to the Quaker practice of diffusing responsibility, the Baptists' approach to leadership had the potential to generate problems for the sect in the colonial context. The significance placed on the office of elder had exacerbated a general crisis over the church's ability to sustain itself in the absence of the founding generation. With an increasing emphasis on the elder, an unsatisfactory leader could seriously endanger the church. Although the evidence is sketchy, John Emblem's term as elder was marred by difficulties that may have added to the church's malaise. In 1695, the church formally objected to Emblem's practice of preaching to other churches without its permission. Three years later, he ran afoul of the law, earning a grand jury presentment for performing the civil ceremony of marriage after his license to do so had expired. The church signaled its dissatisfaction with him, publicly disassociating itself from this activity.[56] Too much was invested in the eldership for the church to survive a poor choice unscathed.

Since leadership positions were shared among a number of Quakers, an unfortunate choice of a leader did not similarly cripple the meeting. In two cases, the Salem meeting initially moved to elevate a man to a position of prominence, only to draw back from what was beginning to seem a problematic choice. Thomas Maule took an active part in reforming the meeting during the 1670s and 1680s. His combative character became increasingly clear as he viciously attacked the mentally unbalanced recanted Quaker William King and then engaged in a pamphlet war with the orthodox establishment.[57] Because he seemed unable to conform to the sect's new quietism, Maule was simply chosen less often for important posts as time went on. Friends overlooked him in spite of the fact that he was one of the wealthiest Salem Quakers of his era.[58] The meeting

---

141–3. Some leaders did have close relations other than children who were disciplined, but no change in their own status followed. See SMM for dealings with Caleb Buffum, Jr., brother of Robert (1713, 1716, 1722); with Jonathan Boyce's father, Joseph (1723); and with Elisha Collins, brother of Zaccheus (1728/9, 1739).

[56] Baptist Record Book, 5 October 1695. Grand jury presentments, 5 October 1697, MAE, 40:472. Benjamin Sweetser et al., Address to the Quarter Sessions, 23 January 1698/9, James Otis Senior Collection, MHS.

[57] Pestana, "William King's 1681 Blasphemy Trial." His publications include *Truth Held Forth and Maintained* ([New York], 1695); *New England Persecutors Mauld with their own Weapons* [New York, 1697]; and *An Abstract of a Letter to Cotton Mather* ([New York], 1701). The Rhode Island Yearly Meeting refused to approve publication of the last of these, an especially abusive pamphlet; RIYM, 1699.

[58] By the turn of the century, Maule's style was so utterly out of step with English Quakerism that John Whiting asserted that Maule did not sound at all like a Quaker and probably was not one; *Truth and Innocency Defended Against Falsehood and Envy* (London, 1702), 151–2. Among those Quakers rated in 1683, Maule owned by far the largest estate; Robert Stone and Josiah Southwick followed with estates one-third as large; calculated from the tax lists in Perley, *History of Salem*, 3:419–22.

was able to shift responsibility away from Maule without causing a rift in the meeting.

The case of sea captain, plantation owner, and merchant Abraham Redwood offers another illustration of the benefits of the flexibility of the Quaker system. Redwood came to reside in Salem in the last decade of his life, after marrying a Rhode Island Quaker who was related to the Collins family of Lynn.[59] The monthly meeting selected him as a representative to the quarterly meeting soon after his arrival. Never again singled out in this way, Redwood had to be treated with for absences during the next decade.[60] Like the Baptist John Emblem, Redwood seemed to have great promise as a leader. After he proved a disappointment, however, the meeting was able simply to pass over him when searching for candidates to fill its posts. By the time relations with Emblem had soured, the Baptists had given him nearly exclusive authority in the church. The Quakers enjoyed a degree of flexibility in choosing and retaining leaders that served them well in awkward situations.

While the Quakers were enjoying the fruits of their more malleable system, the Baptists were becoming increasingly inflexible. By 1738, the Baptists had moved so far from the tradition of artisan preachers and lay leadership that they had become literally unable to function without an ordained minister. When their "worthy & reverend Mr. Elisha Callendar" died, baptisms all but ceased. Three candidates for admission propounded by Callendar before his death had to wait seven months to become members. Elisha's nephew John Callendar, another Harvard-educated Baptist minister, administered the ordinance during a visit from his pulpit in Newport. In addition, preaching by the church's deacons or other lay members was no longer considered adequate. Rather, the church sought the services of other college-educated men, even established church ministers.[61] Whereas his coreligionists had thought of Thomas Goold as a gifted lay person, especially able but not solely qualified to lead, his flock believed that Elisha Callendar had the training and – with his ordination – the unique status that made him alone able to provide for the church.

This dependence on college-educated men brought the Baptists perilously close to the colony's religious establishment. Two decades after hiring a professional minister for the first time, the Baptists had come to think that any learned man – regardless of his denomination – was a better preacher than a

---

59 *Dictionary of American Biography*, s.v. "Abraham Readwood"; *Vital Records of Rhode Island*, 7:27; *Vital Records of Duxbury Massachusetts to the Year 1850* (Boston, 1911), 94. Redwood's wife, Patience Howland Phillips, was the daughter of Rebecca Husey Howland Collins, whose second husband was Samuel of Lynn; Salem Monthly Meeting, Marriage Certificates, 20 August 1695. The *DAB* incorrectly implies that Abraham Readwood, Jr., was the first Quaker of that name, for his less famous father was also among the convinced. The family name later came to be spelled "Readwood."

60 SMM, 26 June, 14 August 1718; 14 January 1724/5; Redwood was given some lesser duties between his appointment as representative and his absences in 1724.

61 Baptist Record Book, 31 March, 9 July, 2 April 1738.

lay Baptist. In 1730, Elisha Callendar's nephew, John Callendar, who was then a member of the Boston church and soon to be the minister of a Newport, Rhode Island, church, had suggested the value some Baptists placed on education when he asserted that "renegades of all sorts are men of No Letters, Education or fortune."[62] The Boston Baptists demonstrated the importance of education for a preacher when, upon Elisha Callendar's death, they asked Boston's orthodox ministers to preach to them in rotation until a replacement could be found. Not surprisingly, these men had little interest in helping a rival church, and the church found that it could not rely upon their cooperation.[63]

Even under normal circumstances, the church's new reliance on an educated ministry was a potential source of difficulties. In search of an education for their more promising sons, the Baptists of necessity sent them to Harvard College for training. There the young men received schooling identical to that of an orthodox minister, developing skills and a style that would distinguish them from the laity. When Baptist church member Ebenezer Phillips ceased traveling down to Boston from Stoneham for worship services, but instead began attending the orthodox church in his home town, he presumably saw little difference in the preaching styles of Elisha Callendar and Stoneham's James Osgood.[64] Furthermore, contacts made at college helped to integrate these future Baptist ministers into the colonial ministerial profession.[65] Their ordinations at the hands of non-Baptist ministers did the same.[66] These conditions fostered the creation of what William McLoughlin has called Baptist statesmen, in contrast to the gadflys, who annoyed the establishment with their criticisms.[67] The dangers inherent in this situation would become obvious only during the ministry of Callendar's successor, Jeremiah Condy, who would align himself with his more conservative colleagues in opposition to the Great Awakening. The church's

[62] Callendar to Nathan Prince, 13 June 1730, Miscellaneous Bound Manuscript Collection, MHS. The "most charitable judgment" that could be made of such men, he continued, was that they professed Christianity for selfish reasons.

[63] Baptist Record Book, 2 April, 2 July 1738.

[64] Phillips, a member since 1722, was treated with in 1737 for entering into communion with Stoneham Church, the first such case on record; Baptist Record Book, 29 May 1722; 21 August, 4 December 1737.

[65] The handful of surviving letters by John Callendar to friends he made at Harvard illustrates this development; Callendar to Nathan Prince, 24 February 1728/9, 13 June 1730, Miscellaneous Bound Manuscript Collection, and Callendar to Benjamin Colman, 24 January 1734/5, Benjamin Colman Papers (both at MHS). For a discussion of the increasing professionalization of the ministry during this era, see James W. Schmotter, "The Irony of Clerical Professionalism: New England's Congregational Ministers and the Great Awakening," American Quarterly 31 (1979): 148–68.

[66] Ezra Stiles thought these ordinations gave legitimacy to the Boston Baptist Church; see The Literary Diary of Ezra Stiles, ed. Franklin Bowditch Dexter, 3 vols. (New York: Scribner's, 1901), 1:156.

[67] McLoughlin, New England Dissent, 282. Although McLoughlin presents this as an urban–rural division, change over time was also a factor, as the case of the Boston church suggests.

resolution of its leadership crisis created new dangers that would temporarily threaten its survival.

Quaker leaders were not in danger of coming into similarly close association with the orthodox community. No member of the Society of Friends received a degree at Harvard College during the colonial period, much less attended – as the promising son of a Baptist family would – in hopes of occupying a place of honor in the sect.[68] According to Peter Folger, who was neither a Quaker nor an admirer of the religious establishment, the sect's most grievous offense had initially been its opposition to "college men."[69] The meeting remained vehemently opposed to a "hireling" ministry and to "sending their children to the Presbeterian schools or to learn in their books."[70] Colonial Quaker leaders in Massachusetts had neither the opportunity nor the inclination to develop such intimate connections with members of the establishment. In 1740, a substantial Friend still had more in common with less prosperous or distinguished members of his own sect than he did with the members of the congregational elite.

Both the Quaker meeting and the Baptist church underwent the process of institutionalization. In particular, leadership went from being more or less informal and spontaneous to structured and routine. The "weighty Friends" of the early eighteenth century, who carefully managed the affairs of the meeting, would have been all but unrecognizable to the first "followers of truth" in Salem, who were swept up in the excitement of the dawning millennium. The colonists who gathered in the meetinghouse on the Mill Pond in Boston's North End to hear a sermon by the learned Elisha Callendar seemingly had little in common with the faithful gathered in one or another private home to listen to the preaching of various artisans and to exhort each other. The momentous changes that had occurred in these years were necessary, as Max Weber suggested, to ensure that these sects would survive.[71]

Yet the routinization of charisma can provide only the general outlines of this trend. The specific circumstances prevailing among Massachusetts Baptists and Quakers gave shape and meaning to the changes that Weber discussed. In each case, the basis for institutionalizing differed. The former followed scriptural precedent in establishing a simple pair of church offices, while the latter implemented a complex system of interlocking meetings and various posts. The in-

---

[68] Furthermore, to my knowledge, no son of a Quaker attended and no graduate went on to join the Society during this period.

[69] Peter Folger, *A Looking Glass for the Times, or the Former Spirit of New England Revived in this Generation* ([Newport?], 1763); reprinted as *Rhode Island Historical Tracts*, no. 16 (Providence, R.I.: 1883), 5–6.

[70] SQM (men's), quoted in RIYM, 1717.

[71] Much of Weber's work dealt with this problem in some form. See, e.g., *Economy and Society*, ed. Guenther Roth and Claus Wittich, 3 vols. (New York: Bedminster, 1968), 1121, 1127–8, 1130–48.

stitutions that were erected upon these two foundations diverged accordingly. With official leadership positions few to begin with, the Baptist system became increasingly hierarchic; ministerial responsibility was eventually concentrated in a single office. The structure of leadership in the Society of Friends prevented a similar concentration of authority but permitted the creation of an elite group that shared most but not all of the power.

The specific historical context for these changes also had an effect. Throughout this period, the Quakers and Baptists remained sects in a colony with an established religion. Their continued existence as alternative faiths was a thorn in the side of that establishment. As the Baptists drifted closer to the orthodox community, they endangered the distinctiveness that made their sect a viable alternative in colonial society. The ordination of Elisha Callendar was applauded then and subsequently for the ecumenical spirit it demonstrated, but the approbation of the orthodox community may have been as much a curse as a blessing for the Baptists, at least in the short run. The Quakers, in contrast, remained aloof, a self-consciously peculiar people. They made their compromises with the world in a general sense, but they did not flirt with the "world's people" among whom they lived. The reform movement that pulled the Quakers into the Society of Friends had seemed a betrayal to many during the 1660s and 1670s. But it succeeded in institutionalizing a unique Quaker community within Massachusetts.

6

Boundaries between sectarians and others

The establishment of two sects in colonial Massachusetts created alternative forums for popular spirituality where none had previously existed. For a generation, an established faith had offered the only opportunity for communal religious expression; now a pair of other choices rapidly became available. Making the decision to abandon orthodoxy, the apostate crossed over a boundary into sectarianism. Yet interaction among orthodox, Quaker, and Baptist took place on the borders between the three faiths, as colonists fought battles and worked for compromises.

In their dealings with sectarians, orthodox colonists freely distinguished between the two sects. In doing so, they revealed a fairly sophisticated grasp of the theological issues at stake. Decades of listening to orthodox preaching and reading the Bible had taught Bay colonists to differentiate between the relatively familiar faith of the Baptists and the more alien one of the Quakers. If the average colonist's commitment to religious homogeneity was less than unwavering, the majority did not vigorously support the development of religious toleration, either. Contrary to the standard interpretation, toleration was not an either/or proposition, but developed partially and unevenly. With time, the boundaries between all three groups would blur, signaling a major change in the organization of colonial life.

The initial creation of sectarian communities was an exercise in defining and crossing boundaries. By publicly declaring their departure from the established faith, Quakers and Baptists moved out of the orthodox fold. In organizing distinctive alternatives beyond the pale of orthodoxy, they introduced an unprecedented situation in which a trio of spiritual options existed. Having labored to forge these new communities, both sects were tenacious in the defense of the options they represented. Largely as a result of the attitudes of ordinary colonists, firm boundaries between orthodox and sectarian were maintained during the latter half of the seventeenth century.

Sectarianism challenged a cherished ideal in seventeenth-century Massachusetts: that town and congregation be synonymous. The gathering of a church was a necessary step in the creation of a new town. Whether a member or not, every resident was required to attend worship services. The focal point of community life was the meetinghouse, where the populace gathered to hear the preaching of the Word. Daily family worship, which revolved around Bible reading, reinforced religiosity as well as familial bonds. Political participation was linked to church membership, so that the brethern of the church were responsible for transacting the business of the town and for serving on the grand juries that brought the transgressions of townsfolk to the attention of the magistrates. The colony's founders had crafted a system that they hoped would promote piety, harmony, and social stability.[1]

Given the pervasiveness of orthodoxy in seventeenth-century Massachusetts society, the presence of sectarian groups had a far-reaching impact. In becoming Quakers or Baptists, colonists abandoned the faith of their neighbors and – in some cases – of their families. In addition, they rejected the spiritual leadership provided by the town's minister. During the first three decades, those men among them who had previously been orthodox church members surrendered the right to participate in local government when they joined a sect. Placing themselves outside the social boundaries of their communities, apostates forged ties that transcended the town and even the colony by entering into sectarian networks that linked them to their coreligionists elsewhere. In effect, they redefined community. Hence, sectarians raised questions about their allegiances to their families and the colony when they rejected the established faith.

In order to create a sectarian community, colonists had to leave orthodoxy. The vast majority refrained from doing so, signaling their commitment to the establishment. The few who did cross that boundary created and sustained new alternatives. Initially, both sects grew largely as a result of individual decisions to abandon the established faith. A modest sectarian immigration to the colony added a relatively small number of members to the Baptist church, and even fewer people to the Quaker meeting.[2] Once a younger generation of Quakers came of age, they began to augment the membership without having to turn their backs on family and friends to do so. But throughout the first eighty years of both sects, a few colonists continued to turn away from the orthodox faith, thereby maintaining sectarian ranks.

The monumental decision to join a sect was presumably never made lightly, but the style in which Baptists crossed the border into sectarianism differed

---

[1] Timothy H. Breen and Stephen Foster discuss the extent of their success in "The Puritans' Greatest Achievement: A Study of Social Cohesion in Seventeenth-Century Massachusetts," *Journal of American History* 60 (1973): 5–22.

[2] Forty-five people, or about 10 percent of all those admitted into the Baptist church prior to 1740, brought recommendations from other, usually English, churches with them; Baptist Record Book. Twenty-five people were clearly Quakers upon arriving in the colony; they probably constituted less than 5 percent of meeting members. This information has been garnered through the reconstruction of the personal histories of known meeting members discussed in Chapter 1, note 50.

from that of the Quakers. Colonists departed from the orthodox fold and moved into the Baptist camp pensively and with caution. Deciding to seek membership in the Baptist church was often an isolating experience, made by a lone individual cut off from contact with other antipedobaptists. Baptists who recorded the details of their decision noted the distress it caused them and the care with which they made it.[3] John Farnum, who was furious when he left Boston's Second Church to throw his lot in with the Baptists, adopted a confrontational style more typical of the Quakers.[4] That orthodox leaders who wanted to discredit the Baptists seized upon Farnum's unusually provocative behavior attested to its rarity. More typically, a sizable group of colonists, apparently unwilling to challenge the orthodox establishment directly, waited until the original charter had been revoked and the colony incorporated into the Dominion of New England before entering into communion with the church.[5]

Some Baptists apparently went so far as to postpone joining the church to avoid angering an orthodox family member. The daughters of William Raymond joined the Baptist church – of which their mother had been a member for decades – within a few years of the death of their orthodox father.[6] James Upham immediately joined the Baptists upon the death of his father Phineas, who had been a church deacon and town representative in Malden.[7] In a variation of this theme, Bostonian Josiah Byles waited until his father's illustrious in-laws, Cotton and Increase Mather, sanctioned the Baptist church by participating in the ordination of its new elder before seeking membership in it.[8]

Side stepping confrontation in this manner was more congenial to the individual who intended to become a Baptist than for those who felt drawn to the Quakers. One of the sons of Quakers John and Hannah Estes awaited his father's death to join an orthodox church, but no documentable case of anyone

[3] T. Goold's narration; "Diary of John Comer," 26–7. Also see Patient, Epistle to *Doctrine of Baptism*. Massachusetts Quakers seldom left first-hand accounts of their convincements. For a nonresident Quaker expressing uncertainty over the decision, see *Some Account of the Early Part of the Life of Elizabeth Ashbridge* (Philadelphia, 1807), 26–32, 19–20.

[4] Case of John Farnum.

[5] Twelve people joined the church in 1686, nine of them after Andros's arrival. That number was exceeded in only one previous year (1681), but admissions that year included a group from Kittery who were preparing to gather their own church. See Baptist Record Book.

[6] Mary and Ruth both married Bacheler (or Batchelder) men early in the 1700s and joined the Baptist church on 7 March 1711 and 7 September 1716, respectively; see Baptist Record Book. William died in 1708. On the Raymond family, see *Dawes-Gates Ancestral Lines*, comp. Mary Walton Ferris, 2 vols. (Chicago: Donnelley, 1931), 2:703–9.

[7] Harold Field Worthley, *An Inventory of the Records of the Particular (Congregational) Churches of Massachusetts, Gathered 1620–1805* (Cambridge, Mass.: Harvard University Press, 1970), 340; Baptist Record Book, 25 September, 8 October 1720; *Journals of the House of Representatives of Massachusetts*, 55 vols. (Boston: Massachusetts Historical Society, 1919–90), 2:1.

[8] The senior Byles married Elizabeth Mather Greenough (daughter of Increase) in 1707. The ordination occurred in 1718, and Byles, along with his spouse, who was a Callendar, joined the church the following year. See Baptist Record Book.

similarly postponing entering the Quaker meeting has come to light.[9] Not only was such conciliation in keeping with the Baptist style, but the act of joining with the church was a less significant aspect of that faith than was the public embrace of Quakerism. Had Ruth Raymond Bacheler, James Upham, or Josiah Byles died without entering into communion with the Boston Baptists, their place among God's chosen would not have been affected. But those who felt called to follow the light failed to live as Quakers at their peril, for it was through their "conversation" that they fulfilled their commitment and became the Lord's people.

Colonists embracing Quakerism displayed a sense of urgency and sometimes even anger, not circumspection. Becoming a Quaker involved a more abrupt break from orthodoxy than becoming a Baptist, and colonists often supported one another in taking this extreme step. In addition, some colonists found the strength to abandon orthodoxy in a fit of rage. Boston inn-holder Nicholas Upshall declared his outrage at the hostile reception accorded the first Quaker witnesses and quickly joined them in their cause.[10] Upshall, the first person in Massachusetts to be convinced, was unusual in that he made his decision in isolation. Others, like John Smith, were similarly propelled into the Quaker faith while angry at the establishment – in Smith's case, the continued incarceration of his wife.

The most dramatic examples of conversions fueled by severe disaffection from orthodoxy occurred in the aftermath of the 1692 witchcraft scare. Rather than Quakerism sparking accusations of witchcraft, as one scholar has recently suggested, the witch controversy led to the growth of Quakerism.[11] Apparently a short time after Sarah Hood Bassett's release from prison – where she had been incarcerated for nine months as an accused witch – she, her husband, her siblings, and their spouses became active in the Salem meeting.[12] Another Lynn resident, Thomas Farrar, Jr., joined the Quaker movement in the wake of the indictment of his father.[13] The devastating experience of the accusation and

---

[9] *Estes Genealogies, 1097–1893*, comp. Charles Estes (Salem, 1894), 11–16. Baptized in Boston within months of his father's death in 1723, Abijah Estes was later received into Salem Church; *Records of the First Church in Salem*, ed. Pierce, 330. This difference between the two sects may reflect a problem with evidence, since Quaker convincements were not recorded in the way baptisms were. However, an extensive prosopography has uncovered numerous cases of intergenerational conflict over the Quakerism of the offspring of orthodox colonists, which suggests that aspiring Quakers were inclined to go ahead in spite of familial opposition.

[10] Jones, "Nicholas Upshall," 21–31.

[11] Christine Heyrman has argued that the Bassett family's Quakerism led to the accusations against them; see "Specters of Subversion," 52. The first evidence that any of them joined the sect comes after the controversy had subsided; SMM, Sufferings, 1697. In addition, Thomas Maule stated explicitly that no Quaker was among the accused; *Abstract of a Letter to Cotton Mather*, 17.

[12] Sarah Hood Bassett was accused but not convicted. Four of her in-laws were also accused; her brother-in-law, John Proctor, was executed at the height of the controversy.

[13] Thomas Farrar was first mentioned in connection with the sect in 1696; Alonzo Lewis, *The*

incarceration of loved ones undoubtedly fortified these colonists as they turned their backs on the community that had launched the campaign against the witches. The circumstances surrounding the convincement of these Lynn Quakers, although extreme, were consistent with the wrenching experience that often accompanied the decision to become a Quaker in early Massachusetts.

Whether colonists left the orthodox faith profoundly disaffected like some Quakers or with the soul searching of the cautious Baptist, once they traversed the border region into sectarianism, they usually remained there permanently.[14] Although converts to either sect were quite unlikely to recant, a few spectacular reconversions were recorded. Quaker William King courted execution by returning from banishment in 1661, only to inform the General Court "how much he, by the rich grace and mercy of God, was now brought to loath & abhorr himself for his sinfull & shamfull practices against authoritie."[15] Another early Quaker convert, John Southwick, returned to the orthodox fold during the last years of his life, long after the death of his Quaker parents and wife.[16] John Farnum, whose dispute with Increase Mather and the North Church had been well publicized by the Baptists' detractors, returned to that church in 1683 during a revival launched by Mather.[17] These were isolated cases, however, for the vast majority of converts did not reenter the ranks of the orthodox.[18]

Nor did they generally move from one sect to another. During the English civil war, serial involvement in various radical sects was fairly common. The same may have been true on the outskirts of orthodox New England.[19] But in

History of Lynn, 2d ed. (Boston, 1844), 144. The fact that he ceased to hold town offices after 1693 suggests that he was convinced around that date.

[14] In a brief sketch of the history of the Salem Monthly Meeting after 1675, Jonathan Chu argues to the contrary; Neighbors, Friends, or Madmen, 161–2. To support his view, he states that Quakers or their near relations joined the Old South Church in Peabody. The two Quakers he identifies (Ann Needham and John Burton) had died by 1711–12. The three relations of Quakers had never been affiliated with the movement themselves. One, Joseph Boyce, was virtually disinherited by his Quaker father in favor of a Quaker son (see ECPR, Joseph Boyce, d. 1695). The recantation of the father of another, John Southwick, had been overlooked by Chu. Easy movement across religious boundaries did not, in fact, occur.

[15] RMB 4, pt. 2:8.

[16] "Town Records of Salem," vol. 2, EIHC, 49 (1913): 140, 148–9. Jonathan Chu would have us view Southwick's term as constable as evidence of a tolerant attitude toward Quakers; yet not only was officeholding by Quakers illegal at this time, of those men whose continued activism in the meeting can be conclusively documented, none served in office. Chu, Neighbors, Friends, or Madmen, 139.

[17] McLoughlin, Introduction to "Baptist Debate," ed. McLoughlin and Davidson, 106; Hall, Life of Increase Mather, 181.

[18] Evidence that sectaries punished those who reversed their allegiance rarely surfaces in the records. Quakers possibly cut off economic ties with Joshua Buffum after he was disowned by the meeting, for he traded exclusively with non-Quakers or family members after 1682; see Joshua Buffum's Account Book, 1672–1704, Essex Institute.

[19] Vann, Social Development of English Quakerism, 23–5; McGregor, "Baptists: Fount of All Her-

Massachusetts, colonists remained committed to the sect they initially joined. Before 1740, only two people are known to have been active in both sects. Charlestown resident Benamuel Bowers's association with the Baptists was short lived and unofficial; he never became a member of the church. Bowers followed an erratic course through the spiritual options available to the seventeenth-century colonist, meanwhile battling energetically and often with the authorities, particularly with his foe Thomas Danforth. Eventually, he may have become more strongly identified with the Quakerism of his wife and daughters.[20] One Baptist church member – a John Farnum, but probably not the same man who had once before recanted his antipedobaptist views – became a Quaker in 1709.[21] No member of the Quaker meeting joined with the Baptists. The marked differences between the two sects organized in Massachusetts militated against easy movement from one to the other; in other areas, where a greater variety of alternatives were available, similar sects presumably drew from the same pool of potential members. And in Massachusetts, the decision to join a sect was not easily made. Once made, it was unlikely to be reversed in favor of either orthodoxy or another brand of heterodoxy.

In making the decision to join a sect, these colonists created not just religiously divided towns but often families riddled with competing spiritual loyalties. A few dramatic examples illustrate this phenomenon. That self-appointed defender of orthodoxy, Edward Johnson, had two adult children involved in sectarian movements before his death.[22] One son of early Quaker convert John Marston, Sr., went on to become not just a member but a deacon in the church that had excommunicated his father.[23] Future Newport, Rhode Island, Baptist church minister John Callendar, Jr., resided from age ten with a stepmother who worshiped and took his half sister to be baptized in Boston's New North Church.[24] Such troublingly divided affiliations were not reserved for the ordi-

esy," 23–63. For a New England example, see Dailey, "Social Network in Seventeenth-Century New England," 43. Catherine Marbury Scot of Rhode Island, known for having converted Roger Williams while a Baptist, later became a Quaker; Jones, *Quakers in the American Colonies*, 25n., 63.

[20] Cadbury, "Early Quakers at Cambridge," 78–81. Also see Danforth's note on the entry for George Bowers to Benamuel Bowers, 28 August 1656, Middlesex County Deeds, Middlesex Registry of Deeds, Cambridge, Mass.; MCC, 25 October 1668; *RMB* 5:153. Bowers, named an overseer in Thomas Goold's will, had to be released from one of his frequent stints in prison to fulfill that trust; see Mary Goold's petition, 22 January 1676/7.

[21] Baptist Record Book, November 1708–June 1709. McLoughlin believes him to have been the same man (Introduction to "Baptist Debate," ed. McLoughlin and Davidson, 106). By 1709, however, that Farnum, if he were still living, would have been over ninety years old. The Baptist-turned-Quaker was more likely his son or one of the other men of the same name in the Boston area; he presumably joined the church between 1696 and 1708, during the gap in its records.

[22] On his daughter, Martha Johnson Amey, who was reported for attending Quaker meetings in Boston shortly before his death, see Moses Paine, Constable's report, 16 March 1673/4, Miscellaneous Bound Collection, MHS. On his son, John, see Wood, *History*, 102.

[23] Perley, *History of Salem*, 2:78–9; *Records of the First Church in Salem*, ed. Pierce, 94.

[24] Holman, "Callendar Family," 15–19, clarifies the fact that John, Sr., married two women named

nary colonial family; even some orthodox church ministers had Baptist relations, including apparently Michael Wigglesworth as well as Increase and Cotton Mather.[25] The tension between loyalties to family and faith created by these
circumstances would contribute to an eventual blurring of the boundaries that
separated orthodox from heterodox in the colony.

These families substituted divided loyalties that were a potential source of
conflict for a shared faith that might have helped to bind them together. The
wills of both Baptist Benjamin Sweetser and former Quaker Joshua Buffum –
whose families included sectarians and nonsectarians – expressed concern over
dissension among their offspring. Buffum was perhaps thinking of his own family of origin; his father's heirs had fought over the estate for years, with his non-
Quaker brothers-in-law suspecting that his Quaker mother kept their shares
for her own use or that of her Quaker sons.[26] No such breach was recorded
among the generation following that of Benjamin and Joshua, so, in these cases,
perhaps parental admonitions were successful. But divisions such as these were,
both men knew, a possible cause of conflict.

Sweetser and Buffum feared the divisiveness that might arise from conflicting familial and spiritual allegiances, because they – like most colonists – knew
that sectarianism represented a profoundly significant alternative to the established faith. As three distinct religious communities initially emerged, the differences among them were clearly visible to most colonists. Entering an illegal
sect was a serious step, because it could bring social disapprobation as well as
legal sanctions down on the head of any colonist foolhardy enough to do so.
Sectarians viewed their decision, once made, as irrevocable; colonists who remained in the orthodox camp were equally certain that joining a sect was a
monumentally defiant act. The barriers that initially separated orthodox from
heterodox were not simply fabricated by the colony's ministers, as sociologist
Kai Erikson has argued.[27] Distinctions between the sects and the established

---

Priscilla and documents the church membership of Priscilla Mann Callendar. On John, Jr., see
Sibley and Shifton, *Sibley's Harvard Graduates*, 7:150–5.

[25] Wigglesworth's sister probably married Benjamin Sweetser (one of their children was named
"Wigglesworth") and joined the church as "Sister Sweetser" a few years after him. Increase
Mather's daughter married Josiah Byles, Sr., whose son became a Baptist church deacon and
brother-in-law of its minister.

[26] Benjamin Sweetser (d. 1716), MCPR; only one son, Samuel (whom Benjamin chose as his
attorney in 1716, see MCC), was a member of the Baptist church; Baptist Record Book, 31
August 1714. Joshua Buffum (d. 1705), ECPR; his children included Quakers Samuel and
Joshua and non-Quaker Damaris Ruck. On the earlier Buffum feud, see Robert Wilson et al.,
Petition, and Mary Buffum Neale's testimony, November 1678, Essex County Quarterly Court
Papers, Essex Institute, Works Project Administration transcription, 30:16; Tamesan Buffum
(d. 1688), ECPR; George Locker et al., Receipt to Caleb Buffum, 29 May 1691, Buffum Family
Papers, MHS.

[27] Kai T. Erikson, *Wayward Puritans: A Study of the Sociology of Deviance* (New York: Wiley, 1966).
By defining deviance as a social construct, Erikson implies that Quakerism, for instance, was
not inherently threatening to the colonial establishment, but was only seized upon as a conve-

churches existed. Ministers, in attempting to contain the sects, continually underscored – and, occasionally, embellished – these distinctions. In doing so, they worked most effectively with issues that ordinary colonists recognized. If they moved beyond the criticisms the populace thought legitimate, ministers quickly found themselves without an audience and modified their arguments accordingly.[28] The boundaries between orthodox, Quaker, and Baptist were created by the colonists themselves, who readily perceived the importance of the divisions that sectarians introduced.

Ultimately, ordinary colonists themselves were responsible for maintaining these boundaries. Concerned orthodox ministers did what they could to prevent interfaith contact. But colonists could choose to defy the ministry. In multiple-faith households, for instance, such contact would have been impossible to avoid. The decision to interact with or to ostracize sectarians was finally in the hands of the people themselves, as Christine Heyrman has pointed out.[29] Massachusetts residents came to a variety of conclusions in making these decisions, from the ostracism advocated by many of their ministers to an easygoing acceptance of the sectarians in their midst. Generally, however, they interacted with Baptists more readily than Quakers, and the border between orthodox and Baptist was heavily trafficked from the first.

On balance, expressions of hostility to Quakerism were initially more common than the reverse, indicating that many colonists appreciated why their leaders had greeted the arrival of the first witnesses in the colony as aggressively as they did. With one exception, scholars have argued that the majority of ordinary colonists held a comparatively benign view of the sect. That the populace opposed the executions has become a commonplace.[30] Yet more direct evidence

nient scapegoat in opposition to which society could be unified. Andrew Delbanco has recently attempted to revive this view; see "The Puritan Errand Re-Viewed," *Journal of American Studies* 18 (1984): 356–7.

[28] The ministerial response to the sects will be dealt with in Chapter 7. For an example that supports the point being made here, see the discussion of efforts to lump Baptists with Quakers, which floundered on the populace's awareness of important distinctions between the two. The ministerial critique of the Baptists then increased in theological sophistication, as more effective criticisms were developed.

[29] In Connecticut, an orthodox woman was granted a divorce from her husband John Rogers, founder of a radical sect; see Anna B. Williams, "History of the Rogerenes," in *The Rogerenes* (Boston, 1904), 142. No similar case occurred in Massachusetts. Heyrman, "Specters of Subversion."

[30] See, e.g., Erikson, *Wayward Puritans*, 120; Bonomi, *Under the Cope of Heaven*, 26–9; Hall, *Worlds of Wonder*, 242. For an early example of this interpretation, see Neal, *History of New England*, 1:310. Christine Heyrman's article, "Specters of Subversion," dissents from this interpretation.

Jonathan Chu has recently attempted to make the case for popular acquiescence to the Quakers' presence by distinguishing between local and central government policy. He believes that fines for nonattendance levied against Quakers were reduced during the mid-1660s because local government chose to defy the policies laid down in Boston. Arguably, the decision to deescalate the conflict was a more general response to the fact that the king was sending inves-

of popular attitudes toward the sect indicates that many ordinary colonists were as appalled by the Quakers as were their leaders. To be sure, some ordinary people, like some leaders, came to believe that the executions had been too extreme a measure, but the fact that they took place without any formal expression of opposition suggests the extent of initial hostility to Quakerism. Although specifying the extent of popular animosity is difficult given the nature of the extant evidence, such hostility seems to have guided the actions of some colonists in their subsequent dealing with local Quakers.

When confronted with a relation who became a Quaker during the early years, some family members demonstrated their complete commitment to orthodoxy, identifying with the establishment fully in the fight against their apostate relative. Edward Gaskill's allegiance to the standing order was so complete that he testified against a number of Quaker heretics in Salem, including his own son, Samuel. Another father provided for disinheriting his son in the event that he continued to hold objectionable views. Mary Shattock Hams wrote to the authorities begging her brother's brief release from prison so that she could escort him to the home of minister John Norton, where she hoped Samuel would be disabused of his Quakerism.[31] These people responded to the specter of a Quaker in their families with just the outrage and horror that the authors of the anti-Quaker legislation would have thought appropriate.

Other colonists also voluntarily expressed hostility toward the sect. Edmund Batter, a member of the Salem elite and a vehement anti-Quaker, was accused of pulling Elizabeth Kitchen from her horse and calling her a "base quaking slut." Many others willingly brought evidence of Quaker transgression to the attention of the authorities.[32] For years after meetings were first held in Salem, local adherents to the sect were conspicuously absent from the courts except when they were being dealt with for sectarian offenses. Having participated in the usual round of debt cases and testimonies about the affairs of neighbors before their convincement, they abruptly ceased to do so afterward.[33] If Salem Quakers were not harassed through the courts as their few coreligionists in Gloucester apparently were, they were excluded from the usual business of the

tigators to look into, among other things, the colony's mistreatment of the Quakers. See Chu, *Neighbors, Friends, or Madmen*, 127.

[31] *EQC* 2:315; occasionally, "Gaskill" was rendered as "Gaskoyne." Felt, *Ecclesiastical History*, 2:218. Petition of Mary Hams, received 17 May 1659, MAE, 11:250.

[32] *EQC* 2:219. Batter may have been a particularly vehement anti-Quaker out of embarrassment: He had relations in the movement, including Henry Phelps (whose son John was his nephew) and Philip Verrin, Jr. (whose brothers referred to Batter as son or brother-in-law); see *EQC* 2:261–2, 1:54; Perley, *History of Salem*, 1:294, 303–4. For residents testifying against Quakers, see periodic mass presentments in *EQC*, vols. 2, 3.

[33] For instance, see references to Joseph Pope and John Kitchen in *EQC*. Michael Shafflin dropped out of the records twice, first after questioning the ordinance of baptism in 1646 and again after joining the Quakers in 1660; *EQC*.

community.[34] In Boston and elsewhere, hostile crowds often gathered at Quaker meetings when a traveling preacher was present.[35] Tensions surrounding the sect may have flared up in 1692: Even though no Quakers were accused of witchcraft, the otherwise problematic execution of Rebecca Nurse may have occurred because of her familial ties to Quakers.[36] In the various ways available to them, ordinary colonists expressed their dislike of Quakerism.

The assignment of public office, which was in the hands of orthodox townsmen, also served to maintain boundaries. The freemen of Salem revealed an awareness of religious affiliations when choosing men to fill offices. Even before Quakers were disfranchised and prohibited from serving, the voters elected no one who had converted to that sect. Orthodox townsmen continued to choose men who had relations involved in the sectarian movement, but only until they demonstrated a personal affinity for the sect.[37] Appointing John Southwick constable upon his return to the orthodox fold may have been intended to test his renewed commitment, for he was required to collect minister's rates and to distrain the goods of Quakers who refused to pay. If so, Southwick passed the test, fulfilling his office until his death part way through his term.[38] The town

---

[34] Heyrman, *Commerce and Culture*, 127–9. Heyrman suggests that the economic status of Salem Quakers declined as a result of economic harassment (128 n.). One of the four wealthy early Quakers she designated (Joshua Buffum) was no longer a Quaker when the tax list of 1700 was compiled (see SMM, 10 October 1682); John Maule failed to equal his father Thomas's level of prosperity because he died two years after his father, leaving a young family (see Collins, Diary, November 1726). Meeting members continued to be slightly wealthier than average; Salem Tax Lists for 1683; Perley, *History of Salem*, 3:419–22; for 1700, *Genealogical Quarterly Magazine* 4 (1903–4): 9–15; for 1721, 1741, Tax List for Massachusetts Towns before 1776. Beyond Salem, the meeting included such comparatively wealthy members as Daniel Bassett and Zaccheus Collins of Lynn and Benjamin Bagnall of Boston.

[35] For instance, *An Account of the Life of . . . John Richardson* (Philadelphia, 1783), 76–7; *An Account of the Life, Travels, and Christian Experiences in the Work of the Ministry of Samuel Bownas*, 2d ed. (London, 1761), 99–102.

[36] Christine Heyrman has suggested that Nurse was suspect as the guardian of John Southwick's son; "Specters of Subversion," 51–2. In making this connection, Heyrman apparently overlooked the fact that Southwick had recanted his Quakerism and served in public office. However, three of Nurse's sons married daughters of Quakers Margaret Thompson and John Smith, which may have tainted the reputation of this otherwise godly woman. *The Ancestry of Sarah Johnson, 1775–1824*, comp. Walter Goodwin Davis (Portland, Maine: Anthoensen, 1960), 53–4, and will of John Smith (d. 1680), ECPR.

[37] John Kitchen ceased to be chosen only after reviling the court in 1662, although his wife had previously been involved in the movement; *EQC* 3:17. Anthony Needham was named corporal of the militia in 1665, although his wife continued to be regularly charged with absences; ibid., 3:290. A number of scholars have treated the 1657 election of Joseph Boyce to the office of selectman as evidence that Quakers were not only voting and holding office in Salem but formed a voting bloc with distinct political interests. Yet the earliest evidence of a Quaker meeting in Salem dates from after the election, and Boyce began attending it only in 1659 or 1660, so the case for the continued political involvement of Salem Quakers is not convincing.

[38] "Town Records of Salem," 140, 148–9.

of Lynn may have been similarly concerned to maintain boundaries between sectarians and nonsectarians when it repeatedly appointed non-Quaker members of the Collins clan to the same post, in effect sending them to distrain goods from their Quaker relations.[39]

Even in the case of the Quakers, however, the attitude of the populace was mixed. Popular anti-Quakerism was not as vicious in Massachusetts as in some other regions; for instance, no Quaker was ever stoned to death by an angry mob, as happened on at least one occasion in England.[40] Nor was the more moderate hostility of Massachusetts colonists universally expressed. Numerous colonists – usually but not always the non-Quaker relations of sectarian offenders – came forward to pay the fines of Quakers who were prepared to undergo more severe punishments rather than comply with the legal system. A handful of orthodox Boston women composed a petition on behalf of their heterodox friend Ann Gillam, reassuring the magistrates that she had not attempted to lead them astray with her views. A petition from the relations of John Chamberlain expressed hopes that he could be persuaded to abandon his newly acquired Quaker beliefs and that he would be treated with mercy in the meantime.[41] Gossip about Quakers originating within the orthodox community was occasionally passed on to the Quakers themselves, and from them, a tidbit sometimes made its way to their coreligionists in England. Quaker journals occasionally report encounters with non-Quakers who received them kindly during their travels; for instance, a non-Quaker living in Ipswich provided a meal for his acquaintance Samuel Collins of Lynn and visiting Friend Thomas Story.[42] Even as late as 1699, however, such incidents were rare enough to be worthy of explicit note.

Not surprisingly, full members of Salem Church were apparently among those least inclined to enter the border region between Quakerism and orthodoxy. In 1681, recanted Quaker William King was tried for blasphemy after Thomas Maule, himself a Quaker, brought his aberrant behavior to the attention of the authorities. Dozens of western Salem residents rallied to King's defense, petitioning the government on his behalf and harassing Maule for his part in the affair. King's supporters included both Quakers and non-Quakers; the latter apparently had no qualms about joining with their heterodox neighbors in de-

---

[39] Joseph Collins seized goods from Samuel Collins, who was either his brother or nephew; he and other Collins men distrained the goods of unrelated Quakers. See SMM, Sufferings, 1708, 1698, 1706, 1707, 1711; and Savage, *Genealogical Dictionary*, 1:434–5.

[40] Michael J. Galgano, "Out of the Mainstream: Catholic and Quaker Women in the Restoration Northwest," in *The World of William Penn*, 125.

[41] For fines paid, see *EQC* 2:314, 3:343. Regarding Gillam, see Mary Warde et al., Petition, MAE, 10:278a. Petition of Henry Chamberlain, Sr., and Henry Chamberlain, Jr., 7 June 1661, Photostat Collection, MHS; the petition does not clarify their relationship to John.

[42] For instance, George Fox heard details of a debate that occurred in one of Boston's churches; see *Secret Works of a Cruel People Made Manifest* (London, 1659), 8. "The Journal of the Life of Thomas Story," ed. William Evans and Thomas Evans, *The Friends' Library* 10 (1846): 110.

fense of an apparently mentally unbalanced blasphemer. However, with one exception, the non-Quakers were not full members of Salem's church. Even after more than two decades with Quakers in Salem, the colonists most actively engaged in the orthodox faith were seemingly unwilling to overlook the religious differences that they – along with their minister – believed significant.[43]

Despite efforts by colonial leaders to consign Baptists to the same marginal position as Quakers, the popular response to members of that sect was more uniformly sympathetic than was the case with the Quakers. During the first years of both sects, orthodox colonists joined together to petition for a change in the treatment each sect was receiving; whereas the 1658 petition regarding the Quakers called for a more rigorous response, a decade later petitioners requested toleration of the Baptists.[44] No evidence remains that colonists personally attacked Baptist converts, as Edmund Batter did Quaker Elizabeth Kitchen in Salem. In fact, Thomas Goold claimed to have been advised by a number of uninvolved colonists to form a new church after relations with the Charlestown Church had reached an impasse.[45] Grand jurors brought far fewer presentments for nonattendance at public worship against the Baptists in their towns. After the concerted effort to crush the church had been abandoned, only one flurry of presentments occurred; the upsurge in Middlesex County during the spring of 1675 was apparently sparked by the publication of one or two Increase Mather treatises on the subject of baptism.[46] During the decade that followed, Boston selectmen began accepting bonds posted by Baptists for "strangers" with Baptist sympathies who wanted to reside there. Leaders who hoped to reinstitute the religious homogeneity of an earlier era were well aware of the contrasting attitudes toward the two sects, advocating that any future campaigns to suppress them target the Quakers first in hopes that the populace could subsequently be convinced to oppose the Baptists as well.[47]

The contrasting popular reception accorded Baptists and Quakers is illustrated by the far greater willingness of non-Baptists to join with Baptists in

[43] Pestana, "William King's 1681 Blasphemy Trial." On Higginson's role in shaping the orthodox community's stance toward the Quakers, see Chapter 7.

[44] William Davis et al., Petition to the General Court, October 1658, printed in Hallowell, *Quaker Invasion*, 153–6; Petition on behalf of Goold.

[45] T. Goold's narration, 50.

[46] The presentments occurred during April, May, and June; see MCC. The preface of Mather's *A Discourse Concerning the Subject of Baptism* (Cambridge, 1675) was dated second month (i.e., April). The month of the publication of his *The first Principles of New England concerning the Subject of Baptisme* (Cambridge, 1675) is not known, but it, too, may have appeared early in the year, having been written some years earlier and revised during the preceding year; see Thomas Holmes, *Increase Mather: A Bibliography*, 2 vols. (Cleveland, 1931), 256. These were the first publications on the subject since 1665. King Philip's War, which would have no apparent effect on presentments, did not begin until late June.

[47] "Bonds for Security of Boston Strangers, 1670/1–1700," Photostat Collection, MHS. *The Diary of Samuel Sewall, 1674–1729*, ed. M. Halsey Thomas, 2 vols. (New York: Farrar, Straus & Giroux, 1973), 1:29–30.

submitting petitions to the government during the seventeenth century. On the one hand, Baptists and non-Baptists participated in petitioning efforts regarding such relatively inconsequential matters as loaf bread baking in Boston (1671, 1679), the creation of a new town in western Massachusetts (1674), regulations on butchering (1693), and a timber building erected in defiance of Boston regulations (1697).[48] On the other hand, petitionary efforts that included Quakers and non-Quakers were comparatively rare and were reserved for issues of paramount importance. In a fight over the disposition of common lands in 1678, a sizable mixed group petitioned the General Court for assistance against the Salem selectmen. In response, the selectmen attempted to belittle the petition by pointing out that Quakers, "men against government and learning," were among those making the complaint.[49] Forming political partnerships with Baptists apparently did not involve this liability. Only pivotal issues, such as control over common lands or the impending capital trial of a neighbor, encouraged orthodox Salemites to reach across religious boundaries to join with Quakers in petitioning the government during the seventeenth century. Less pressing issues brought Baptists and non-Baptists into association.

A few orthodox colonists were so comfortable with antipedobaptism that they considered inaugurating a policy of open communion. In a handful of churches in England, advocates and opponents of infant baptism worshiped together. Some Woburn Church members were apparently prepared to discuss a request made by John Pierce that he be allowed to continue in communion with them despite his antipedobaptism.[50] The idea was opposed, perhaps initially by Woburn minister Thomas Carter as well as by other church members. The proposal was subsequently branded "scandalous" by a number of other ministers asked to give their advice on the matter.[51] After Pierce's request had been denied, Woburn-area Baptists took the unusual step of continuing to attend the weekday lectures given by Carter. Despite their inability to work out a compromise, Baptists clearly perceived the orthodox community in Woburn as espe-

---

[48] John Man et al., Petition, 2 June 1671, Photostat Collection, MHS; Thomas Skinner et al., Petition to the General Court, 28 May 1679, ibid.; Daniel Gookin et al., Petition to the Governor, 27 May 1674, ibid.; Richard Chearrin et al., Petition, 14 June 1693, MAE, 69:90; Roger Kilcup et al., Petition, 6 April 1697, Miscellaneous Bound Manuscript Collection, MHS.

[49] *EQC* 7:74–5; Selectmen of Salem versus Proprietors, 1678, SCC, filed under 1724.

[50] See McLoughlin's account in *New England Dissent*, 84–9. The Baptist Record Book does not contain an entry for Pierce's baptism, which was mentioned in "Questions and Answers on Baptism," and in testimony by Thomas Pierce and Matthew Johnson, [1679], MCC. Pierce is, however, subsequently referred to as a member; Baptist Record Book, 10 March 1678/9. On English practices, see Tolmie, *Triumph of the Saints*, 24–7; Christopher Hill, *A Turbulent, Seditious, and Factious People: John Bunyan and his Church, 1628–1688* (Oxford: Oxford University Press [Clarendon Press], 1988), 292–5, 90–1.

[51] "Questions and Answers on Baptism" has been attributed to Samuel Willard and the accompanying note to Increase Mather. Whether a formal council of churches was held – as McLoughlin states (*New England Dissent*, 85) – is unclear from these documents.

cially amenable to them, a fact that may be traceable to that church's comparatively radical bent.[52]

Limits to the larger community's willingness to accept Baptists did exist initially, however. A number of towns used the practice of "warning out" against Baptist church members who wanted to take up residence; not only widows such as Elizabeth Watts, but also men who were able to support themselves and their families such as Thomas Osborne were informed that they were not welcomed as inhabitants.[53] Although the change was not so decisive as in the Quaker case, Baptists were temporarily less likely to appear in court on matters of public concern than they had been prior to the founding of their church. Most churches would not consider even a more limited form of open communion in which opponents of infant baptism publicly expressed their views but refrained from affiliating themselves in any formal way – such as by rebaptism – with like-minded Christians.[54] Edward Johnson may have used the threat of disinheritance against his Anabaptist son, just as a number of orthodox fathers of Quakers did.[55] In an individual effort to maintain boundaries, William Raymond entered into full communion with the local established church well into middle age, but only seven weeks after his wife of eleven years had joined the Boston Baptist Church.[56] Marriage to the daughter of a Baptist elder apparently did not give Raymond pause, but her own affiliation with the sect encouraged him to formalize his commitment to orthodoxy. Acceptance of Baptists was not complete, despite a greater willingness to countenance their presence.

When dealing with the Baptists, the orthodox community was divided in more complex ways than it was with regard to Salem's Quakers. The saints of Salem seem to have been less likely to involve themselves with the Quakers than townspeople who were not members of the church. Active supporters of the Baptists, such as those who signed the 1668 petition, were drawn from both groups within the orthodox community. Their advocacy of the Baptists' cause indicated not a general lack of involvement with the established faith but rather a concern over specific issues. Surprisingly, given the scholarly emphasis on the link between sectarianism and the development of religious liberty, very few

---

[52] MCC, 15 June 1675. On Woburn, see Chapter 2.

[53] Watts was warned out of Charlestown, 3 January 1686; Osborne out of Billerica, 19 December 1676. Elizabeth Russell, the widow of John, Sr., may have been the woman warned out of Charlestown on 16 December 1678. See MCC.

[54] McLoughlin, *New England Dissent*, 87. In 1725, minister Nathaniel Appleton suggested to John Comer that he remain in communion with Cambridge Church despite his antipedobaptism. George Selement misread this as a suggestion that Comer hold dual membership, although Appleton clearly intended an open communion arrangement. See "Diary of John Comer," 32–3; Selement, *Keepers of the Vineyards: The Puritan Ministry and Collective Culture in Colonial New England* (Lanham, Md.: University Press of America, 1984), 88.

[55] Wood, *History*, 102; MCC, 15 June 1675. John gave up his new faith only until his father's death.

[56] Baptist Record Book, 2 October 1692; *Dawes-Gates*, comp. Ferris, 2:708–9.

colonists supported the sectaries on these grounds: Only one or two people publicly defended both sects, out of a desire for general toleration in the colony.[57] More of the Baptists' supporters wanted toleration extended only to such inoffensive dissenters as they believed that sect to contain. Others were distressed over the decision to extend baptism to the grandchildren of visible saints and sympathized with the sect's more restrictive view of the ordinance. At least one petitioner continued to advocate the causes of the English commonwealth, defending the Baptists and opposing any endorsement of royalism.[58] The views of Baptist supporters covered the gamut from a dissatisfaction with the colony's intolerance to a staunch commitment to its traditionally restrictive church membership.

In their willingness to interact freely with the Baptists and their comparative hesitation with regard to the Quakers, the larger community demonstrated its appreciation of the differences among the three faiths. The affinity between orthodox and Baptist beliefs and religious forms rendered that sect both comprehensible and – for some, at least – congenial. The Quaker faith, however, was disturbingly different. The Quakers held beliefs that lay people as well as clergy found abhorrent and advocated such radical practices as public preaching by women. A crowd in Newbury made its hostility to female preaching clear in the opening decade of the eighteenth century, "calling for a Dram" so loudly that Lydia Norton – despite her "strong manly voice" – could not be heard. Around the same time, a "rude mob" in Boston drowned out the preaching of Sarah Clements.[59] Even the spatial organization of Quaker meetings, in which the faithful sat facing each other rather than forward and where no special space was reserved for the preacher, demonstrated the radicalism of the Quakers.[60] The sect continually emphasized its sense of separateness by observing testimonies that required Quakers to comport themselves in peculiar ways. These features of the Quaker movement could engender profound hostility and – especially among the orthodox saints – lasting suspicion. In responding to the two sects as they did, ordinary colonists revealed that they recognized Re-

---

[57] Colonel Thomas Temple, who tried to intercede on behalf of the Quakers and signed the petition in support of the Baptists, offers the most striking example. See Willem Sewel, *History of the Rise, Increase and Progress of the Christian People* (London, 1722; reprinted in 2 vols., Philadelphia, 1855), 1:425. Also see Hooten, Something Concerning my travell, 204.

[58] Petition on behalf of Goold suggests limited toleration. On the baptismal issue, see Holifield, *Covenant Sealed*, 182, and idem, "On Toleration in Massachusetts." Two North Church members refused to attend when Seaborne Cotton, Increase Mather's relation and a royalist sympathizer, was preaching there; one or both of them also signed the petition in support of the Baptists. Hall, *Life of Increase Mather*, 71, 73–4.

[59] For instance, Roger Clap especially objected to Quaker pretenses to holiness and perfection; *Memoirs*, 17. *Life of Bownas*, 99–102; *Life of Richardson*, 76.

[60] Eventually, Quaker elders would sit at one end of the room, although the others continued to face the center. When that innovation occurred in Massachusetts and whether a platform for the elders was built during the colonial period is not known.

formed Protestantism even when they saw it in the guise of an antipedobaptist church and that they knew Quakerism to be doctrinally at odds with their own faith.

The social geography of sectarianism contributed to the perception that Quakers were profoundly alien. Because the Quakers created an overlapping religious and familial network in western Salem and, eventually, the bordering section of Lynn, they were somewhat insulated from their non-Quaker neighbors. And they were more visibly connected to their coreligionists, receiving "strangers" as visitors on a regular basis. These circumstances encouraged orthodox colonists to view them as outsiders. The Baptists, however, lived scattered among orthodox colonists and, in some cases, interacted on a regular basis only with people who did not share their faith. Further, the Baptist church had little contact with and, until the 1760s, no formal ties to other Baptist churches. As a result, Baptists did not advertise their commitment to an alternative religious community in the way that Quakers did. Many Baptists had no choice but to traverse the border between their own faith and that of the orthodox community.

The geography of these sectarian movements may have facilitated the Baptists' somewhat better reception in another way as well, for the collection of minister's rates was not the volatile issue in Boston that it could be in Salem or Lynn. In the latter towns, heads of households were taxed to raise the funds for the minister's salary. When confronted with a refusal to pay, the town had to distrain goods equal to the amount in question or to increase the rates of other residents to make up the difference. This situation fostered confrontation and resentment.[61] Although the Baptists' move into Boston, the seat of the colonial government, could be seen as particularly provocative, they were, in a sense, choosing the path of least resistance. Rather than being rated, residents there contributed voluntarily toward the minister's support; both nonattendance and failure to contribute were difficult to police. Boston Baptists thereby sidestepped the problems associated with sectarians' refusal to support the established faith.[62]

When Quakers and Baptists reached out to the larger community, they contributed directly to the formulation of the contrasting attitudes that greeted them. Participating in a propaganda campaign for the support of the orthodox community, both sects competed with ministers and – to a lesser extent – magistrates who presented their own interpretation of sectarianism. The energy with which they entered the battle and the manner in which they fought it

---

[61] SMM, Sufferings, provides examples of the distraining of goods to support the minister of Lynn around the turn of the century; by this time, the practice in the larger town of Salem had apparently ceased.

[62] McLoughlin, New England Dissent, 278. Other church members, living scattered through various towns, were in circumstances similar to that of the Quakers, of course, but their smaller numbers limited the pecuniary harm their refusal to pay could cause their orthodox neighbors.

helped to shape the populace's attitudes toward them. The Quakers' approach cast the relationship in stark, divisive terms, while the Baptists were characteristically conciliatory.

Quaker tactics were typically strident and aggressive. Much of their public witnessing during the first two decades – going naked for a sign, interrupting court sessions and worship services, memorializing the executed witnesses – was intended to criticize the establishment for a non-Quaker audience. They favored two criticisms in particular: the injustice of the Quaker executions and the self-serving nature of ministerial opposition to the truth of the light. Dismay over the executions did eventually become widespread, a shift the Quakers themselves labored to further. The latter point – that "hireling" ministers were primarily concerned with defending their financial interests when they attacked Quakerism – was a favorite of Thomas Maule, who gleefully exploited widespread quibbling over clerical salaries in making his denunciations. In his hands, even an offer of open communion made to Boston's Baptists became an effort to increase Cotton Mather's income.[63] As far as the magistrates were concerned, townsfolk ought to know better than to repeat a rumor spread by a Quaker that John Higginson had more grain than his family could use.[64] By making the case in thoroughly antagonistic terms, the Quakers encouraged those who were not prepared to reject their faith and their leaders to dismiss the sect instead.

The Baptists asked only to be tolerated, and they did so in a manner well calculated to elicit sympathy. Their appeals to the public were made only rarely. The classic instance occurred during the struggle over the use of their new meetinghouse in 1679–81. The authorities, belatedly discovering their intention to use the building as a place of worship, resorted to ordering the door nailed shut after quickly passing a law requiring a permit to erect a meetinghouse. On the following Sabbath, the church met outside next to the structure despite inclement weather.[65] The event was staged to earn the sympathy of the residents of Boston's crowded North End, by suggesting that the law-abiding and basically harmless Baptists were being mistreated by the authorities. Suffering willingly and in full view of the orthodox community, the Baptists made a symbolic bid for acceptance. Colonists who responded favorably had only to doubt the wisdom of a specific policy rather than to reject altogether the establishment that instituted that policy. By asking for less, the Baptists were more likely to receive what they wanted.

---

[63] Maule, *Abstract of a Letter to Cotton Mather*, 15–16. Also see *EQC* 7:110.

[64] *EQC* 5:355–6, 360; the Quaker in question was not otherwise mentioned in connection with the sect, however.

[65] On the meetinghouse controversy, see Baptist Record Book, 1679–80; *RMB* 5:271–2; "Increase Mather's Diary," 408; Isaac Backus, *Church History of New England, from 1620 to 1804* (Philadelphia, 1839), 121; Wood, *History*, 137–41.

The boundaries that separated sectarians from the remainder of colonists eventually blurred. The Baptists, who had neither been viewed nor had seen themselves as total outsiders, were the first to become better integrated into the larger community. By the 1730s, on the eve of the Great Awakening, few prejudices remained to prevent them from participating freely in most aspects of colonial life. Even the comparatively exotic Quakers came to be more fully accepted by midcentury. The suspicions they aroused as well as the substantive differences that divided them from the larger community established limits to the degree of assimilation that was possible during the years prior to 1740. Compared to the earlier period, however, relations between Quakers and the orthodox had also eased noticeably.

Officeholding among sectarians serves as one example of the change occurring between 1690 and 1720. Sectarians were eligible to hold public office under the charter of 1692. The prospect of having some of the onerous duties assigned by the town meeting every year taken over by sectarians was understandably tempting. In Boston, nonsectarians quickly began choosing Baptists for various lesser tasks. Baptists there continued to hold offices in accordance with their social status and numbers in the town. Voters apparently felt some qualms about choosing Quakers initially, however.[66] In Lynn, the freemen selected only a few Quaker converts at first. They chose those who were recently convinced but who had a history of service, such as Samuel Collins; a number of them were – perhaps intentionally – given the office of constable, which led to conflicts over the collection of Jeremiah Shepard's salary. After fighting over the matter during the 1690s, the town dropped it by refraining from choosing Quakers as constables for decades.[67] In the 1710s, officeholding by Quakers rose to levels commensurate with their numbers in the local population. And, by the 1720s, Quaker men – especially Zaccheus Collins – were holding the office of selectman regularly.[68] With that, Quakers surpassed Baptists, who had neither the wealth nor the numbers to be chosen selectmen in Boston. The highest office held, however, was fittingly reserved for a Baptist church member, who served as representative for his town, Sandwich. Even so, he resided

---

[66] Elections were held on or around 25 March every year. See the results in *BTR*, vols. 7, 8, 12, 14, and in *Records of ye Towne Meetings of Lyn, 1691–1783*, 7 vols. (Lynn: Lynn Historical Society, 1949–71), vols. 1–7.

[67] For fights over the minister's rate, see *Towne Meetings of Lyn*, 1:40–1, 45. Subsequently, Quakers and Baptists in Boston might be chosen for the chore of collecting ministerial rates in order to force them to pay occasionally for a substitute; see *BTR*, 8:109, 181, 186; 12:155, 244; 16:64. Since numerous orthodox church members paid fines rather than accept the unpopular post, this periodic fining of sectaries seems to have been an effort to spread the burden of an onerous job. This practice meant that joining a sect was not an easy way out of all responsibility for supporting public worship. Also see SMM, February 1716/17.

[68] Lynn Quakers did not stop participating in politics after 1734, although William McLoughlin suggests that Friends generally did so at the time; see *New England Dissent*, 595n.

in a region typically outside of the scope of the church, in heterogeneous and comparatively tolerant Plymouth County.[69] Long-standing differences in community perceptions of Baptists and Quakers continued in force for some years into the new century, but suspicion of even the Quakers declined in significance with time.

This blurring of boundaries occurred for a variety of reasons, including changes within all the groups involved and in the transatlantic context of colonial life, as well as the impact of the unavoidable contact between sectarians and their nonsectarian neighbors. As the Baptists and even the Quakers relinquished some of the more extreme features of their early movements, they were more easily accepted into the larger community. The former gradually took on many orthodox church practices, which lent them a respectability they had previously lacked. Especially after 1718, when they chose a learned man to serve as their elder, their church seemed more like Boston's other religious societies. The Quakers, who not only did not have a single learned minister but who also continued to sanction preaching by women, would never blend in with the colony's other faiths. But they did drop other of their more radical practices: Of special significance on this score was their confrontational public witnessing. The Quakers had changed, as apologists for the executions found it increasingly necessary to point out.[70]

The orthodox community was more inclined to accept Baptists and even Quakers in the eighteenth century for various reasons, some of them contradictory. By this time, other groups appeared more threatening to those who sought to defend New England's religious traditions. During the 1680s, Boston crowds expressed animosity toward the first Anglicans to worship in the town, offended by the political power that the Church of England men flaunted in commandeering the Third Church of Boston for their services. A series of wars beginning in 1689 against French Canada sparked renewed anti-Catholic sentiment that would last until the Revolution.[71] Even while community prejudices were being directed at these powerful groups, some colonists were embracing a comparatively liberal attitude toward religious differences. The elite was exposed to latitudinarianism at Harvard, and those of more modest social status demonstrated cosmopolitan inclinations when they began snapping up the mildly disrespectful *New England Courant*.[72] Both animosity toward these comparatively

[69] See *Journals of the House of Representatives*, 3:4.   [70] Cotton Mather, *Magnalia*, 2:451–3.

[71] Carl Bridenbaugh, *Cities in the Wilderness: The First Century of Urban Life in America, 1625–1742* (New York: Ronald Press, 1938), 70; Alfred F. Young, "Pope's Day, tar and feathers and Cornet Joyce, Jun.: from ritual to rebellion in Boston, 1745–1775" (paper delivered at Anglo-American Historians' Conference, Rutgers University, 1973).

[72] On the *Courant*, see Miller, *Colony to Province*, 333–44. Admittedly, the paper was probably most popular when opposing inoculation, but even then it took swipes at Cotton Mather and other local dignitaries. On latitudinarianism, see Norman Fiering, "The First American Enlightenment: Tillotson, Leverett, and Philosophical Anglicanism," *NEQ* 54 (1981): 307–44.

powerful religious groups and the trend toward liberalism fostered acceptance of Baptists and, to a lesser extent, Quakers.

The transatlantic context in which these changes were occurring directly encouraged greater toleration of differences in a number of ways. During the first half of the eighteenth century, residents of Massachusetts port towns came into contact with traders and sailors from throughout the Atlantic basin. These connections inevitably exposed colonists to previously unfamiliar faiths and attitudes. Eastern Massachusetts gradually became more cosmopolitan, even though it was, at the same time, painfully aware of the provincialism of its own efforts at mimicking British sophistication. Among those with ties to the colony were the Quaker grandees of the middle colonies. That members of the Society of Friends had launched such successful colonization ventures as Pennsylvania and were able to govern them well helped to undermine negative images of Quakers that had been developed in the early days of the sect. The people of Boston, Salem, and, to a lesser extent, Lynn had a growing number of compelling reasons to rethink their traditional hostility to sectarianism.

Closer to home, the continued presence of these sects in the colony for a half-century without any alarming results further relaxed tensions. Once sectarianism had been a fact of colonial life for over a generation, the dire predictions about the insidious impact it would have became questionable. Quakers, for instance, had been declared "malignant & assiduous promoters of doctrines directly tending to subvert both our churches & state," while Baptists were supposedly "opening a doore for all sortes of abominations to come in among us."[73] Although early-eighteenth-century Massachusetts may not have been all that the magistrates of the mid-seventeenth century could have wished, both church and state were still more or less intact. More importantly, whatever the hopes of orthodox leaders, cutting off all contact across religious lines had proved impossible. Familial ties and long-standing relationships among neighbors often continued in force regardless of such differences. Despite the evidence of those who sided with the establishment against their Quaker relations, loyalty to family must have been an especially strong force for change. Over the years, many colonists displayed the same loyalties as John Farnum's wife, who vigorously defended her husband to Increase Mather even though she could not follow him into the Baptist faith.[74] In a society in which shared faith was to serve as a unifying force, colonists carved out neutral spaces where extrareligious interaction freely occurred. Decades of circumventing spiritual barriers minimized the significance of such differences.

The softening of boundaries was at once demonstrated and furthered by the existence of peripheral groups of colonists associated but not fully involved with the orthodox, Baptist, and Quaker faiths. This development first occurred within the orthodox community, as increasing numbers of colonists failed to seek church

[73] *RMB* 4, pt. 1:451; 4, pt. 2:374. [74] Increase Mather, Diary, 11 December 1665.

membership. This pastoral and ecclesiastical problem – which raised questions about how to involve more people in the church and how to bring them under church discipline in the absence of more energetic involvement – took on added urgency when orthodoxy faced competition for the allegiances of these colonists. The halfway covenant allowed the progeny of church members to enter into a formal relationship with the church without seeking full membership themselves. After its introduction, three relationships to the church were possible – full membership, partial membership as a "child of the church," and attendee. Persons in the latter two categories were potentially passive participants in the orthodox establishment.[75]

Even farther out on the periphery of the establishment were those colonists who failed to affiliate themselves with any faith. Nonattendance at worship services of any sort clearly occurred in colonial Massachusetts, although very little is known about it. All the houses of worship in Boston combined had a seating capacity insufficient for its burgeoning population. New towns and those in frontier regions often went without ministers. Even when attendance was possible, an unknown number of colonists did not take part. Some of the surviving evidence suggests that, despite laws mandating attendance, not all of those who shunned worship services were called before the courts.[76] The halfway covenant and group covenant renewals failed to sweep all of the colonists not affiliated with a sect into an orthodox church, which further softened the distinctions between the three groups.

The Baptist movement similarly included some colonists who were not actively involved as members of the church. Evidence of this peripheral group is sketchy, for they neither joined the church nor were generally punished for their association with it. When constables came to early church meetings to gather names of attendees, they invariably listed some nonmembers. Among those representing the Baptist side in the 1668 debate were a number of men who were affiliated with but never members of the church.[77] Possibly these people were fully committed to antipedobaptist principles but felt themselves unworthy of church membership. In that case, they were the Baptist equivalent of the devout nonmember of any orthodox church. Some of them may have been indifferent to the principles that distinguished the two faiths, as Samuel Willard suggested when he remarked that they attended Baptist meetings sim-

---

[75] Morgan, *Visible Saints*, ch. 4; Pope, *Half-Way Covenant*. For a welcome study of how the reform was implemented in one church over time, see Mary Macmanus Ramsbottom, "Religious Society and the Family in Charlestown, Massachusetts, 1630–1740" (Ph.D. diss., Yale University, 1987).

[76] David Hall mentions these facts, although he does not systematically address the question of nonattendance; see *Worlds of Wonder*, 16–17. Also see Gildrie, *Salem*, 85–6. As an example of failure to prosecute, Cassandra Southwick's "usual absences" were only punished when she became associated with Quakerism; *EQC* 2:49.

[77] The meeting described in the opening of Chapter 2 offers one example of nonmembers attending during the early period. Of the debate participants, neither John Thrumble nor Benamuel Bowers joined the church; see "Baptist Debate," ed. McLoughlin and Davidson, 106–7.

ply because these were more conveniently located than those of the established church.[78] Others may have come only to satiate their curiosity about the movement. Evidence of this marginally involved group surfaces again in the eighteenth century, but whether it existed throughout the church's early history cannot be determined from the surviving records.[79]

The Quakers were the last to develop this sort of peripheral group of worshipers. Early meetings of the sect included a few people who failed to make a firm commitment to Quakerism.[80] Either they were simply curious as well as daring enough to attend a meeting to satisfy that curiosity or they experienced second thoughts after throwing themselves into the movement initially. Subsequently, attendance apparently contracted to include, with rare exceptions, only those who identified themselves as Quakers.[81] By the 1690s, non-Quakers were again attending meetings, not to disrupt but to sit in respectful silence. Public Friend John Fothergill first commented on the presence of non-Quakers at a meeting in Boston in 1706, and by 1722, he was having difficulty making arrangements to talk with his coreligionists there alone.[82] The practice eventually became widespread, especially when a traveling Friend was slated to speak. When the populace first began to show an interest in hearing, rather than heckling, the preaching of traveling Quakers, magistrates and ministers labored to prevent them from doing so. Official opposition finally subsided.[83] Members of the larger community also went to Quaker weddings increasingly as the century progressed; the 1737 union of two wealthy Boston Quakers was held in the First Church meetinghouse because the "vast Concourse of People of all Perswasions who came to see the Solemnity" could not be accommodated in the sect's own edifice.[84]

By the eighteenth century, the colonists' penchant for "gadding" to sermons – as critics of the English Puritan movement had derisively put it – had come

---

[78] Willard, *Ne Sutor Ultra Crepidam*, 22.

[79] In 1739, when Jeremiah Condy was ordained, the brethren clearly expected his weekday lecture to draw a non-Baptist audience; see Baptist Record Book, 1 October 1739. Three years later, an apparent nonmember was permitted to build a pew; ibid., 18 July 1742. By Samuel Stillman's day, the church boasted a sizable unbaptized congregation.

[80] The meeting described in Chapter 1 included some people who were not permanently involved in the sect.

[81] One exception was Charles Hill, who, although not a Quaker, "always went to the Quakers meeting and . . . scorned to go to hear old Higgenson" preach; *EQC* 7:110.

[82] For a 1699 meeting that attracted respectful passersby, see "Life of Thomas Story," 109. *An Account of the Life and Travels, in the Work of the Ministry, of John Fothergill* (London, 1754), 32, 124.

[83] "Life of Thomas Story," 175; Fothergill, *Account*, 32; James Dickinson, *A Journal of the Life, Travels, and Labour of Love in the Work of the Ministry* (London, 1745), 148. After the Great Awakening, the authorities would actually facilitate the popular desire to attend such events; see, e.g., *Memoirs of the Life and Gospel Labours of Samuel Fothergill* (Liverpool, 1843), reprinted in *The Friends' Library*, ed. Evans and Evans, 9 (1845): 160–2, and "Mary Weston's Journal," 50–1, transcribed by John Eliot, LSF.

[84] *New England Weekly Journal*, 9 August 1737. Also see *Boston Evening Post*, 8 August 1737.

to encompass the religious meetings of the heterodox. Massachusetts culture remained deeply religious, if not as completely focused on the peculiarities of the New England way. Listening to sermons or to a rare public debate of religious topics[85] was, among other things, a form of entertainment in this society. In search of social and intellectual stimulation as well as, perhaps, religious edification, colonists breached barriers between the various religious organizations. Out of curiosity, at least, they attended the worship services or – in the case of the Baptist church – eventually the weekday lectures of sectarians.[86] In the very different environment of the early eighteenth century, they carried on a practice begun in the early years of the colony's history, when their ancestors had eagerly attended the lectures offered by the ministers of neighboring congregational churches. John Cotton, Thomas Shepard, and John Davenport would have looked upon the practice with the same horror that high church Anglicans felt toward lay Puritans who hungered for godly preaching during the early seventeenth century.

The Boston Baptists, far more than the Salem Quakers, relished the opportunities created by the relaxation in interfaith relations during the early eighteenth century. Beginning in the early 1700s, the Baptist church apparently participated regularly in the days of fast and thanksgiving called by the orthodox community.[87] A number of Baptist men worked as schoolmasters, trusted to teach the children of orthodox parents. Baptist church deacon Shem Drowne, a metalsmith, was hired to make weathervanes to adorn numerous public buildings, including Faneuil Hall and a number of congregational meetinghouses.[88] Had they been offered it, Quakers would not have welcomed the opportunity to take so active a part on the periphery of orthodoxy. As a matter of principle, they apparently continued to ignore, even if they ceased to defy, fast and thanksgiving days.[89] They kept their children out of town schools and tried to maintain their own institutions. They accepted work from non-Quakers, but they avoided actually laboring on the meetinghouses of other faiths. By mutual agreement, the Quaker community steered clear of the religious life of other colonial residents.

---

[85] The Baptist debate attracted "a great concourse of people" in 1668; *RMB* 4, pt. 2:373. Such public debates were far more common in England.

[86] The lectures scheduled in 1739 after Condy was ordained may have been an innovation or simply the rescheduling of an ongoing event; see Baptist Record Book, 1 October.

[87] A note from Cotton Mather to "My worthy friend, Elder Mr. Ellis Callendar, Elder of a Church of Christ in Boston" asking for Baptist participation in a day of thanksgiving was quoted by Wood, *History*, 196. As Mather observed, "We are well assured of the welcome which a motion of such a nature will find with you."

[88] Sibley and Shifton, *Sibley's Harvard Graduates*, 5:512, 9:443–4; Wood, *History*, 241. Robert Bishop and Patricia Colbentz, *A Gallery of American Weathervanes and Whirligigs* (New York: Dutton, 1981), 6–9, 14.

[89] *EQC* 5:63. In his diary, Zaccheus Collins regularly noted the calling of such days by the governor, but mentions no observance of them by Quakers; see, e.g., 3 July 1755.

Nothing captures this difference between the two sects better than patterns of book ownership. While the Baptists bought books that attested to their sense of themselves as part of a larger community of English Reformed Protestants, the Quakers' reading demonstrated their continued insularity. Baptists whose estate inventories listed book titles owned many of the same works as orthodox colonists. Only occasionally did they have books defending the tenets peculiar to their faith.[90] When the church's pastor, Jeremiah Condy, opened a book-shop, he carried a particularly varied stock.[91]

In contrast, Quakers owned only Bibles or works written by members of their own sect, including manuscript copies of Quaker sermons preached else-where.[92] The meeting fostered this exclusivity by establishing a lending library of Quaker books in 1714. Supplemented over the years by gifts and purchases, the collection came to number at least two dozen titles, of which George Fox's *Journal* was apparently in the greatest demand.[93] Although they might welcome non-Quakers into their meetings for worship, Salem Monthly Meeting members did not perceive themselves as having much in common with other colonial faiths. The modest acceptance they were accorded by the middle decades of the eighteenth century – which did represent a radical change from their place in colonial society seventy years earlier – went about as far as the Quakers themselves were willing to go in their relations with "the People in General."[94]

The changing relations among orthodox, Baptist, and Quaker attested to the transformation of the politics of religion in Massachusetts. By their continued presence in the colony, Quakers and Baptists gradually undermined the ortho-dox establishment, encouraging ordinary colonists to make their own peace with sectarians. In their dealings with Quakers and Baptists, these colonists revealed that they appreciated the doctrinal differences between their own faith and that

---

[90] For instance, see Joseph Callendar (d. 1767) and Shem Drowne (d. 1774), SCPR. Six of the older titles were included in the orthodox libraries described in "Three Early Massachusetts Libraries," *CSMC* 28 (1930–3), 107–75. Joseph Callendar owned Thomas Crosby's *History of the English Baptists*, the only specifically Baptist book among those inventoried. The American Antiquarian Society copy of John Walton's *Vindication of the True Christian Baptism* (Boston, 1738) formerly belonged to Josiah Byles. The 128 books in Elisha Callendar's library were not individually listed but included Baptist as well as non-Baptist works, many of them given to him by Thomas Hollis; see Elisha Callendar (d. 1738), SCPR, and Hollis's letters in "Documents from the Harvard University Archives, 1638–1750," ed. Robert W. Lovett, *CSMC*, vols. 49, 50 (1975), esp. 49:303, 50:445.

[91] Elizabeth Carroll Reilly, "The Wages of Piety: The Boston Book Trade of Jeremy Condy," in *Printing and Society in Early America*, ed. William L. Joyce et al. (Worcester, Mass.: American Antiquarian Society, 1983), esp. 126–31.

[92] See Joseph Buffum (d. 1731) and Ezekial Fowler (d. 1736), ECPR. Among Samuel Collins's papers is a summary of a sermon apparently preached at Bristol by T. Willson, dated 1694; LHS.

[93] SMM, May 1714, November 1715, May 1716, March 1724/5, April 1729. The meeting began to monitor the circulation of Fox's *Journal* after some members kept it too long; May 1720.

[94] Collins, Diary, 4 September 1756.

7

The politics of religious dissent

After the efforts to rid the colony of sectarianism failed, orthodox leaders turned their attentions to containing the threat posed by the sects. The battle was no longer fought primarily by the colonial government – which was restrained by royal as well as some popular displeasure over the initial persecution – but was taken up instead by the colony's ministers. The latter were not only freer to act because of the unofficial nature of their role in imperial politics; they also felt particularly responsible for the souls of their parishioners and the fate of the New England way. As they shouldered responsibility for policing the boundaries between orthodoxy and sectarianism, ministers – led by John Higginson of Salem – unhappily acknowledged that the problem of dissent had more to do with popular attitudes than with state policy.

To a far greater degree than has been previously appreciated by historians, the Quakers and the Baptists actively shaped the changing orthodox response to their presence. Taking their cue from the sectaries themselves, leading clergymen developed two distinct strategies to shield their flocks. The first of these, which involved casting sectaries as aliens, followed from the Quakers' approach to the orthodox establishment. The Baptists provided the inspiration for the second tactic, which focused on educating the populace. The ministers' emphasis shifted over time, as they responded to changes in the broader political context and they reversed their position on which sect posed the major danger to orthodoxy.

Although impelled to tolerate the presence of dissenters, the colonial elite did not easily relinquish its vision of a religiously unified society. Despite later efforts by such New England apologists as Cotton Mather to minimize the extent of early support for intolerance, the uneasy truce worked out in the 1670s did not usher in an era of equanimity based on widespread support for religious toleration.[1] Colonial leaders, who would have preferred to squelch sectarians altogether, clearly felt compelled by royal pressures and changing circumstances in the colony to adopt a more tolerant approach. After the traditional strategies designed to rid the colony of sectaries had proved untenable, con-

---

[1] For instance, Cotton Mather, *Parentator* (Boston, 1724), 57.

cerned ministers focused their energies on uniting the populace in opposition to the two objectionable groups. If an orthodox colony was no longer possible, at least the orthodox majority could shun the heretical minority. Keeping the seriousness of the sectarian threat before the people, the religious leaders consciously defined the godly community in contrast to these intruders. Antisectarianism became a rallying point for a religiously unified majority.

Salem minister John Higginson first developed this strategy to counter the influence of Quakers in his town. His two-part program was designed to reclaim as many apostates as possible and to emphasize the distinctions between godly orthodox and wayward sectaries.[2] After a series of conciliatory gestures in the early 1660s enticed only one or two Quakers back into the orthodox fold, the others were excommunicated. At about the same time, the church publicly renewed its covenant – to which had been appended a new anti-Quaker clause.[3] Higginson supported those church reforms, such as the halfway covenant and covenant renewals, that would pull more of Salem's adult population into active participation in the church. At one point, he toyed with the idea of dropping the conversion relation as a prerequisite of church membership, another reform that would expand participation in the established faith. Throughout, he preached repeatedly and vigorously against the sect. Even the marginally involved could be made to feel that they were a part of this invigorated orthodox community, when contrasted with the provocative and ostracized Quakers.[4]

Higginson's approach was widely publicized when he delivered the election-day sermon in 1663, the year after he finished putting his program into place. *The Causes of God and His People in New England* offered a concise statement of the logic behind Higginson's methods: Accept minor differences of opinion within well-defined limits and work to bring all colonists within those boundaries.[5] Significantly, Higginson's sermon developed what would prove to be a

[2] For the various elements of Higginson's program, see *EQC* 2:193, 225; *Records of the First Church in Salem*, ed. Pierce, 91, 93–4, 5; "Letter to [?] about Higginson's election sermon before the General Court and Davenport's Discourse," 6 June 1663, MHS; Besse, *Sufferings*, 2:210–11; Maule, *New England Pesecutors*, 32; and George Fox, *Something in Answer to a Law Lately made* [London, 1679], 19. In addition to the efforts enumerated in this paragraph, Conrad E. Wright has suggested to me that the church vote on 10 September 1660 may have been innovative in limiting charitable contributions to the "poor of the Church," thereby excluding the Quakers from benefits that had previously been distributed to all destitute residents of the town; see *Records of the First Church in Salem*, ed. Pierce, 87.

[3] See Gildrie, *Salem*, 51, for earlier revisions by Hugh Peter repudiating separatist views.

[4] Historians of Salem have long debated whether a particular local leader was "hard" or "soft" on Quakerism. In general, my interpretation agrees with that of Richard Gildrie (*Salem*, 136–7, 143–8). He believes, however, that Quakerism contributed to declension by causing doctrinal confusion and encouraging flexibility, while I see Higginson using the Quakers to create clarity and a new basis of unity within the establishment.

[5] John Higginson, *The Cause of God and His People in New England* (Cambridge, 1663). This is the oldest published election-day sermon extant. In his efforts to solidify orthodoxy, Higginson also provided the town with a more harmonious past; he transcribed the church records into a new

favorite technique for calling the orthodox to action – the theme of declension.[6] Ministers all over New England, in hopes of encouraging renewed vigilance on the part of their congregations, would follow Higginson in depicting New England society as having abandoned the first generation's standards of godliness.[7] The presence of the Quakers served Higginson's cause both as a sign of decline and as an outside reference point against which a newly inspired populace could define itself.

During the years that followed, other ministers and churches adopted Higginson's approach to sectarianism. Seventeenth-century pulpit harangues against Quakers and Baptists were rarely designed to dissuade those who were seriously considering apostasy; ministers would counsel people who required their assistance in private pastoral visits.[8] Rather, these sermonic denunciations presented sectarians as aliens, demarcating the division between godly and heterodox.[9] The colony's clerics placed the devastation wrought by King Philip's War in 1675–6 within this framework, citing the presence of sectarians as one of God's reasons for sending that ultimate alien, the barbarous heathen, against his people.[10] In towns that were particularly imperiled by the sectarian menace – as Lynn was by Quakerism in the mid-1690s – ministers set aside days of fasting and prayer to rally the community "that the spiritual plague might proceed no further."[11] Members of the orthodox community reaffirmed their commitment to the established faith individually, when they brought their children forward for baptism, and collectively, when they restated their support for the church covenant in ritual renewal ceremonies. This "resurgence of baptismal

---

book with all references to the conflict surrounding Roger Williams's brief ministry deleted. See Baughman, "Excommunications," 89–90.

[6] Perry Miller credited Higginson with establishing the declension motif in this sermon; "Declension in a Bible Commonwealth," in *Nature's Nation* (Cambridge, Mass.: Harvard University Press, 1967), 24. Also see Bozeman, *To Live Ancient Lives*, 311–12.

[7] For a similar interpretation of the rhetoric of declension, see Stout, *New England Soul*, 80.

[8] For instance, see Cotton Mather's description of Thomas Thatcher rooting out Quaker books and counseling those who were in danger of succumbing to the sect; *Magnalia*, 1:444–5.

[9] Examples can be found in Jonathan Mitchell, *Nehemiah on the Wall in Troublesome times* (Cambridge, 1671), 27; [Increase Mather], *The Necessity of Reformation* (Boston, 1679); Daniel Denison, *Irenicon, or a Salve for New England's Sore* (Boston, 1684); James Allin et al., *The Principles of the Protestant Religion Maintained* (Boston, 1690). Perry Miller characterized the tract by Denison as "a wise, sane, level-headed plea for toleration" (*Colony to Province*, 140–1); Denison, however, declared Quakerism a violent, and Anabaptism a sly, assault by Satan (190–1).

[10] Increase Mather, *A Brief History of the Warr with the Indians* (Boston, 1676), reprinted in *So Dreadfull a Judgment: Puritan Response to King Philip's War, 1676–1677*, ed. Richard Slotkin and James K. Folsom (Middletown, Conn.: Wesleyan University Press, 1978), 18; *RMB* 5:244; [Mather], *Necessity of Reformation*. Only Ipswich minister William Hubbard openly dissented from the view first championed by Mather and endorsed in the 1679 synod; Hall, *Faithful Shepherd*, 240–3; see also, Increase Mather, Diary, 10 August 1676.

[11] Lynn minister Jeremiah Shepard, quoted in Alonzo Lewis, *The History of Lynn* (Boston, 1829), 142. On Shepard's campaign against the Quakers, also see Parsons Cooke, *A Century of Puritanism . . .* (Boston, 1855), 443, 98.

piety" was linked to the sectarian presence, for it served to demarcate those who were in covenant from those who were not.[12] Occasionally, churches that were currently free from the influence of sectarianism covenanted specifically against it, as was the case with the Ipswich Church and the "evils of Quakerism" in 1678.[13] Using the Quakers and Baptists to strengthen the cohesiveness of the orthodox community, pastors made the best of an unwelcome situation.

Orthodox leaders spread damning gossip about the sects and compared them to other evildoers in an effort to promote the perception that their adversaries were dangerous extremists. Making the most of early Quaker statements that the inward light superseded the Bible and ignoring modifications in the sect's position since that time, ministers often informed lay people that the Quakers refused to acknowledge that the Scriptures were the Word of God.[14] The tale of Increase Mather's abuse at the hands of Baptist convert John Farnum circulated widely, helping to counter inclinations to view the Baptists in a more positive light. Both sects were likened to the Anabaptists of Munster, who had advocated free love for the faithful and death to all nonbelievers. A pamphlet on the events at Munster, reprinted in Cambridge just after the Baptists gathered their church, served to associate the new church with that debacle.[15] The continued use of the term "Anabaptist" to refer to the Boston church helped to keep that connection alive. Meanwhile, New Englanders linked the Quakers to a host of other satanic agents, including papists, witches, and Indians.[16]

The portrayal of sectarians as outsiders proved most effective with the Quakers, for whom it had originally been developed. Quakerism, as the more radical departure from orthodoxy, had always earned especially vicious epithets. Initially, official pronouncements by the General Court described them as "wicked and dangerous seducers" and "incorrigible rogues & enemies to the common peace."[17] Given this understanding of the sect, Quakers could easily be depicted as alien. The extremism of the early movement and the Salem community's clannishness also enhanced the image of Quakerism as far beyond the pale.

---

[12] Holifield, *Covenant Sealed*, 226; he covers the sacramental renaissance generally in ch. 7.

[13] Thomas Cobbett to Increase Mather, *CMHS*, 4th ser., vol. 8 (1868): 290.

[14] *The Life and Correspondence of William and Alice Ellis*, ed. John Backhouse (London, 1849), 132.

[15] Norton, *Heart of New England*, 53–61; *RMB* 4, pt. 1:385; "Baptist Debate," ed. McLoughlin and Davidson, 108–9; Willard, *Ne Sutor Ultra Crepidam*, 23–6. Guy de Bretz, *The Rise, Spring, and Foundation of the Anabaptists* (Cambridge, 1668); the work was originally published in French in 1565, and, according to the preface, an English reprint had previously appeared under a different title.

[16] "Antipedobaptist" finally replaced "Anabaptist" in Cotton Mather's *Brethren Dwelling Together in Unity* (Boston, 1718), although the latter continued to be used occasionally for years after that; see "List of Annabaptists, 1761," Newton, Mass. Papers, 1749–1869, AAS. Governor Bradstreet to James Martin, 27 March 1683, in *Calendar of State Papers: America and West Indies, 1681–Feb. 5. 1685*, ed. J. W. Fortescue, 11 (1898): 411–12; Humphrey Norton, *New England's Bloody Ensigne* (London, 1659), 7; and *EQC* 2:219.

[17] Norton, *Heart of New England*, 82 (mispaginated); *RMB* 4, pt. 2:3.

New England authors continued to bandy about what one Quaker deemed these "monstrous misrepresentations of Friends" for years after similar diatribes against Baptists had ceased.[18] Already in the years before 1684, the published works of ministers more frequently contained such attacks on Quakers than on Baptists.[19] After the charter was revoked, such references to the Baptists ceased altogether, but those to Quakers did not. With the political situation demanding circumspection, Increase Mather adopted a more indirect approach to damning Quakerism, repeating stories of the murderous debauchery of the Long Island Ranters in his exceedingly popular *Essay for the Recording of Illustrious Providences* (1684). Dubbing them the "singing and dancing Quakers," Mather linked this group – which reportedly staged sacrificial killings, danced naked, and otherwise worshiped the devil – to the Quakers themselves.[20] Similarly, Cotton Mather would associate Quakers first with witches and then also with Satan and Indians in pamphlets published five and fifteen years later.[21] The Mathers wanted to remind New Englanders of the alien nature of Quakerism even after it had become impolitic to do so directly.

This theme was developed so effectively that the alien Quaker assumed a symbolic significance in the colony. In order to criticize legal proceedings against Cambridge young people who had been gathering late at night to eat and drink, a Watertown man ridiculed the standards for their comportment by saying "ere long the young men must pass by the mayds like quakers and take no notice of them." Associating official policies with Quakerism did not have the desired effect of undermining those policies in this case, but such was clearly the intention of this colonist.[22] On another occasion, newly arrived English dance master Francis Stepney tried to defend his own objectionable conduct by arguing that he was not as terrible as the Quakers with whom the magistrates sought to link him. Found guilty of "prophane and wicked speeches tending to blasphemy in saying there was as much divinity in some playes as in some of the old Testament . . . and reviling of authority, saying the Authority here were but shoemakers and taylors," Stepney failed to persuade the magistrates that he ought to be forgiven his excesses simply because they paled in comparison with those of the Quakers.[23]

---

[18] *Account of the Life of John Fothergill*, 32.

[19] I have been able to locate six attacks on Baptists and nine on Quakers for the period from 1659 through 1684; two of the pamphlets deal with both sects.

[20] *An Essay for the Recording of Illustrious Providences* (Boston, 1684), 340–56.

[21] *Memorable Providences Related to Witchcraft and Possession* (Boston, 1689), app. *Decennium Luctuosum* (Boston, 1699), 162–85. Also see Richard Slotkin, *Regeneration Through Violence: The Mythology of the American Frontier, 1600–1860* (Middletown, Conn.: Wesleyan University Press, 1973), 130.

[22] Abraham Arrington, quoted in Roger Thompson, *Sex in Middlesex: Popular Mores in a Massachusetts County, 1649–1699* (Amherst: University of Massachusetts Press, 1986), 88.

[23] Francis Stepney, "Reasons for Appeal, 4 February 1685/6," and Isaac Addington, "An Answer to what is given by Mr. Francis Stepney, 2 March 1685/6," both in SCC. Increase Mather

To be likened to the Quakers, as Stepney had been, was a profound insult. In 1690, Cotton Mather was declared a "semi-Quaker" for his views on the Lord's Supper. The erstwhile Quaker turned Anglican George Keith tarred Boston minister Samuel Willard with the brush of Quakerism in 1704, suggesting that his theological arguments advanced that sect's cause. In combating deism, Increase Mather dismissed the belief that salvation was readily available by noting its similarity to Quaker tenets. Years later, during the Great Awakening, Charles Chauncy would invoke this rhetorical strategy, equating revivalists with Quakers.[24] Anabaptism – only rarely used in a similar way during the seventeenth century – was then likely to be coupled with Quakerism. For example, while imprisoned for disobeying his master, Job Tookie went to great pains to counter the aspersion his master had cast upon his father – that he was an "Annybaptisticall Quakeing Rogue."[25]

The association of Quakers as aliens continued for so long in large part because the Quakers themselves enhanced that image by adopting a provocatively defiant stance toward the colonial establishment. Their audacious disregard for the authority of the colony's magistrates and ministers was most marked during the first twenty years of the sect's existence in Salem. A letter to Governor John Endecott written by two incarcerated Quakers, Mary Southwick Trask and Margaret Thompson Smith, captures the extent of early Quaker disrespect. Having been in prison for eighteen months, the pair wrote describing the retribution in store for the governor. The two women described Endecott and "the rest of the Rulers" as "cruel . . . hard-hearted . . . unjust." Under the spell of the evil ministers, the magistrates "are greedily swallowing the polluted waters that come through the stinking channels of your hireling Masters, unclean spirits."[26] This declaration was a far cry from the beseeching petition Endecott must have expected from two young wives and mothers who had been kept from their families for over a year. Trask and Smith's failure to adopt the supplicants' role was typical of the Quakers, and their strident tone was standard fare during these emotionally charged early years.[27]

Between 1660, when Trask and Smith penned their letter, and 1680, when

---

responded to the interest in "mix't dancing" with *An Arrow out of the Quiver of the Scriptures* (Boston, 1684; 1686).

[24] [Henry Glover], *Essay to Discover the Principle Cause of the Anger of God, against New England* (Boston, 1690?), 1–2, 3, 5, 6; Mather, *Little Flocks Guarded*, 75. George Keith, *A Refutation of a Dangerous & hurtful Opinion Maintained by Mr. Samuel Willard* [New York, 1702], 6–7. Increase Mather, *A Discourse Proving the Christian Religion* (Boston, 1702), A3. Charles Chauncy, *Enthusiasm described and caution'd against* (Boston, 1742), 4; and *Seasonable Thoughts on the State of Religion in New England* (Boston, 1743), 80–1, 86, 173, 217.

[25] *EQC* 8:336.   [26] Bishop, *New England Judged*, 453–7.

[27] Elaine C. Huber discusses a similar letter by imprisoned English Quaker women; " 'A Woman Must Not Speak': Quaker Women in the English Left Wing," in *Women of Spirit: Female Leadership in the Jewish and Christian Traditions*, ed. Rosemary Ruether and Eleanor McLaughlin (New York: Simon & Schuster, 1979), 159–60.

the proreform faction succeeded in gaining control of the meeting, the Quakers remained openly dismissive of the dignity of the colony's leaders. Once the worst of the persecution had passed, local Quakers continued to castigate the authorities for the executions of 1659–61. Although, as Jonathan Chu has pointed out, the government distinguished between resident and foreign Quakers during the initial confrontation and treated the former with far less severity, Massachusetts Quakers did not acknowledge this distinction.[28] They thought of the martyrs as their compatriots and the injustice done them as their own. Before Salem Quakers stopped haranguing Essex County magistrates late in the 1660s, the innocent lives snuffed out needlessly at Boston was a favored topic. Whenever one of the "chief persecutors" died, local Quakers noted the details of his death, checked them for signs that God had been punishing him for his role in the atrocities, and passed on the more sensational accounts to English Friends who sometimes saw them into print.[29]

Calamities that befell the colony were interpreted by the Quakers as providential signs of God's displeasure with the persecution. They thought King Philip's War a clear indication of divine outrage on this score.[30] One of their number, probably Salem Quaker Edward Wharton, erected a monument in Boston to the martyred witnesses, which included the following inscription: "Though here our Innocent Bodyes in silent Earth do lie, Yet are our Righteous Souls at Rest, our Blood for Vengance Cry."[31] Everything from the witchcraft scare of 1692 to the failure of wheat and peas to grow in Boston, the Quakers blamed on the executions.[32] In making these interpretations, sectaries participated in what David Hall has described as the politicization of the doctrine of providence.[33]

Wharton's memorial, with its vengeful inscription, was one of the last public

---

[28] Jonathan Chu, "The Social Context of Religious Heterodoxy: The Challenge of Seventeenth-Century Quakerism to Orthodoxy in Massachusetts," *EIHC* 118 (1982): 119–50; and idem, *Neighbors, Friends, or Madmen*, esp. ch. 4.

[29] For instance, Bishop, *New England Judged*, 463–5.

[30] Dublin Quakers may not have agreed with the Salemites' interpretation; they donated provisions to the colony to aid those who had been impoverished by the war. Felt, *Ecclesiastical History*, 2:603.

[31] E[dward] W[harton], *New England's Present Sufferings under their cruel Neighboring Indians Represented in two Letters, lately Written from Boston to London* (London, 1675), 4–5. The pamphlet by the person who erected the monument has been consistently attributed to Wharton. Arthur Worrall recently suggested that Scituate Quaker Edward Wanton could have authored it but offered no reason to doubt the accepted attribution; *Quakers in the Colonial Northeast*, 207 n.33. In one of the two 1675 editions, the inscription appears at the end of the work rather than on page 5, with a slight variation in the wording. The version of the inscription recorded in "Increase Mather's Diary," 401, slightly differed yet again.

[32] Maule, *Truth Held Forth*, 175–6; *A Journal of the Life, Travels and Labours in the Ministry of John Griffiths* (London, 1779); reprinted in *The Friends' Library*, ed. Evans and Evans, 5 (1842), 341.

[33] Hall, *Worlds of Wonder*, 94–5. I would argue, however, that providence was already being used as a political tool (whether by English kings or New English ministers) before radicals seized upon it to support their cause.

attacks launched by local Quakers. Within five years, Wharton had died and the Salem meeting had turned away from such provocative tactics in favor of quietism. English Quakers, having already abandoned such methods by the time the pamphlet describing the incident appeared, ordered that it "be made wastepaper of."[34] In the future, the violent tone taken by Wharton, Trask, and Smith would fall into disuse among Salem Quakers. The last of their number publicly to denounce local leaders would be Thomas Maule, who published a series of increasingly vituperative tracts around the turn of the century. His polemical approach and unseemly insults ultimately earned him the censure of local – rather than London – Quakers. By that time, New Englanders were policing themselves for violations of the sect's testimony against violence.[35]

The later Quaker style – less vitriolic, but still distant – was captured in a second sectarian letter to a Massachusetts governor. Half a century after Trask and Smith castigated John Endecott, "antient and often ill" Salem Quaker Richard Estes wrote to Governor Joseph Dudley with a suggestion for quelling God's obvious anger at the colony. A self-described "lover of righteousness and a friend to all men," Estes reopened the sensitive subject of the Quaker executions with the approbation of the Salem Monthly Meeting. With reference to the punishments David suffered for the ill-treatment of the Gibeonites, Estes informed Dudley that "the shedding their blood hath been ye Chief thing that hath Acationed ye judgment of ye Lord on New England." The sixty-four-year-old weaver and slaymaker felt that a public condemnation of the law ordering banishment on pain of death and a public acknowledgment of the wrong that had been done to the deceased were in order.[36] Possibly inspired by the investigation into the witchcraft trials of 1692 conducted in Salem in 1710–11, Estes hoped that the government would make amends for yet another indefensible act. Needless to say, Estes – even though he would live for another quarter century – would never see the colonial government comply with his directive.[37] Although his tone was more respectful, Estes followed in the tradition of early Quakers as he judged and advised the authorities. Even in 1711, Estes did not approach the governor of Massachusetts in the same way as other colonial artisans. This stance in turn contributed to the effectiveness of presenting members of his sect as outsiders.

The Baptists, in contrast, were not so readily contained within the sectarian-as-alien theme. In part, this resulted from the very nature of that sect's dissent

[34] Quote from the minutes of the Morning Meeting in London, in Joseph Smith, *A Descriptive Catalog of Friends' Books,* 2 vols. (London, 1867), 2:878.

[35] RIYM, 1699. As late as 1690, four Massachusetts ministers declared that "many New England Quakers are far from quiet"; Allin et al., Preface to *Principles,* A5. Presumably, they were thinking of the recent past or exaggerating from Maule's case.

[36] Richard Estes to Joseph Dudley, SMM, 14 November 1711.

[37] Chadwick Hansen, *Witchcraft at Salem* (New York: Braziller, 1969), 217–19. Estes died in January 1736/7; Noyes, *Genealogical Dictionary,* 224.

from orthodoxy. Since infant baptism was widely considered to be a difficult issue, ostracizing those who dissented over it could seem excessive. This impression only increased with the passage of time, as the church became less iconoclastic and more respectable. Sweeping statements that cast Baptists as evil aliens could prove ineffective or even counterproductive when delivered to an audience disinclined to view them in such harsh terms. And since Baptists had long been fairly well integrated into the English dissenting community, denunciations of that sect were far more likely to earn the colony unwanted negative publicity there.[38] As late as 1680, Governor Simon Bradstreet confidently declared to English officials that Quakers were not Christians, a statement he did not make of the Anabaptists.[39]

Despite their comparatively benign character, the Baptists were not readily acceptable to the defenders of orthodoxy. Urian Oakes admitted that Baptists were not as bad as Quakers but advocated the need for continued vigilance against them when he commented: "It argues but an ill spirit & very low esteem of the Truth when a man dreads no Error, but that which will damn him." William Hubbard, who is credited with being the only leading New Englander openly to favor a more tolerant approach to sectarians during the 1670s, believed that the "neglect or disuse" of infant baptism would mean the end of the Christian religion. Other commentators suggested that the Baptist threat was actually the more serious of the two. And these attitudes would prove tenacious: As late as 1722, some colonists remained ready to declare Baptists heterodox.[40] That the heavy-handed tactics used against the Quakers eventually proved ill suited to the Baptists only underscored the insidious nature of the Baptists' challenge.

Unlike the Quakers, the Baptists did almost everything in their power to hamper efforts to dismiss them as pariahs. At the outset, Thomas Goold inaugurated the practice of downplaying the radicalism of the Baptists' position. Stretching the truth somewhat, he and other converts repeatedly claimed that only one, relatively minor point, their position on baptism, divided them from the established church.[41] Even in asserting their right to gather a church, the

---

[38] See Backus, *History*, 1:311–15; John Westgate to Increase Mather, *CMHS*, 4th ser., vol. 8 (1868): 579–80. Daniel Neal's sympathies went out primarily to the Baptists; *History of New England*, 2:353, 356, 367. On one of the letters dealt with by Backus, see Francis J. Bremer, "When? Who? Why?: Re-evaluating a 17th-Century Source," *PMHS* 99 (1988): 63–75.

[39] Letter to the Committee of Trade and Plantations, 18 May 1680, Public Records Office (CO5, 904), Kew, Great Britain.

[40] Urian Oakes, Preface to Mather, *Divine Right of Infant-Baptisme*, A3; William Hubbard, Epistle Dedicatory in *The Happiness of a People* (Boston, 1676), n.p.; Simon Bradstreet to Richard Baxter, in "Woodbridge–Baxter Correspondence," *NEQ* 10 (1937): 582–3; Thomas Hollis to Benjamin Colman, *Harvard College Archives*, 423.

[41] For example, see "Baptist Debate," ed. McLoughlin and Davidson, and McLoughlin's discussion in the Introduction, 98–9. Increase Mather declared this an outright lie; Preface to Willard, *Ne Sutor Ultra Crepidam*, 4.

Baptists used highly respectful language; the tactful and conciliatory tone adopted for the first time in their 1665 statement to the General Court was obviously intended to make the bitter pill of an Anabaptist church a little easier for the authorities to swallow.[42] As part of these efforts, Baptists tried to disassociate themselves from the Quakers in response to the orthodox tendency to lump them together. Mary Goold was clearly thinking of the Quakers when she wrote that the Baptists "did not disturb neither churches nor courts, neither by word nor by action, but desire to live quietly and peaceably among them."[43] Within a decade and a half of the founding of the church, the Baptists sought to make amends for some of the excesses of the early years: The church finally reviewed John Farnum's by then infamous case, concluding that his carriage had indeed been "offensive and unchristian" and requiring him to apologize to his former brethren in Boston's North Church.[44] With such conciliatory gestures, the Baptist church labored to improve its relations with the orthodox establishment.

While the Quakers seized upon King Philip's War as an opportunity to remind the larger community of its history of persecution, the Baptists responded instead with offers of assistance. The authorities did not want sectarians involved in the war effort, presumably because they thought heretics could not be trusted.[45] As a result, Baptist William Turner, who had been a sergeant in Oliver Cromwell's New Model Army, was not at first permitted to participate. When the situation became desperate, however, he was granted a captain's commission. With fellow Baptist Edward Drinker serving as lieutenant, Turner's company fought a pivotal battle in May 1676 at the falls in northwestern Massachusetts that now bears Turner's name.[46]

Henceforth, the Baptists frequently cited Turner's death in the battle and the importance of that engagement for the subsequent English victory as evidence of the great sacrifice they had made and were prepared to make for the good of the colony. John Russell, Jr., could not refrain from observing that, despite the ill treatment they had received, the Baptists had been "some of the

---

[42] SCC, [24?] October 1665.   [43] [Mary Goold's account.]

[44] John Russell, *A Brief Narrative of some Considerable Passages Concerning the First Gathering and further Progress of a Church of Christ, in Gospel Order in Boston . . . Commonly (though Falsely) called by the name of Anabaptist* (London, 1680); reprinted in Wood, *History*, 160–2.

[45] No Quakers served in any Salem company during the war according to lists compiled by George Madison Bodge, *Soldiers in King Philip's War* (Boston, 1891); yet there is no firm evidence that they were persecuted as a result of their failure to participate. In *The Present State of New-England with respect to the Indian War* ([London, 1675], reprinted in *Narratives of the Indian Wars, 1675–1699*, ed. Charles H. Lincoln [New York: Scribner's, 1913], 24–50), the author claimed that some New England Quakers were "forced to run the gantelop [gauntlet?]" for their refusal to "go out on Command" (44). The account does not specify where this incident occurred; there is no indication that it involved Salem-area Quakers.

[46] Bodge, *Soldiers in King Philip's War*, 232–5, 241–7; McLoughlin, *New England Dissent*, 74. Turner's heroism could also be used to put an end to any lingering associations between Anabaptism and pacifism, an association discussed by Gura, *Glimpse of Sion's Glory*, 116.

principal Instruments to subdue the Barbarous Heathens." The positive impact
of Turner's heroics on the sect's image was not immediate, however. Increase
Mather recorded news of Turner's near death by drowning just before the
battle as an "observable Providence" intended as a judgment against Anabaptism. He thought God made his point with particular clarity on this occasion,
noting the connection between "dipping" – that is, baptism by immersion –
and drowning. Mather neglected to record Turner's victory and death, however.[47] Clearly, the changes the Baptists sought would come only slowly.

When discussing the cause of the war in which Turner lost his life, the
Baptists took an entirely different tack than the Quakers. Whereas the Quakers
consistently cited the colony's sufferings as proof that God was enraged at the
murder of his innocent lambs, the Baptists refrained from making similar statements about the role of the persecution they had endured. In fact, Russell was
willing to see his church given some responsibility for divine wrath if the orthodox community acknowledged its share of the burden. In the face of diatribes
claiming that the toleration extended to both sects had caused the devastating
conflict, Russell calmly suggested a fair and reasonable middle ground that the
Quakers disdained.[48] In this area, as in so many others, the Baptists sought
conciliation and the Quakers demanded justice.

The different perspectives that they brought to their relationships with the
establishment are evident in the petitions written by members of both sects.
Quakers rarely petitioned the government. The role of supplicant was not one
that individual Quakers or the local Quaker meeting was ever likely to adopt.
The dearth of Quaker petitions as well as the tone of the few that were written
further attest to the sect's defiant stance. Baptist petitions provide a contrast
with those of the Quakers, in both their number and their general tone. The
Baptists' determination to appease the defenders of orthodoxy colored the petitions presented to the authorities by individual Baptists and by the church as
a whole. Comfortable with the role of supplicant, members of that sect assumed
it more frequently.

The few surviving petitions from the Quakers bear the customary opening,
"The Humble Petition of the People Called Quakers," but these documents
are far from humble. The 1707 petition by Samuel Collins and Walter Newberry to the governor and council about goods seized to pay taxes for the support of the ministry opens with a polite request for relief. However, this request
is immediately followed by a threat: The Quakers would be forced to "trouble

---

[47] Russell, *Brief Narrative*, 167. "Increase Mather's Diary," 402. However, the volume of diarial
references to sectarians all but ceased after 1680–1; only during George Keith's 1702 visit do
they recur again in comparable numbers. See the bulk of the diary, which is still in manuscript
(Mather Family Papers, AAS).

[48] Russell, *Brief Narrative*, 167–8. Like Russell, Rhode Island Baptist Samuel Hubbard thought
the war had been caused by a general lack of godliness; he wrote that New Englanders "have
not so turned to the Lord as ought to be, and his displeasure is broke forth in the country by
the natives"; quoted in Backus, *History*, 1:327.

our superiors at home" if the matter was not quickly redressed. Characterizing the official policy as "very hard and unreasonable," the pair reminded the authorities that despite the favored status their churches enjoyed in the colony, in England both the Quakers and "those under whom wee suffer are but a licensed People," all dissenters from the Church of England.[49] With its confident tone and thinly veiled threats, this petition was not the sort of plea the colonial government was accustomed to receiving from the gunsmiths and minor merchants of Massachusetts. It was, however, typical of the Quakers' few requests for changes in government policy.

During the first years, Baptist petitions were couched in the most submissive language. Petitioners humbly acquiesced to the wisdom of the authorities in incarcerating them. They hinted that they might someday be persuaded that their own position on baptism was erroneous, as when three church members "humbly beseeched" the General Court, "Let there be a bearing with us, til you shall reveal otherwise [regarding the efficacy of infant baptism] to us." They frequently offered to pray for the recipients of their pleas. They begged for mercy and apologized for bothering the magistrates at all. They appended the flattering description "honored" to most references to the magistrates and the court. In a 1670 petition, William Turner even called the General Court "the servants of Christ."[50] Entreaties submitted by these Baptists could not have differed more from the pronouncements of the first Quakers.

Later petitions by the Baptists continued in the same vein.[51] Of all the extant petitions they composed, none was more self-effacing or obsequious than that prompted by an indiscretion committed by their church elder in 1698. After more than three decades of laboring to present themselves as dutiful subjects, the church was dismayed to find that John Emblem was performing marriages without a license. Clearly distressed because this transgression of the "wholesome laws established by our honorable authority . . . gives ground for the justifying such charges" as were commonly made against it, the church condemned Emblem's transgression. The church firmly disassociating itself from him: "We do noe waies desire to justify, butt hereby declare our detestacon Against such pracktices." And it begged the court to overlook Emblem's activities. Apologizing profusely for his misconduct in his name, the petitioners even announced that Emblem "laies himself att your feet in hopes of ye Acceptance

---

[49] Samuel Collins and Walter Newberry, Petition, 21 January 1707/8, MAE, 11:235. See also Benjamin Bagnall et al., Petition to Governor Shirley, received 2 June 1748, ibid., 12:454. Richard L. Bushman (*King and People in Provincial Massachusetts* [Chapel Hill: University of North Carolina Press, 1985], 49) describes the typical petition and its humble tone.

[50] Quotes from Thomas Goold et al., Petition to the General Court, 14 October 1668, MAE, 10:220; William Turner, Petition to the General Court, 27 October 1670, ibid., 228. Also see John Russell, Sr., Petition to the General Court, October 1672, ibid., 231. For an exception, see John Pierce, Statement, 16 December 1679, MCC; even he hoped that the court would bear with him and pray for him.

[51] For example, see James Bound et al., Petition, 26 September 1739, MAE, 12:92.

of this his true & unfeigned Acknowledgementt [of his evil]."[52] This statement indicates how far the Baptists were willing to go in seeking congenial relations with the establishment. As a result, Cotton Mather never found cause to complain of Baptist ingratitude, as he did of the Quakers.[53]

The irony of the contrasting stances adopted by the Salem meeting and the Boston Baptist Church is that they are the reverse of our general understanding of these two religious groups. Quakers, known for their pacifism, seem unlikely to have "a Judging Censuring Reviling spirit," as one opponent described it.[54] Although Salem adherents to the sect did eventually move toward verbal non-violence, they remained willing at least to censure, if not to revile. Their militant style was reminiscent of an Old Testament prophet. The primary characteristics of the colonial Baptists, according to most histories, was their unrelenting advocacy of the separation of church and state.[55] Far from badgering the authorities constantly on this or any other issue – as their coreligionists would do in the later colonial period – the Boston church adopted a conciliatory tone toward the religious and civil authorities. In contrast to the Quakers' prophetic harangue, the Baptists imitated the example of the patient, long-suffering Christ. Their very presence and that of the Quakers undermined the religious establishment, but the Baptists seemed content with that. They labored to avoid otherwise challenging the authorities whenever possible.

The sectary-as-alien theme, which had never been well suited to the Baptist case, fell into disuse in the early years of the eighteenth century. In the context of imperial politics, open displays of intolerance had become increasingly unacceptable. The colony's record of persecution eventually contributed to the revocation of the original charter. Under the new provincial government established in 1692, the established church was permitted to maintain its traditional position of preeminence, and leading ministers began singing the praises of the religious liberty that the colony enjoyed. In this climate, dismissing other dissenters from the Church of England as unassimilable aliens was impolitic.[56]

---

[52] Benjamin Sweetser et al., Address to the Quarter Sessions, 23 January 1698/9, James Otis Senior Collection, MHS. See also grand jury presentments, MAE, 40:472. Despite the church's assurance that Emblem was contrite, three members but not the elder himself signed the letter.

[53] *The Serviceable Man* (Boston, 1690), 35.

[54] Roger Williams to John Trockmorton, ca. 23 July 1672, *The Correspondence of Roger Williams*, ed. Glenn La Fantasie, 2 vols. (Hanover, N.H.: Brown University Press/University Press of New England, 1988), 664.

[55] The most important recent example of this approach can be found in McLoughlin, *New England Dissent*. Denominational histories have traditionally emphasized this aspect of the Baptists' history, beginning with Isaac Backus, *History*.

[56] Bruce Tucker discusses the transatlantic political context in "The Reinterpretation of Puritan History," *NEQ* 54 (1981): 481–98; and idem, "The Reinvention of New England, 1691–1770," *NEQ* 59 (1986): 315–30. Also see Lawrence Stephen Earley, "Endangered Innocent, Arrogant Queen: Images of New England in Controversies over Puritan Persecution, 1630–1750" (Ph.D. diss., University of North Carolina, 1975).

The politics of dissent within the colony also became further complicated under the new charter. The number of sectaries under the jurisdiction of Massachusetts shot up with the inclusion of the old Plymouth Plantation within the bounds of the colony. The mechanisms for isolating sectaries would never be as effective in that region, with its tradition of a heterogeneous religious culture. And sectaries there – especially Quakers – added substantially to local agitation for legal reforms.[57] Anglican church services – introduced in Boston under Edmund Andros while the colony was incorporated into the short-lived Dominion of New England – continued to be held after Andros's government fell in 1689. The Church of England presented the colonial leaders with a special set of difficulties, since the political connections of the small but growing Anglican community rendered it powerful beyond its numbers. The suggestion, which English dissenters had long been making, that all dissenters should unite to counter the Anglican threat became more compelling with the introduction of the Church of England in various towns.[58]

With the sectarian-as-alien strategy no longer useful, the colony's leading ministers did not simply give up the fight against the sects, however. They had long since abandoned the goal of a religiously unified society, and some of them – especially in comparatively cosmopolitan Boston – were beginning to develop creative ways of dealing with diversity.[59] Under the provincial charter, they continued to face the challenge of keeping the established faith at the center of community life. Part of their program for doing so involved addressing the criticism of orthodoxy that adherents of other faiths presented to the colonial populace. Educating colonists about the theological distinctions that elevated orthodoxy over other faiths proved a better tactic in the battle against sectarianism in the eighteenth century. Just as the Quaker threat had shaped the sectarian-as-alien theme used in the preceding century, the Baptist faith was instrumental for the development of this educational program.

For years, orthodox ministers had been paying special attention to the somewhat hazy boundary between the established and Baptist faiths. They had begun cautioning their congregations to avoid the errors of Anabaptism years before the Boston Baptist Church had been founded. The halfway covenant,

[57] J. M. Bumstead, "The Pilgrims' Progress: An Ecclesiastical History of Southwestern Massachusetts, 1620–1776" (Ph.D. diss., Brown University, 1965), 33–4, 53, 55–9; and idem, "A Well-Bounded Toleration: Church and State in the Plymouth Colony," *Journal of Church and State* 10 (1968): 278–9.

[58] For this argument, see Thomas Hollis to John Leverett, *Harvard College Archives*, 447. A New English example of this alliance occurred when one of the Baptist elders joined the committee of religious and civil leaders that orchestrated the overthrow of the dominion government; David S. Lovejoy, *The Glorious Revolution in America* (New York: Harper & Row, 1972), 240. On the spread of Anglicanism, see John Frederick Woolverton, *Colonial Anglicanism in North America* (Detroit: Wayne State University Press, 1984), 112–15.

[59] See, e.g., Middlekauff, *The Mathers*, 305–19.

widely debated on the eve of the church's founding, brought these issues into stark relief. When discussing the proposed extension of baptism, concerned clergy frequently commented on whether the reform would help or hinder their continuing efforts against the Anabaptist heresy.[60] In making the case for the change, pamphleteers might dismiss their opponents' views as Anabaptism, but they also labored to explicate covenant theology in order to show that infant baptism was, in fact, mandated by Scriptures.[61]

An educational campaign had been one component of the fight against the Baptist church at least since 1668, when the government had hosted a public debate with church members and others who were "anabaptistically" inclined. Tracts defending the "divine right of infant baptism" – as Increase Mather's 1680 publication unequivocally termed it – addressed the questions raised by antipedobaptists in detail. The defenders of orthodoxy frequently highlighted specific contrasts, as when they accused Baptists of cruelty to parents who were denied the solace of bringing a child into the church. This charge, although undoubtedly effective, was at the top of a slippery slope, for the Quakers could hurl similar accusations against the established faith; visiting Quaker George Keith did just that in 1690.[62] Every time a minister preached a sermon on baptism, parental obligations, or the covenants, he contributed to the cause. The ministers urged one another to reach out to a wider audience by publishing simple statements – "adapted to the meanest capacity" – explaining how best to defend the orthodox position.[63]

After the turn of the century, educational efforts by the ministry became more systematic. Beginning with Cotton Mather's *Baptistes* in 1705, the Boston press issued numerous catechisms intended to prevent the spread of the sect's views. These guides were designed to assist the believer in fending off the arguments made by Baptists. Ministers often used a question-and-answer format, with a pastor responding to the queries of a confused but respectful parishioner.[64] Others – such as William Williams, who issued a pair of tracts in

---

[60] [   ] Russell, "Antisynodalia," [1672]; and anonymous essay fragment regarding the 1662 synod, both in Mather Family Papers, AAS.

[61] [Richard Mather], *A Defense of the Answer and Arguments of the Synod* (Cambridge, 1664), 13; Mitchell, *Answer to the Apologetical Preface*, 5–6, 7, 27, 37.

[62] Urian Oakes, Preface to Mather, *Divine Right of Infant-Baptisme*, ii; John Allin, quoted in "Baptist Debate," ed. McLoughlin and Davidson, 109. In *The Pretended Antidote Proved Poyson* ([Philadelphia, 1690], 114), Keith deemed their willingness to accept the damnation of infants "cruel & hard-hearted."

[63] Simon Bradstreet to Increase Mather, 20 April 1681, *CMHS*, 4th ser., vol. 8 (1868): 477, stated, "Three sheets of paper, well filled by a dexterous & able hand . . . would profit the world more than all Dr. Owen, Mr. Baxter, Mr Hughs, etc. have written" in defense of the Sabbath (against which Bradstreet believed Anabaptists and others argued). George Curwin quoted by Benjamin Wadsworth, *The Bonds of Baptism* (Boston, 1717), preface.

[64] Cotton Mather, *Baptistes* (Boston, 1705; 2d ed., 1724). See, e.g., idem, *The Man of God Furnished* (Boston, 1708); Benjamin Wadsworth, *Some Considerations About Baptism* (Boston, 1719).

1721 – wrote on the related issues of the responsibilities of parents and children inherent in the orthodox approach to baptism.[65] In 1719, Boston presses began producing pamphlets favoring infant baptism written in response to pro-Baptist publications that had been issued elsewhere.[66] For the next twenty-five years, only one or possibly two works offering the other side of the argument were published on Boston's presses.[67]

The ministry never launched a similarly sophisticated educational campaign to combat Quakerism.[68] The only Massachusetts cleric who offered to educate the laity against the "manifold heresies and blasphemies" of Quakerism was the incomparably prolific Cotton Mather. In a 1691 diatribe aimed at then Quaker missionary George Keith, who had been trading insults with Massachusetts leaders for two years, Mather included a lengthy list of assertions the orthodox could use to ward off Quaker proselytizers.[69] In contrast to tracts intended to counter Anabaptism, Mather made no effort to persuade the uncertain; rather, he simply asserted orthodox positions as if they constituted self-evident refutations of Quakerism. In 1708, he produced an ambitious catechism intended to arm the "man of God" with arguments against all the errors (and then some) that he might conceivably confront in the colony, including Quakerism, Socianism, Pelagianism, Antinomianism, Anabaptism, and Sabbatarianism.[70] With the exception of the indefatigable Mather, Massachusetts ministers did not prepare written guides refuting Quakerism comparable to those on antipedobaptism.

Although detailed refutations of the sect's tenets were not generally produced by Bay colony authors, publications by others were occasionally issued from Boston presses. After Roger Williams wrote an account of a 1672 public disputation that he had with three Quakers in Rhode Island, Massachusetts

---

[65] William Williams, *The Obligations of Baptism, and the Duty of Young People to Recognize Them* (Boston, 1721); idem, *The Duty of Parents to Transmit Religion to their Children* (Boston, 1721).

[66] Joseph Lord, *Reason Why, Not Anabaptist Plunging But Infant-Believer's Baptism Ought to be Approved* (Boston, 1719); Peter Clark, *The Scripture Grounds of the Baptism of Xtians Infants . . . Asserted* (Boston, 1735).

[67] A 1723 reprint of John Norcott's popular *Baptism Discovered Plainly and Faithfully* may have been published in Boston; McLoughlin suspects that publication was sponsored by the Boston church (*New England Dissent,* 317). In 1738, John Walton's *Vindication of the True Christian Baptism* was certainly reprinted in Boston. Another reprint of Norcott's work in 1747 would begin an avalanche of Baptist tracts.

[68] In 1659, the General Court ordered the publication of a broadside on Quakerism; both it and a longer document circulated at the same time in manuscript focused on justifying the executions, however. *RMB* 4, pt. 1:384–90.

[69] Mather, *Little Flocks Guarded,* title page, 59–94.

[70] Cotton Mather, *The Man of God Furnished, The Way of Truth Laid Out* (Boston, 1708), 72–81; see the second essay, "Supplies from the Tower of David." Two years before, Mather completed another anti-Quaker tract, "New And Remarkable Discoveries"; but, as it was never published and no manuscript copies are extant, the nature of that effort can only be surmised from its somewhat sensational title. See "Diary of Cotton Mather," 7:571–2.

governor John Leverett paid to have *George Fox Digg'd Out of His Burrowes* published in Boston. Leverett later gave copies of the tract to his friends.[71] In 1682, Samuel Sewall arranged for the publication of an account of a minister's dealings with Quakers on the island of Bermuda. A second anti-Quaker effort by a Rhode Islander, Pardon Tillinghast's *Water Baptism* (1689), may have also been issued in Boston. An elder in a Providence Baptist church, Tillinghast wrote to defend the ordinance of baptism generally against the Quaker belief that only baptism by the spirit was required of God's people.[72] In 1709, the indomitable George Keith was finally published by a Boston press. Written during Keith's Anglican phase, *A Serious Call to the Quakers inviting them to return to Christianity* had appeared in three editions in London before a Boston printer issued it. Just as some Massachusetts authors wrote to help the laity ward off Baptists, Keith intended *A Serious Call* to be used by people who found themselves confronted with Quakers: "All Good Christians are desired to have this sheet in their Houses, and as they have opportunity, to shew the Poor Deluded Quakers their Errors."[73]

As the cases of Williams, Keith, and possibly Tillinghast indicate, Massachusetts leaders willingly accepted the assistance of odd allies in their battle against Quakerism. Under normal circumstances, these three men would not have been published in Boston. Williams, who had previously been banished for his dangerous religious and political views, still had a tense relationship with the Massachusetts government. Yet Williams would win the praises of even Cotton Mather for his able defense of the "main principles of the Protestant religion."[74] If Tillinghast's work was published in Boston, it predated any other Baptist tract by at least thirty-four years.[75] That the Anglican George Keith was called upon to assist in fending off the Quakers was equally surprising. Significantly, the edition of Keith's tract produced in Boston omitted direct references to the Anglican clergy as well as a spirited effort to excuse Keith's previous stint as a Quaker, suggesting the limits of the colonial elite's readiness to

[71] (Boston, 1676). Williams's title puns on the names of two prominent English Quakers, George Fox and Edward Burroughs, neither of whom had participated in the debate. For Leverett's role, see *Correspondence of Roger Williams*, 689–90. Cambridge minister Thomas Shepard inscribed on the title page of his copy (now owned by the John Carter Brown Library) "given me by ye honorable Jno Leveret, Governor of ye Massachusetts, 30:6:77." George Fox correctly asserted that Leverett was not ashamed of his role; *Something in Answer to a Letter* (London, [1678?]), 1.

[72] Sampson Bond, *A Publick Tryal of the Quakers in Barmudas* (Boston, 1682). Tillinghast, *Water Baptism Plainly Proved by Scriptures* ([Boston]: 1689), responded to a "paper" by then-Quaker George Keith.

[73] *A Serious Call*, 4th ed. (Boston, 1709), 16. Keith claimed that Boston printers refused to publish one of his earlier works for fear of offending the ministers; *A Journal of Travels from New-Hampshire to Caratuck* (London, 1706), 2. Presumably, he was referring to *A Reply to Mr. Increase Mather's Printed Remarks* (New York, 1703).

[74] Mather, *Magnalia*, 2:433.

[75] That is, assuming that Norcott's 1723 *Baptism Discovered* was issued in Boston. Otherwise, John Walton's *Vindication* (1738) was the next Baptist tract published there.

countenance a lesser evil in warding off a greater one. Even these cases, in which Boston presses produced works aimed at combating specific Quaker ideas, affirmed the predominant image of the alien Quaker; for only in fighting these heretics would the orthodox ally themselves with such unlikely associates as Keith, Williams, and Tillinghast.[76]

The urgency of isolating Quakers from the larger society declined as a result of changes within the Salem Quaker community itself. Arguably, so little energy was expended educating the populace against the Quaker threat because there was simply no need. Presenting the sect as antithetical to the New England way proved an effective strategy initially. By the turn of the century, when local Quakers had abandoned their evangelical fervor and become inward looking, they were making no serious effort to expand their sect. Since colonists were unlikely to arrive at Quaker tenets in isolation from the influence of the already convinced, the possibility that the error would spread was minimal. Under these circumstances, painstakingly disproving specific Quaker beliefs only served to broadcast them. With antipedobaptist sentiments circulating more widely – even in the absence of evangelical efforts on the part of individual Baptists – ministers realized that point-by-point refutations, which might do some good, surely could do no additional harm. Once the clergy dropped the Quaker-as-alien theme, they simply gave up attacking the sect altogether.

As the assaults on Quakerism sputtered to a halt, the battle against the Baptist faith had to be carried on. In the early eighteenth century, colonists were as likely to toy with Baptist beliefs as they had been in Thomas Goold's day. Ministers labored to convince them that the established faith accurately expressed God's plan for his people. Despite their continued vigilance, the number of Baptist converts began to increase slowly in the late 1730s. A number of new churches were gathered with the help of the Boston Baptist Church during the years just before the Great Awakening.[77] This trickle of Baptist conversions would turn into a veritable flood after the revival. When that happened, established church ministers would continue to use the strategies they had developed to combat the influence of the Boston Baptists – issuing pamphlets, preaching sermons, and counseling privately those in danger of apostasy. Only the vigorousness of this competition for souls would be new.

With these conflicts still in the future, relations between the establishment and the sects attained an equilibrium of sorts by 1730. The legal persecution of the sects had largely passed.[78] Ministers no longer publicly derided either

---

[76] Samuel Bond, whose tract Sewall published in 1682, may have been another odd ally, for he apparently left Boston after delivering a plagiarized sermon; see Hutchinson, *History*, 1:361.

[77] These churches were gathered by former members of the Boston church who sought help with establishing a new church as they were dismissed from the one in Boston; see Baptist Record Book, 3 August 1735, October 1740, 4 November 1741.

[78] Such Quaker testimonies as pacifism continued to lead occasionally to conflict between that sect and the authorities; see Worrall, *Quakers in the Colonial Northeast*, ch. 8.

the Quakers or the Baptists. An ecumenical movement within the transatlantic English dissenting community that encompassed Baptists, if not Quakers, had been popular for some time among some Massachusetts religious leaders.[79] The cosmopolitan Boston minister Benjamin Colman took this tendency to an extreme, refusing to participate in the 1718 ordination of Elisha Callendar because he deemed the Baptists insufficiently ecumenical – despite the fact that he clearly approved of the change in interchurch relations that the event marked.[80] These liberal tendencies were generally balanced by a determination on the part of ministers to promote their own faith in competition with others. The orthodox had finally taken the advice given by their English brethren during the previous century: With the passage of the 1727 law granting relief from ministerial taxation, sectarians were accorded treatment befitting fellow Protestant dissenters from the Church of England. Indeed, this legislation granted colonial dissenters a better arrangement than English nonconformists had.[81]

These comparatively amiable relations created an unforeseen problem for the orthodox establishment. In the context of improved relations, the intolerance of the early years appeared increasingly unjustifiable. Dutch Quaker Willem Sewel added to these difficulties by reopening the subject of the executions in a history published in London in 1722.[82] The fact that colonial leaders had initially defended the continued suppression of sectarianism by citing the words and deeds of the first generation of colonists only made matters worse, for the veneration of the founders served as a major component in their campaign to foster social unity.[83] Cotton Mather, who was bent on defending the reputations of his ancestors, labored to persuade his audiences that early sectarians – especially the Quakers – were thoroughly unlike their contemporary counterparts. Even Mather eventually dropped this strategy, apparently concluding that his presentation of the staid Quakers as dangerous radicals or raving lunatics was not persuasive.[84]

Yet in a sense, Mather was right. Both sects had changed remarkably in the

---

[79] See Fiering, "The First American Enlightenment." For an early statement signaling a willingness to include Baptists, see Mather, *Surest Way*, 15–16.

[80] Benjamin Colman to Robert Wodrow, 23 January 1719/20, in "Some Unpublished Letters of Benjamin Colman, 1717–1725," ed. Niel Caplan, *PMHS* 77 (1966): 113. A number of Baptists apparently appreciated Colman's ecumenism, seeking him out to solemnize their marriages when the Baptist church elder was unable to do so; *The Manifesto Church: Records of the Church in Brattle Square, Boston . . . 1699–1872*, ed. Ellis Loring Motte (Boston, 1902), 232, 245.

[81] McLoughlin, *New England Dissent*, ch. 13; Thomas J. Curry, *The First Freedoms: Church and State in America to the Passage of the First Amendment* (New York: Oxford University Press, 1986), 89–90.

[82] Sewel, *History of the Quakers*.

[83] Thomas Shepard, *Eye-salve or a watch-word from our Lord Jesus Christ unto his church* (Boston, 1673), 24–5. Stout deals with the glorification of the ancestors, *New England Soul*, 54–6, 67–8.

[84] For an instance of Mather's efforts, see *Magnalia*, 2:451–3.

PART III

Culmination

8

Denomination and sect,
1740–1780

During the late colonial period, both the Boston Baptist Church and the Salem Quaker meeting experienced a crisis in their relationships with the larger society. In the Baptists' case, the church's traditionally accommodating stance created difficulties during the Great Awakening. Only gradually did the church recover from the malaise that overcame it during the 1740s and 1750s, finally forging a denominational identity that undergirded its penchant for accommodation with a newfound strength. The Quakers, who had not previously felt welcomed into colonial society, first confronted opportunities for integration in the post-awakening years. Rather than follow the Baptists in recasting themselves as a denomination, the Quakers rejected these opportunities for social and religious intercourse during the revolutionary years. They chose to remain sectarians. By the end of the colonial period, the Baptists and the Quakers emerged from these ordeals firmly committed to diametrically opposed conceptions of their identities.

Few Massachusetts churches suffered greater upheaval as a result of the Great Awakening than did the Boston Baptist Church. By the early 1740s, the church identified so thoroughly with the establishment that it became caught up in the struggles that divided the orthodox community. Although the Great Awakening would ultimately foster the spread of the Baptist faith, the oldest Baptist church in the colony was traumatized rather than rejuvenated by the revival experience. The troubling implications inherent in the church's accommodating approach played themselves out during the revivals and the years that followed. Only in the mid-1760s did the Baptist church begin to recover. Under the direction of a new minister, the church was finally able to maintain both its traditional stance of accommodation and its viability as a distinctive religious organization. The Baptists assumed the characteristics of a denomination.

The Boston Baptist Church entered the 1740s primed to reject the predestinarian doctrinal emphasis, the religious enthusiasm, and the social leveling of the Great Awakening. In the late 1730s, the brethren had chosen as their new minister the urbane and liberal Jeremiah Condy, a young man with many ties to Boston's ministerial elite and the polish acquired during a stint in Great

Britain.[1] They seemingly found these traits particularly desirable, for they went out of their way to choose Condy over the less illustrious Edward Upham. Although both men had received educations at Harvard and had undergone believer's baptisms, the church preferred the better connected and more sophisticated Condy over the more readily available Upham.[2] In making its selection, the church chose a man who would be disinclined to endorse revivalism.

Apparently a substantial number of church members were similarly disinclined. As the revival was sweeping through Boston, Condy – responding to criticisms of his pulpit message – asserted that the majority of members did not want him to preach the doctrine of election.[3] This drift away from the Reformed position among at least some church members may have been connected to a compatible shift in the composition of church membership. Leading Boston families had been experiencing unprecedented multigenerational conversions. If a belief in predestination was consistent with the church's traditionally atomized membership, a departure from that position may have been linked to this group's unusual conversion patterns, explaining and giving legitimacy to them. These Boston Baptist families included most of the church's lay officers, and they strongly supported both Condy's theological views and his ministry.[4]

In the months preceding the call to Condy, the church had signaled its discomfort with lay leadership – which would be an important point of contention during the revivals. With the untimely death of Elisha Callendar in March 1738, the Baptists were without an elder for the first time in two decades. Despite a history of preaching and baptisms by lay officers, the church did not function again fully until Callendar was replaced with Condy. The brethren contracted with Edward Upham, a Harvard-educated church member searching for a pulpit, to preach; they also tried, without noteworthy success, to arrange to have Boston's congregationalist ministers deliver the second Sabbath sermon in rotation.[5] Baptisms all but ceased; three candidates propounded by Callendar before his death were baptized months later by Elisha's nephew John Callendar

---

[1] Sibley and Shifton, *Sibley's Harvard Graduates*, 8:20–30. Condy's theological liberalism was made apparent in two published sermons, *The Godly and Faithful Man Characterized* (Boston, 1747), and *Mercy Exemplified in the Conduct of a Samaritan* (Cambridge, 1767).

[2] Baptist Record Book, 2 April, 20 August, 12 October, 24 December 1738. On Upham, see Sibley and Shifton, *Sibley's Harvard Graduates*, 9:443–8.

[3] Albert H. Newman, *A History of the Baptist Churches in the United States* (New York: Christian Literature, 1894), 256.

[4] These family connections are described in Chapter 5. Only one member of either of these two leading families, Abiah Callendar Doane, was among the vocal opposition to Condy; see Baptist Record Book, 17 January, 14 February 1743.

[5] McLoughlin states that the Boston ministers complied with the request (*New England Dissent*, 293); the entry in the Baptist Record Book that he cites for this information (31 March 1738) makes no mention of these ministers. The only reference to them (2 April) states that they were to be asked but not whether they complied. When Upham's three-month contract was renewed, his duties were expanded to include the afternoon sermon as well, which suggests that the non-Baptist Boston ministers had not, in fact, been cooperative.

on a pastoral visit from his Newport church.[6] The assumption that only learned and ordained men were qualified to provide leadership – clearly conveyed in these actions – would dictate the church's rejection of the efforts of some revivalists to empower the laity.

With Condy at its helm and the majority of the church members who resided in Boston supportive of his theological liberalism and pleased with his genteel personal style, the Boston Baptist Church eventually emerged as an opponent of the Great Awakening. No evidence remains of the reaction that Condy and his flock had to the first preaching tour of George Whitefield, which inaugurated a series of revivals in eastern Massachusetts. Like others who would ultimately oppose the Great Awakening, the Boston Baptists may have been receptive at the outset. Pious people from across a broad spectrum of opinion welcomed the upsurge in religiosity that Whitefield's initial visit brought. With the ecumenical bent typical of eighteenth-century religious liberals, Condy may well have applauded Whitefield's own ecumenism, for the "grand itinerant" – though himself an Anglican – consciously preached a nondenominational message and explicitly included Baptists among those who could be truly saved.[7] Subsequently, the radical potential of the revivals become apparent, as leading revivalists broadcast their criticisms of the unconverted, lay exhorters took to the road to preach, and some converts displayed signs of "enthusiasm."[8] By this stage, if not earlier, the Boston Baptist Church was officially in the anti-revival, or "Old Light," camp.

As in many Old Light churches, a schism tore the Boston Baptist Church apart, because a faction within it was unwilling to dismiss the revival movement.[9] In 1742, this group stopped attending worship services and began to criticize Condy and the church openly. They believed the church had been corrupted by Arminianism, by which they meant a belief that a person could bring about his or her own salvation through good works. Condy, they averred, "softens, moderates and explains away the guilt, malignity, corruption and depravity of human nature exactly as the high Arminian clergy forever do." Four brethren sent a letter to the church demanding that Condy state his views on the interlocking theological issues that lay at the heart of their disagreement. Not only did Condy refuse to discuss their objections, but the church proceeded to discipline the members of this disgruntled faction.[10]

In July 1743, Condy's critics joined with other Bostonians to gather another Baptist church, one that they claimed was the true heir of the church founded

---

[6] Baptist Record Book, 2 April, 9 July 1738.

[7] The Continuation of the Reverend Mr. Whitefield's Journal (London and Boston, 1741), 49.

[8] Edwin S. Gaustad, The Great Awakening in New England (Gloucester, Mass.: Peter Smith, 1965), ch. 5.

[9] Ibid., 120; Wood, History, ch. 11.

[10] Baptist Record Book, 1742–3. Portions of the letter are quoted in Backus, History, 2:421, and Wood, History, 240–1.

in Charlestown nearly eighty years before. As many as a dozen members of
Condy's church – probably at least 10 percent of the total number – participated in the exodus during the 1740s.[11] The new church, which chose Boston
artisan Ephraim Bound as its elder, upheld theological positions reminiscent of
the founding generation of Baptists and of seventeenth-century Reformed
Protestants generally. Presenting the Baptists who remained in Condy's church
as usurpers, the schismatics tried to claim the name "First Boston Baptist Church"
for themselves. As the 1742 letter to Condy's church declared:

> Their godly ancestors, the first founders of said church, were strict Calvin-
> ists as to the points aforementioned [eternal election, original sin, grace in
> conversion, justification by faith, the Saints perseverance], nor would they
> by any means, as we can prove, suffer a Free Willer or Arminian, if they
> knew a person to be so, to join with the church.[12]

Indeed, Goold and his companions would probably have found the new church,
which met in private homes to hear the evangelical exhortations of a leather
breechesmaker, more congenial than Condy's church, which met in the meetinghouse by the Mill Pond to listen to the learned discourse of the liberal and
sophisticated Condy. Tellingly, schismatic Ruth Bound echoed Thomas Goold's
statement to the representatives of orthodoxy when she informed Condy's church
that she refused to meet with it any longer because "the text 'come out from
among them and be ye separate' had been much on her mind."[13]

In the anomalous position of an Old Light Baptist church, the church suffered more than the loss of these members in the years following the schism.
Admissions dropped off sharply. Having admitted eighteen new members during the four years from his ordination until the schism, Condy would wait another thirteen years before surpassing that number.[14] Bostonians inclined toward
antipedobaptism were far more likely to join the rival church; it grew to 120
communicants by 1765, while the first church shrunk to half that size.[15] And
Bostonians whose primary concern was hearing liberal Christianity preached
might attend any number of other Boston churches, most of them more vigorous and all of them more respectable than Condy's antipedobaptist church.[16]

---

[11] Wood, *History*, 240–2; McLoughlin, *New England Dissent*, 320–2. The second Baptist church's
records are no longer extant, but Thomas Ford Caldicott (*A Concise History of the Baldwin Place
Baptist Church* [Boston, 1854], 20) reported that the founding members numbered seven (which
was standard in New England) and were soon joined by twenty-six others.

[12] Wood, *History*, 240–1.   [13] Baptist Record Book, 23 November 1742.

[14] Baptist Record Book, 1739–56. By contrast, the second four years of Elisha Callendar's ministry
witnessed a two-thirds increase over the first four years; ibid., 1718–26.

[15] Wood, *History*, 242. Bound's church attracted some communicants from beyond Boston, as the
first church had formerly done. For certificates of two Lynn members, see *Towne Meetings of
Lyn*, 5:12.

[16] One of the few staunchly Old Light churches in Boston was that of Mather Byles, whose half-

During the same period, members who lived outside Boston – the "country" brethren as Condy described them – gradually ceased to contribute toward his support.[17] Along with the cancellation of his poorly attended weekly lectures in 1742, these developments marked a substantial loss of income for Condy, who turned his attentions to an alternative career as a bookseller.[18] Early in 1751, Condy requested dismissal from his position as minister, eager to devote all of his time to this comparatively lucrative and intellectually stimulating endeavor. Thirteen years passed before Condy's request was complied with, during which time he continued as the church's uninspiring and occasionally absent minister.[19] While a plethora of Baptist churches were springing up all over the colony in the wake of the New Light movement, the original Particular Baptist church in the colony was, ironically, in decline.[20]

The problems the Boston Baptist Church experienced arose directly out of its seventy-five-year history. The church had slowly moved away from many of the practices and principles that had characterized it initially. Unable to produce a second generation of suitable leaders and perhaps impressed by the more learned discourse of John Myles, the Oxford-educated minister who preached to them briefly in the 1670s, the church experienced a leadership crisis late in the seventeenth century. Not until the ordination of Elisha Callendar in 1718 would it succeed in producing an acceptable leader from its own ranks. But Callendar's ordination heralded other troublesome developments, for his Harvard training and the participation of neighboring congregationalist ministers in his ordination signaled a growing dependence on the orthodox community. With worship services becoming more structured and a formally educated and ordained leader installed over the church, the Baptists abandoned a tradition of "mechanic" preaching, that is, by artisans, and deemphasized – at least – the role of lay prophecy. To make the transformation complete, a group of leading families became uncomfortable with the doctrine of limited redemption, preferring a more inclusive religious body over a strictly pure church.

brother Josiah was a deacon in Condy's church; Gaustad, *Great Awakening in New England*, 55–6.

[17] Baptist Record Book, 17 February 1750/1. These people never officially terminated their relations with the church.

[18] Ibid., 31 October 1742. See Reilly, "Wages of Piety," 83–131. Condy's account book dates from 1758, by which time his business was well underway. Reilly speculates that he entered the book trade after he appealed to the church to release him in 1750 (actually 1750/1). In all probability, he began his business even earlier and, by 1751, was ready to expand it to support himself and his family fully. See ibid., 83n.

[19] Baptist Record Book, 17 February 1750/1, August 1764–January 1765. Condy spent a year in London in the early 1760s, during which time he arranged to have "his friends" preach to the church; see Reilly, "Wages of Piety," 87, and Baptist Record Book, 8 June 1760.

[20] C. C. Goen, *Revivalism and Separatism in New England, 1740–1800: Strict Congregationalists and Separate Baptists in the Great Awakening* (New Haven, Conn.: Yale University Press, 1962), ch. 6. At his death, Condy's obituary suggested that he was abused because he refused to conform to fashion; *Boston Weekly News Letter*, 1 September 1768.

In calling the erudite Jeremiah Condy to serve as their minister, this core group within the church openly declared their preference for liberal theology and amiable relations with the established churches.[21]

In the 1740s, the Boston Baptists were forced to confront the implications of these changes. The church no longer represented a distinct alternative to colonial orthodoxy and therefore did not reap the rewards of upheaval within the ranks of the established faith. Indeed, the Baptist church was so completely integrated into the orthodox fold that the religious divisions that wracked the larger community similarly affected the Baptists. Far from benefiting from a crisis in colonial religious life – a crisis that might well have redounded to their benefit – the Baptists fought among themselves as did their congregational neighbors.

Only during the revolutionary era would the church recover from its experience as an Old Light Baptist church, achieving a balance between its traditionally amicable relations with the orthodox community and its own distinctive identity. With a new minister, an unprecedented opportunity to participate in denominational activities, and a renewed commitment to Reformed Protestant principles, the church was able to adjust to its circumstances as one denomination among many in late colonial Boston. During these years, the First Boston Baptist Church emerged as a viable competitor in Boston's spiritual marketplace, with many of the characteristics of a denomination.[22]

One reason for the church's prosperity was its new, charismatic minister, Samuel Stillman (1765–1807).[23] Although perhaps not as socially polished as Jeremiah Condy, Stillman was college educated and highly respectable. He had a modestly evangelical preaching style. Under Stillman, the church reaffirmed its commitment to those doctrines – "Election, Effectual Calling, [Perseverance] in Grace to Glory and Justification by the Righteousness of Jesus Christ" – that had been deemphasized during Condy's ministry.[24] After twenty years of declining membership, the church's fortunes were reversed. Stillman's evangelical style successfully competed with Boston's other preachers, drawing in new members – including many from the rival Baptist church – and a sizable unbaptized congregation. The church experienced sustained growth as well as occasional major revivals throughout Stillman's four-decade-long ministry.[25]

---

[21] Condy's attitudes toward the larger community (as well as his abhorrence of quarreling) are captured in his letter to Mitchell Sewall, 14 February 1737/8, Curwin Family Papers, AAS.

[22] Sidney Mead outlines these characteristics in "Denominationalism," 103–33. The church's records first used the term in July 1765, Baptist Record Book.

[23] "Biographical Sketch of the Author's Life," in *Select Sermons on Doctrinal and Practical Subjects, by the late Samuel Stillman* (Boston, 1808), v–xx.

[24] The quotation is taken from First Boston Baptist Church to the Warren Association, 31 August 1770, Backus Papers, ANTS. Early in his ministry, Stillman preached a series of sermons on the human propensity to trust in personal righteousness and the need for total reliance on God; see Samuel Stillman, *Four Sermons* (Boston, 1769).

[25] Baptist Record Book, 7 July 1765; Wood, *History*, 244–302. According to Isaac Backus, Still-

With so many other Baptist churches in the colony competing for new members in outlying areas, the members drawn in by Stillman's preaching tended to be local residents. Unlike earlier generations of church members, these people were able to participate actively in the community life of the church.

The Baptists were able to balance this competitive evangelizing against continued congenial relations with their non-Baptist neighbors. No incident captures the extent of the church's rapport with the larger community better than the temporary merger of its worship services with those of the congregational New Brick Church for six months in 1771.[26] Because the burgeoning Baptist congregation had outgrown its almost century-old meetinghouse – a fact that offers one indication of Stillman's success as an evangelist – the brethren decided to erect a new structure on the site of the old one. During the period between the demolition of the old building and the completion of the new, they arranged to meet in Ebenezer Pemberton's church with Stillman and Pemberton dividing the preaching to the combined congregation between them. Apparently without qualms about leaving his flock in the hands of this New Light Congregationalist, Stillman visited Philadelphia briefly during these months.[27] From 23 June until 15 December 1771, according to the Baptist church records, the "two Societies maintained a happy Union & Friendship."[28]

In another display of the church's rapport with the larger community, Stillman and many of his parishioners entered enthusiastically into the patriot cause. At a time when other Baptists were using the revolutionaries' need for popular support to pressure them into guaranteeing the separation of church and state, Stillman was speaking publicly on the patriots' behalf, and many church members were enlisting.[29] While in Philadelphia during the siege of Boston, Still-

man's success led to a rise in anti-Baptist publications between 1765 and 1773; *History*, 2:419–20. During Stillman's ministry, the church fared better than its Boston rival; see Caldicott, *Concise History*, 42.

[26] Also consider Stillman's unprecedented request that a candidate for admission arrange to be dismissed from her local congregational church; Baptist Record Book, 5 July 1772.

[27] John Boyle, "Boyle's Journal of Occurrences in Boston, 1759–1778," *NEHGR* 84 (1930): 271. On Ebenezer Pemberton, a Harvard-trained New Light who itinerated through New England from his New York City pulpit during the awakening and took over the New Brick Church in 1753, see Frederick Lewis Weis, *The Colonial Clergy and the Colonial Churches of New England* (Lancaster, Mass.: Society of the Descendants of the Colonial Clergy, 1936), 162; and Gaustad, *Great Awakening in New England*, 25.

[28] Baptist Record Book, 14, 31 May; 8 December 1771.

[29] Stillman's patriotism was praised in a poem Ezra Stiles copied into his diary under the heading "Ludicrous descriptions of the Boston Ministers as to Liberty about 1772"; *Literary Diary of Ezra Stiles*, ed. Dexter, 1:491–2. For his patriot activities, see Wood, *History*, 268, 272–3. As many as 40 church members – out of a total membership in 1777 of only 137 – fought on the patriot side; *Massachusetts Soldiers and Sailors of the Revolutionary War*, 17 vols. (Boston: Wright & Potter, 1896–1908), lists participants; "A List of all the Baptist churches in New England," 1777–82, comp. Isaac Backus, Backus Papers, ANTS, provides the number of members in

man preached to the Continental Congress, giving a funeral sermon for delegate Samuel Ward, a Rhode Island Baptist.[30]

The Baptists' identification with the larger community was not complete, however, for they were also conscious of themselves as members of a distinctive religious community. For the first time in its history, the First Boston Baptist Church engaged in various denominational projects. Coincident with Stillman's ordination, New England Particular Baptists began to create denominational organizations; Rhode Island College was founded in 1764 and the Warren Association – the first formal association of Calvinist Baptists in New England – three years later. After a century of isolation, the church entered into these organizations energetically, sending representatives to the Warren Association meetings and supporting the newly founded college.[31]

Pulled in various directions, Samuel Stillman and the First Boston Baptist Church successfully navigated a middle course during the revolutionary period. An evangelical in comparison to Jeremiah Condy, Stillman refrained from the emotionalism of some revival preachers. Generally his auditors concurred; according to one critic, Stillman expressed amazement on a rare occasion when he witnessed an emotional display in response to his preaching. Apparently only Sarah Drowne Condy found him too evangelical for her tastes.[32] A member who complained about the conservatism of the church was also a rarity. The expanding membership overwhelmingly approved of Stillman's approach.[33] As a patriot as well, Stillman adopted a moderate tone, in contrast, for instance, to the radical John Allen, who was preaching to the Second Boston Baptist Church in 1772–3.[34] With similar moderation, Stillman and some lay members occasionally supported the efforts of Baptists who were militant on the question of

1777. (In comparison, as few as two and perhaps only as many as four can be identified as Loyalists.)

[30] *Letters of John Adams, Addressed to his wife*, ed. Charles Francis Adams (Boston, 1841), 1:93 (spine title: *Adams Letters*, vol. 3). Adams used the term "Anabaptist" to refer to Stillman.

[31] McLoughlin, *New England Dissent*, ch. 27.

[32] *The Life, Conversion, Preaching, Travels, and Sufferings of Elias Smith* (Portsmouth, N.H., 1816), 284; according to an appalled Smith, the man apologized afterwards. On Condy, see Wood, *History*, 253. Her objections may have been fueled by resentment over Stillman's success, which far exceeded that of her husband. In any case, she returned to the church four years later; Baptist Record Book, 31 August 1770.

[33] Brother Beriah Curtis stayed away from worship services because he objected to the rating of the pews and the idea that the ministry was a "divine" institution. He also wanted to see lay prophecy and foot washing instituted; Baptist Record Book, 31 August 1770. Pews were linked to subscriptions in the last year of Callendar's ministry; ibid., June 1737. When lay prophecy was phased out is unclear, but it presumably occurred by the time of Callendar's ministry and helps to explain the church's failure to rely temporarily on a lay preacher to replace him in the pulpit after his death.

[34] John M. Bumsted and Charles E. Clark, "New England's Tom Paine: John Allen and the Spirit of Liberty," *WMQ*, 3d ser., 21 (1964): 561–70.

church and state, but they never led the fight. Predictably, Stillman would support the new federal constitution.[35]

Stillman, however, was not another Jeremiah Condy in his eagerness to get along with the larger community. Unlike Condy, he consciously identified with the Baptist cause. For instance, when chosen to preach the 1779 election sermon, Stillman laid out the Baptist position on church and state, apparently turning to his more militant fellow pastor, Isaac Backus, for assistance in drafting these passages. According to William McLoughlin, the publication of Backus's *Government and Liberty Described* (1778) may have led the legislature to ask a Baptist to preach. If Stillman, both a patriot and a moderate among the Baptists, seemed the more acceptable choice to deliver the prestigious sermon than the openly critical Backus, he did at least discuss the issue in his sermon.[36] In Stillman, the First Boston Baptist Church had found a leader who combined Condy's respectability and learning with a pride in his uniquely Baptist identity.[37]

With this moderate approach, the church hit upon a solution to the problems that had erupted during Condy's ministry. The Baptists continued to enjoy the good relations with their congregationalist neighbors that they had come to prize. At the same time, they maintained the principles that distinguished them within Boston's Reformed Protestant community. During these years, the church conformed as closely to Sidney Mead's definition of a denomination as Mead had thought possible for the colonial period; the church functioned as a voluntaristic institution with a strong sense of its common concerns and objectives, a revivalistic, even missionary bent, and a pietistic theological orientation.[38] Accepting the relative religious pluralism of prerevolutionary Boston, the Baptist church worked to improve its place in the new order. The Baptists threw themselves into the friendly competition for souls behind an engaging leader. The survival of their church ultimately depended on their success in this competi-

[35] All the pamphlets Backus produced in support of the separation of church and state from 1778 to 1783 were printed for and/or sold by Phillip Freeman, Boston bookseller and Baptist church member. This fact alone raises questions about McLoughlin's argument that rural and urban Baptists were divided on this issue; see especially his introduction to *Truth is Great* in *Isaac Backus on Church, State and Calvinism: Pamphlets, 1754–1789*, ed. William McLoughlin (Cambridge, Mass.: Harvard University Press, 1968), 399. On the Warren Association's Grievance Committee, Stillman was active in many protests.

[36] *Backus on Church, State and Calvinism*, ed. McLoughlin, 346. The preceding year's sermon had attacked the Baptist position.

[37] Significantly, Stillman developed his approach in the more pluralistic southern and, especially, middle colonies, not in eastern Massachusetts, where denominationalism was just beginning to emerge after midcentury. For comparison, see Richard W. Pointer, *Protestant Pluralism and the New York Experience: A Study of Eighteenth Century Religious Diversity* (Bloomington: Indiana University Press, 1988).

[38] Mead, "Denominationalism"; see especially his discussion of the selection of leaders, 114–15.

tion rather than on their ability to withstand persecution or ostracism, as in days gone by. Under Stillman, the church finally discovered a strategy for survival that was suited to its traditionally accommodating temperament.

Like the Baptists, the Salem Quakers struggled to redefine their place in society during the late colonial period. For them, however, the Great Awakening was ultimately of little consequence. In contrast, the revolutionary upheaval of the 1770s forced the meeting to confront its relationship to non-Quakers and its commitment to distinctive sectarian testimonies. During these years, Salem-area Friends adopted a vigorous program of self-reformation, purging their meeting of those who refused to conform to strict standards for appropriate conduct. In contrast to the Baptists, the Quakers reasserted their separatist stance. The Salem Monthly Meeting joined with Friends in other colonies in choosing sectarianism.

While the Boston Baptist Church was torn apart by the divisions that resulted from the Great Awakening, Salem Monthly Meeting members were no more than fleetingly touched by the revivals. During the early stages of the awakening, Friends were occasionally in the huge crowds that listened to such famous itinerants as George Whitefield and Gilbert Tennent.[39] The nondenominational message conveyed by these preachers and their criticisms of the colony's religious establishment undoubtedly helped to account for the Quakers' unprecedented presence at such gatherings. Having satisfied their curiosity about the revivals and concluding that revivalists only "pretent to be leade and gided by the spirit of god," Friends apparently ceased attending these meetings. Young Quakers who subsequently experienced a renewed commitment to their own faith may have been influenced by the heightened religiosity in the broader community, but they remained strictly within the bounds of Quakerism.[40] The Salem meeting experienced neither schism nor apostasy as a result of the revivals.

The Quakers passed through the religious awakenings of the early 1740s comparatively unscathed, in part because of the theological differences that continued to separate their own faith from that of other colonists. The revivalists' reliance on the Reformed Protestant doctrines of limited atonement and the need to acknowledge one's sinfulness were at odds with fundamental Quaker beliefs.[41] In fact, on the eve of the awakening, some meeting members were

---

[39] Collins, Diary, 22 September, 6 October 1740; 22 January 1740/1.

[40] Ibid., December 1741, 11 March 1741/2. Collins ceased mentioning Friends' attendance at revival meetings after the first two months of 1741.

[41] For one Rhode Island woman who did leave the Quaker faith during the revivals and the distress her obsession with sin caused her parents, see *Memoirs of Miss Susanna Anthony*, comp. Samuel Hopkins (Worcester, Mass.: 1796; revised edition, Clipstone, 1802), esp. 23, 31, 37–8. To the extent that the awakening heightened commitment to reformed theology, it amplified the divisions between Quakers and the establishment. On the doctrinal differences between Friends

suspected – apparently by mistake – of having "given into the principles of [the] universal redemption of the whole creation of mankind notwithstanding they go of the stage of this world in sin and rebilion & unreconciled to god." More inclined to err in the opposite direction from that favored by revival preachers, Friends would prove immune to their message.[42] Any affinity some of them might have felt for the universalist position put them in no danger of flirting with other colonial religious groups in the 1740s, since open advocacy of that view was still well in the future.[43] Along with the meeting's traditionally aloof stance, these doctrinal differences served to keep them uninvolved in the awakening that proved so harmful to the Baptist church.

Not the Great Awakening but the Revolution challenged the Salem Quakers. Unlike during the revivals, the issues at stake in the later conflict were not primarily religious; doctrinal differences were more likely to be subsumed than highlighted in the conflict with Britain.[44] In contrast to earlier wars, which were presented to colonists from the first as military endeavors, the revolutionary struggle began as a political problem in which Quakers could play a role as readily as anyone else. Having been marginally involved in colonial politics for generations by the 1760s, Massachusetts Friends participated in the initial discussions of British policy. As these became highly charged, Quakers were in danger of abandoning their traditionally aloof stance. Throughout the conflict, Friends found military and political developments so engrossing that they had to remind one another repeatedly not to follow the news of the world's affairs too avidly. Once imperial relations took a turn for the worse and armed conflict began to seem possible, Quakers had no choice but to step back from the "commotion" if they were to maintain their pacifism.[45]

As the crisis in imperial relations was unfolding, Salem Friends confronted the implications of their situation. Concluding that some meeting members were identifying too thoroughly with the concerns of "the world's people," the

and New Lights, see "An Abstract of the Journal of Edmond Peckover's Travels in North America and Barbadoes," *The Journal of Friends Historical Society* 11 (1904): 104; Frederick B. Tolles, "Quietism versus Enthusiasm: The Philadelphia Quakers and the Great Awakening," *Pennsylvania Magazine of History and Biography* 69 (1945): 26–49.

[42] SMM, September, November 1739; SQM (men's), April, September 1740.

[43] Charles Chauncy's *Salvation for All Men* (Boston, 1782) was the first published statement of this view by someone identified with the establishment. Also see Marini, *Radical Sects in Revolutionary New England*. Some Friends would flirt with Unitarianism in the next century; Frederick B. Tolles, "The New-Light Quakers of Lynn and New Bedford," *NEQ* 32 (1959): 291–319.

[44] This is not to deny the importance of religious affiliation in dictating an individual's political stance, since many members of minority faiths were inclined to loyalism, as were most Anglicans. However, even in those cases, the issues were largely political rather than religious.

[45] Epistle to SMM, SQM, November 1777, Quaker Miscellaneous Collection, 1770–9, LHS; Minutes, Committee for Sufferings, New England Yearly Meeting (formerly RIYM), January 1782. Jeremiah Hacker to John Pemberton, 14 April 1775, Pemberton Papers, microfilm copy, Friends Library, Swarthmore College, Swarthmore, Penn., 27:128.

meeting decided to reassert its aloofness by underscoring Quaker distinctiveness. By the mid-1770s, Friends had agreed to crack down on overt violations of the peace testimony, to discipline others who failed to live by the light of truth, to tighten membership standards in order to eliminate nominal participants from the meeting, and to orchestrate the manumission of all slaves held by meeting members.[46] In making these changes, the meeting sought to reinforce the boundaries that had traditionally separated it from the rest of society, boundaries that had become less distinct in recent years. Like other American Quaker meetings during the preceding few decades, Salem Friends reformed themselves in response to their perception of their condition.[47]

The revolutionary crisis directly challenged the Quakers' peace testimony. Despite a 1700 statement issued by the yearly meeting against fighting, drilling, and paying taxes that financed wars, New England Quakers had traditionally adhered only loosely to the pacifistic principle. They had paid taxes that indirectly supported war but had always agreed that militia drilling (or "learning war") as well as fighting were unconscionable.[48] Although Salem Quaker men had found it relatively easy to abide by these guidelines during the various eighteenth-century imperial wars, many of them were sorely tempted to fight for independence. In a 1774 letter to his brother Ezra, Stephen Collins vigorously expressed patriotic sentiments that British abuses had inspired. A year later, the Rhode Island Yearly Meeting received reports that some Lynn Quakers had cooperated when called upon to serve in the town watch.[49] In 1775-6, a number of meeting members took up arms against the British.

The Salem Monthly Meeting – confronted with the specter of a fighting Quaker – was compelled to deal with this apostasy.[50] During the first years of armed hostilities, four men were disowned for fighting or otherwise engaging in martial affairs. A larger number were disciplined for conduct "contrary to known principles"; in some cases, this was clearly a reference to lapses from pacifism.[51] These men had gone beyond the compromises that the meeting had

---

[46] SMM, 1772–83. James, *A People Among Peoples*, 247–9.

[47] On the middle colonies, see Marietta, *Reformation of American Quakerism*.

[48] SMM, 17 June 1700. Worrall explains the compromise legislation first passed in Massachusetts in the 1750s to raise extra taxes from Quakers to make up for their refusal to serve in times of war; *Quakers in the Colonial Northeast*, 137–9. Salem Quakers did not protest the tax in the way that the Nantucket Quakers did, although they did discuss it; see SMM, October 1756, January 1757, March 1758. On the Quakers' inability to agree to oppose such taxes during the Revolution, see Worrall, *Quakers in the Colonial Northeast*, 141–6.

[49] Stephen Collins to Ezra Collins, 19 May 1774, Collins Family Papers, filed with Northey Family Papers, Essex Institute; Committee for Sufferings to Lynn Friends and to SMM, both dated 12 July 1775; also SMM (men's), October 1775.

[50] A schism among southeastern Massachusetts Quakers resulted from this issue; see Arthur F. Mekeel, "Free Quaker Movement in New England During the American Revolution," *Bulletin of the Friends Historical Association* 27 (1938): 72–82.

[51] SMM (men's), December 1775; June, September, December 1776; March 1777. The Nichols

been willing to endorse in the past, and their coreligionists felt compelled to renounce them.

Disciplining men who defied the peace testimony was only one aspect of a larger campaign within the Quaker meeting to reinvigorate the sect's sense of commitment. Having already concluded that Friends needed to redouble their efforts to "live by the light of truth," the monthly meeting had begun stepping up discipline on a variety of offenses even before the men who were participating in "war affairs" were disowned. The number of cases handled by both the men's and women's monthly meetings began to rise in the early 1770s, peaking in the men's meeting in 1776–7 and in the women's in the two following years.[52] During the decade beginning in 1773, the two meetings acted upon an astounding eighty-eight cases, ultimately disowning fifty people (thirty-two men and eighteen women). The reason for the action went unrecorded in a large number of instances, with the men's minutes proving particularly reticent. With possibly one exception, the recorded offenses committed by women related to marriage.[53] They were deemed guilty most frequently of "marrying out" of the meeting (which entailed failure to arrange approval for an impending marriage, usually – but not always – because the intended spouse was not a Quaker); some were charged with "too early a birth" after marriage (which revealed that a couple had transgressed meeting regulations by indulging in premarital intercourse). Men were disciplined for a wider range of offenses, including – in addition to those relating to marriage – drunkenness, spousal abuse, and participation in war affairs.[54]

Such a sharp rise invariably raises the question, did the number of offenses multiply or did the meeting's concern over them simply increase? The handful of cases that focused exclusively on "too early a birth" were unprecedented, indicating that young Quakers were participating in a societal trend toward rising numbers of bridal pregnancies.[55] The war itself may have exacerbated

---

brothers (disciplined in August 1776) fought, and Ichabod became a war hero; Susan Farley Nichols Pulsifer, *Witch's Breed: The Pierce-Nichols Family of Salem* (Cambridge: Dresser, Chapman, & Grimes, 1967), 39. John and Joseph Dean (March 1777) also fought; *Massachusetts Soldiers and Sailors*, 4:610–11.

[52] SMM (men's), 1772–83, and SMM (women's), 1772–82.

[53] In thirteen of forty-one cases, no transgression was recorded. Twenty-one women married out, six of whom were pregnant at the time; two more had gone only so far as "keeping company out of unity" when the meeting dealt with them. Another four had too early a birth, and one was deemed guilty of undefined "indecent behavior."

[54] From 1773 through 1782, forty-seven men's cases were recorded, with twenty-eight listing no cause. Marrying out and premarital pregnancy accounted for only four apiece. Involvement in the war was cited in seven cases. One man, who was drinking excessively, was declared a "disorderly walker"; another mistreated his family; a third "lived in Conformity to the Corrupt Customs and fashens of the World." Finally, Jonathan Buffum left the meeting angered because he believed Friends were mistreating his wife Sarah, who had herself been disciplined.

[55] For example, SMM (men's), May 1773, March 1774. Too early a birth had never previously been listed as a cause for discipline. This lack of cases apparently did not arise from a failure to

objectionable behavior on the part of the Quakers, as it did briefly and with less significant consequences among the Baptists, presumably because the hostilities disrupted the usual patterns of family and community life.[56] The temptation to disregard the sect's pacifistic stance was presumably stronger during a war of resistance than it had been during earlier wars fought far from eastern Massachusetts at the behest of imperial officials; local Quakers passed through those conflicts with relative ease. In addition, disowning a sizable number of men skewed the sex ratio in the meeting, which inadvertently encouraged women to seek mates outside of it. That the peak in cases handled by the women's meeting followed that in the men's and consisted largely of marriage-related offenses suggests that the two trends may have been linked in this way. More meeting members may have been acting in unacceptable ways, a shift that would explain an upsurge in discipline.

However, heightened concern that members conform to traditional norms also contributed to the sharp increase in disciplinary measures. A number of Friends, including prominent meeting member Ebenezer Pope of Boston, asserted that discipline had been lax and called for its more widespread and consistent application.[57] Some of the people who were disowned were, in fact, long-time miscreants; William Gray, for instance, had failed to attend meetings, live with his wife, or provide for his family for an extended period.[58] Questionable activities that had once been common were abandoned during this period as well. Lynn Quaker men ceased to serve in the office of constable in 1771, a post the meeting had previously acknowledged to be problematic but which Friends had continued to hold sporadically for many years. And Abner Hood was following in the footsteps of the late Zaccheus Collins – who had been a well-respected meeting leader – when he agreed to accept the post of selectman, but his fellow Quakers labored to dissuade him and finally threatened to take action against him if he held the position again.[59] New standards or at least

discipline those guilty of bridal pregnancy; of fifty-seven Salem Quaker couples married prior to 1750 whose dates of marriage and birth of first child are known, no clear case of bridal pregnancy emerges. For the period from 1750 until 1774, one couple (out of thirty-two for whom births were recorded locally) had a child seven months after marrying; either the meeting knew this to be a premature birth or simply ignored the possible infraction that the timing suggested. On the general trend, see Daniel Scott Smith and Michael S. Hindus, "Premarital Pregnancy in America, 1640–1971: An Overview and Interpretation," *Journal of Interdisciplinary History* 5 (1975): 537–70.

56 After the Boston Baptists were reunited in 1776, having been scattered for over a year during the hostilities with the British, a number of disciplinary cases had to be addressed. See Baptist Record Book, 1776–7. I know of no study of a Massachusetts church during this era that treats this issue, so it is unclear whether the trend extended beyond these two sects.

57 Ebenezer Pope to the monthly meeting elders, 4 June 1775, Purintan Family Papers, Correspondence, LHS; also Sarah Buffum to same, 8 September 1773, Buffum Family Papers, Correspondence, LHS.

58 SMM, July 1773; also October 1775, October–November 1782.

59 On constables, see SMM, February 1716/17; and *Towne Meetings of Lyn*. On selectmen, see SMM (men's), June 1782; and Henry Oliver to Abner Hood, 17 April 1780, LHS.

an unprecedented effort to uphold old standards also contributed to the meeting's expanding activism. Reinvigorated discipline helped to carry the sect through perilous times; for it served, as the Rhode Island Yearly Meeting pointed out in 1776, "as a hedge about us."[60]

In addition to repairing this hedge by enforcing long-standing rules, the Salem meeting actually raised standards for members' behavior during this period by taking a strong stand on the long-unresolved issue of slaveownership. Slaveholding had never been as widespread among Salem Friends as in wealthier meetings located in colonies where slavery was a more important institution, but the meeting in Salem had been similarly unable to agree on a satisfactory resolution of the problem.[61] After dealing with the question in a desultory fashion for years, the Salem Monthly Meeting vigorously applied itself to ending the practice beginning in 1775. By February 1778, all Quaker slave masters had been persuaded to manumit their slaves, and the resulting papers of manumission were read aloud at the monthly meeting. With this measure, the Salem Monthly Meeting surpassed both the Newport Quaker meeting and their non-Quaker neighbors in the movement to end slavery.[62] Their reforming zeal encouraged them to move beyond their traditional standards for sectarian behavior and to expect more of themselves on such issues as slaveholding. Their newfound opposition to this oppressive institution helped to demarcate the boundaries that protected them from the "world's people."

Nowhere is the Salem Quaker concern for reconfirming their separate identity during the revolutionary era more apparent than in the new standards for sectarian membership that were instituted. Whereas earlier converts simply attended meetings for worship and demonstrated their convictions by living as Quakers, now prospective members were examined and formally accepted into the meeting. These procedures had been in use for some time in other meetings and had been familiar to local Quakers for decades. They had been utilized on an earlier occasion when one aspiring member who appeared suspect for some reason had been subjected to careful scrutiny.[63] But only during the ref-

---

[60] Quoted by James, *A People Among Peoples*, 251.

[61] Of sixty-five Salem Quakers whose probate records contain inventories, five owned a total of eight slaves at the time of their deaths. See ECPR for Josiah Southwick (1692), Robert Stone (1694), Samuel Gaskill (1725), Daniel Southwick (1733), and Zaccheus Collins (1770). Collins reportedly owned two additional slaves at some time in his life; see Lewis and Newhall, *History of Lynn*, 344. The slaves owned by West Indian plantation owner Abraham Redwood (d. 1728/9), who resided briefly in Salem, were not listed in ECPR.

[62] SMM (men's), October 1772, March 1775, March 1776, February 1778. The question of slavery was first raised by the monthly meeting in March 1717/18 and very seldom for forty-five years after that date. Also see RIYM, 1743, 1744, 1769, 1770, 1771, 1773. It is unclear from the meeting records how many slaves were freed in the 1770s. Two cases were listed separately; the remainder were manumitted as a group in 1778, and the number went unrecorded. Massachusetts residents would continue to hold slaves into the next decade, as would wealthy Newport Quakers; Lorenzo Johnston Greene, *The Negro in Colonial New England, 1620–1776* (New York: Columbia University Press, 1942), 42; and James, *A People Among Peoples*, 229.

[63] SMM, October 1759, January 1760. Perhaps Benjamin Bickford had previously been an ortho-

ormation of the 1770s did the meeting systematically institute the practice. Demonstrating the extent of their commitment to these policies, Friends denied an applicant's request for membership for the first time in 1777.[64]

Not only were new members screened, the meaning of membership took on increasing sophistication.[65] The basis for an individual's right to claim a place in the meeting was refined, with the term "birthright membership" introduced into the meeting records.[66] The clerk began carefully keeping vital records in order to ensure that future generations of birthright members could be easily identified. This new concern to document familial ties to the meeting also led the clerk to transcribe genealogies into the record book and may have guided some Quaker parents in choosing names for their children.[67] For the first time, a parent was held responsible for an offspring's failure to remain a member; Abigail Bassett received a committee visit after she consented too readily to her daughter's marriage out of the meeting. Those without a legitimate claim to membership carefully verified their place in the meeting; two men applied after discovering that they did not qualify under the new guidelines, despite having been active as Friends for some time. Even people who were disowned enjoyed a right to appeal unfavorable decisions under the newly articulated system.[68] The Salem Monthly Meeting emerged from the revolutionary period with its membership as well as standards for the conduct of members more clearly defined than ever before.

In responding to the threat of accommodation by purging their own ranks in this way, the Friends in Salem, Lynn, and Boston were contributing to a tradition of periodic reformation within the sect. Such reform efforts had become a regular feature of American Quakerism, with the largest one to date being the campaign in the middle colonies that had fueled the withdrawal of Friends from politics during the 1750s.[69] Reformation was not solely or even primarily

---

dox church member; in any case, he was required to compose a "paper" before being accepted into the meeting. Also see ibid., February 1745/6, for the only other early instance of a man applying for membership in the meeting; an immigrant into the area, he may have brought the practice with him.

[64] SMM (men's), January 1767, April 1771, June 1773, April 1775, May 1776, July 1777. SMM (women's), September 1778; February, December 1780; May 1782.

[65] The need to identify Friends in good standing so that they could be granted military exemptions helped to spur this development; see Moses Brown to James Pemberton, 18 February 1777, Pemberton Papers, 29:141.

[66] SMM (men's), September 1783. During the preceding decade, the meeting had begun using a related phrase, "had his or her education among Friends," with regard to the children of Quakers; see e.g., SMM (men's), December 1775; SMM (women's), March 1783. Marietta discusses this phrase in *Reformation of American Quakerism*, 69–70.

[67] SMM (men's), December 1783; e.g., Children of Isaac and Anna Estes Hacker, 1773–99, SMM, Births and Deaths, 1709–1818, p. 81. Joseph and Elizabeth Southwick named a daughter Cassandra for the first Quaker convert in their clan (and reputedly in Salem generally); see SMM (women's), May 1783.

[68] SMM (women's), June 1778. SMM (men's), April 1779, September 1783.

[69] See esp. Richard Bauman, *For the Reputation of Truth: Politics, Religion, and Conflict among the*

sparked by renewed hostilities toward Friends, as some scholars have suggested. In many – if not most – cases, members of the society came to feel that
they had become too involved in the affairs of the world and that the "hedge"
that protected them was in need of repair.[70] Once this realization had become
widespread, the meeting acted to reinvigorate sectarian discipline and to disown
those who refused to conform. Despite the loss of some members – who, in the
case of the Salem Monthly Meeting, were predominantly men – the meeting
emerged from this flurry of reform activity rejuvenated.

The idea that a single reformation of American Quakerism occurred over-
looks not just the periodic nature of these reform movements but also the importance of local circumstances for launching them. The reforms adopted in
Pennsylvania in 1750, although dramatic, were not the first nor would they be
the last.[71] Traveling Friends and meeting epistles tried to carry the reforming
impulse in one region to others but rarely succeeded, at least to the satisfaction
of the former. Changes were implemented only when Friends in a given locale
perceived a need for them.[72] At such a time, they borrowed freely from practices and procedures developed by other meetings or created new ones to suit
their needs.[73] Reformation came two decades earlier to Pennsylvania because
Friends there had cause for concern about their compromises with the world
sooner.

Pennsylvania Quakers, 1750–1800 (Baltimore: Johns Hopkins University Press, 1971); and Marietta, *Reformation of American Quakerism.*

[70] James, *A People Among Peoples,* 239–41; Marietta, *Reformation of American Quakerism,* 55–6. As
the case of the Salem meeting attests, societal animosity inadvertently helped to fortify the community's sense of solidarity and to obviate the need for additional testimonies that would serve
to distinguish Friends from others. Massachusetts Quaker scruples were fairly easily accommodated by the revolutionary government; see, e.g., Minutes, Committee for Sufferings, March
1778. For an exception, according to Jo Anne McCormick, see "The Quakers of Colonial South
Carolina, 1670–1807" (Ph.D. diss., University of South Carolina, 1984), 66, 79, 202–3.

[71] Carol Hagglund, "Disowned without Just Cause: Quakers in Rochester, Massachusetts During
the Eighteenth Century" (Ph.D. diss., University of Massachusetts, 1980); and McCormick,
"The Quakers of Colonial South Carolina," discuss reform in two other meetings outside of
the middle colonies. Bauman treats the Pennsylvania reformation as occurring in two phases;
see *For the Reputation of Truth,* 160. The later Hicksites movement can be seen as another
(though ill-fated) effort at reform; see H. Larry Ingle, *Quakers in Conflict: The Hicksite Reformation* (Knoxville: University of Tennessee Press, 1988).

[72] Even endorsement of a specific practice by the local yearly meeting did not ensure its adoption.
For instance, in 1717, the men's monthly meeting held an extended discussion about whether
to let "strangers" from "beyond the bounds of this monthly meeting" attend business meetings
without first presenting a certificate, only to discover after arriving at a decision that the practice
was "strictly forbiden in our Records of Discipline" compiled by the yearly meeting; SMM,
May 1717. This incident should remind us not to assume that behavior necessarily follows from
the rules intended to guide it.

[73] Although Pennsylvanians did not play the pivotal role in launching the reformation in Massachusetts that some scholars have attributed to them, Quaker meetings beyond Massachusetts –
especially in Pennsylvania and England – did contribute practices that were instituted during
the 1770s by Salem-area Friends. In particular, procedures having to do with membership were
imported.

In Massachusetts, Friends gained acceptance far more slowly, never achieving the political power and social prestige that their coreligionists enjoyed in Penn's colony. Conditions in the northern colony – including the history of persecution, the efforts of the authorities to isolate the sect and to fortify the orthodox establishment against the threat it represented, and the theological doctrines that differentiated the Quakers from the majority – all served to keep the sect apart. By midcentury, however, the boundaries between the Salem meeting and the world had begun to grow hazy.[74] In this respect, the Great Awakening indirectly contributed to the Quaker reformation in that it fractured the orthodox community and furthered contact across religious boundaries. By the 1760s, one Bostonian was able to remark of the sect, "At present they are esteemed of good morals, friendly and benevolent in their disposition, and I hope will never meet with any further persecution on account of their peculiar tenets or customs."[75] On the eve of the Revolution, in other words, the Quakers were seen by some of their fellow colonists as simply another denomination. During the Revolution, they confronted and rejected this vision of their relationship to the larger community, as some of their coreligionists had done in Pennsylvania earlier and others were doing in various colonies during this period.[76]

In order to render the middle colony reform movement all of a piece with the later campaign in New England, scholars have asserted that the northern meetings actively resisted making needed changes for two decades. Traveling Friends who spoke critically of their New England coreligionists provide the primary evidence that reformation was long overdue by 1770.[77] Yet visitors to

---

[74] To give but one example, in 1742, when Charles Chauncy wanted to denounce revivalists by linking them to Quakers, he thought it necessary to explain why early Quakers were considered threatening; by this time, the Quaker as alien had lost its currency as a symbol. See *Enthusiasm described*, 4.

[75] Hutchinson, *History*, 1:205.

[76] In his 1780 letter to Abner Hood, Henry Oliver laid out the logic behind the denominational approach only to reject it in favor of withdrawal from the world.

[77] Worrall, *Quakers in the Colonial Northeast*, ch. 5; and Byers, *Nation of Nantucket*, 262. Marietta's account assumes that the reformers' assessments were invariably accurate and that the fault lay entirely with their unreceptive auditors; see, e.g., *Reformation of American Quakerism*, 38–42. Visitors often provided contradictory assessments of the state of a meeting; for some examples, see Selleck, *Quakers in Boston*, 50–2. The explanation offered for the delay is that reform had to await the deaths of an older generation of intransigent leaders; the evidence for this is a comment Samuel Forthergill made regarding elderly Friends in New York. See Worrall, *Quakers in the Colonial Northeast*, 82; Byers, *Nation of Nantucket*, 262; and James, *A People Among Peoples*, 248.

These works assume that Quakers everywhere acknowledged a clear standard for conduct and readily recognized divergence from it. In fact, standards changed over time with the introduction of new testimonies or the refinement of existing ones. As in the case of John Woolman, whose opposition to slavery led him to boycott such everyday items as cotton cloth, witnessing could always be carried beyond what the society deemed necessary.

the region had been admonishing the meeting to exercise greater care in following the light of truth since the seventeenth century; their exhortations served to
heighten the commitment of the faithful. As with the jeremiads by established
church ministers that they resembled, these statements, if taken at face value,
paint an unduly negative picture of the state of affairs in a given meeting. After
the Revolution as before it, visitors came to Massachusetts in order to exhort
Friends there, not because reform had failed but because such admonitions
were part of the evangelical role of the Public Friend.[78]

Despite the criticism leveled at them by traveling visitors and by later historians, the Quakers of Salem, Lynn, and Boston had accomplished what they
had set out to do with their reform movement. They were able to pass through
the American Revolution without being absorbed into the society at large. At
the cost of a reduction in membership, most notably in Boston, the Salem
Monthly Meeting renewed its sense of itself as a self-consciously sectarian en-
tity.[79] Those who could not live by the light of truth to the satisfaction of the
meeting were probably not turned away completely; wayward believers may
have been able to attend meetings for worship even though they were no longer
counted among the members.[80] More rigorous standards for official membership in the meeting maintained an ideal for Quaker behavior that effectively set
the sect apart. In the very different circumstances of late-eighteenth-century
Massachusetts, the Quakers had to work harder at keeping themselves separate.
During the revolutionary era, they chose to do just that.

By rejecting opportunities for interdenominational rapport in order to return
to the isolationism of a sect, Salem Friends acted in accord with their own
century-long history. Because Quakerism initially represented a radical departure from the established faith, the colonist who joined this sect decisively rejected the religious culture that informed the spiritual lives of most Bay colonists. In Salem, the Quakers created a tight-knit sectarian community that helped
to compensate for the hostility to which they were subjected. Even as relations
with some of their non-Quaker neighbors and relations improved, they maintained their distance from the colonial establishment. Well into the eighteenth
century, Quakers thought of themselves and were perceived by other colonists
as alienated from the larger community. Attitudes toward the sect relaxed only

---

[78] "Journal of Joshua Evans," *Friends Miscellany* 10 (1837): 55; *Memoirs and Journal of Hugh Judge*
(Byberry, [Penn.], 1841), 198. For similar postreform criticisms leveled at Nantucket Friends,
see Byers, *Nation of Nantucket*, 265–6.

[79] The Boston weekly meeting, always the smallest of the three, would be canceled in 1808; Selleck, *Quakers in Boston*, 79. From 1776 until 1800, marriage certificates granted by the monthly
meeting ran two to one in favor of residence in Lynn over Salem, with only one Bostonian (out
of a total of 138 brides and grooms residing in the three towns) marrying; see Marriage Certificates, 1776–1800, SMM.

[80] Nonmembers continued to attend meetings during this period; "Journal of Joshua Evans," 55;
Memoirs of the Life, Travels, and Religious Experiences of Martha Routh (York, 1822), 73, 97. Presumably, former members were free to participate on the fringe of the meeting if they so chose.

in the late colonial period, when changes in the orthodox community helped to minimize the radicalism of the Quaker alternative. Opportunities for acceptance, which came late to the Quakers, remained modest. By ignoring these opportunities, Salem Friends resumed their traditional position in Massachusetts's altered spiritual landscape.

The Boston Baptist church, in embracing rather than rejecting denominationalism, similarly continued on its unique path. The Baptist faith had never represented the severe break with orthodoxy that Quakerism had. In fact, conversion often occurred in isolation from other proponents of the sect, in a dialogue with the orthodox faith. As a result, this sectarian movement was geographically dispersed, unlike the highly concentrated Quaker community in Salem. The common ground shared by the Baptists and the orthodox increased in importance with time, as the former drifted toward the latter in matters of church polity and, especially, leadership. Baptist converts, adopting a fairly familiar faith and living scattered among non-Baptists, earned acceptance from the larger community more readily. From the first, Baptists courted this acceptance.

In the late colonial period, after passing through a period of crisis, the Baptists settled on a new strategy for surviving while accommodating. In the 1740s, the Baptists seemed to have succeeded too well in winning acceptance. Having long striven to become better integrated into the larger community, the Boston Baptist Church had the misfortune of making great strides toward this goal on the eve of the revivals. Caught up in a wider trend toward liberal Christianity, the church was ill prepared to respond positively to the evangelical movement of the early 1740s. Unlike the Quaker meeting, which hardly deigned to notice the excitement among its neighbors, the Boston Baptist Church was torn apart by the revivals. The church recovered from this ordeal only when it struck upon the denominational alternative. Under Stillman, the Baptists retained their favored status in the larger community while recovering a measure of their earlier distinctiveness by establishing a denominational identity. While the Quakers returned to the sectarianism that had initially defined their own and the Baptists' official position in the colony, the Baptists eagerly seized upon the new option that revolutionary Massachusetts offered.

The Salem Monthly Meeting and the First Boston Baptist Church elected different roles for themselves at the end of the colonial period. The choice the Baptists made paved the way for the cooperation and competition that would characterize interdenominational efforts during the early nineteenth century (and beyond). The Quakers' backward-looking approach also had a future, for it anticipated the various utopian sects that would withdraw from society to pursue a unique religious vision. In moving into the postrevolutionary era, both the Baptists and the Quakers followed paths that were consistent with their more than century-old histories.

Index

187